French and Indian War Notices
Abstracted from Colonial Newspapers
Volume 4: September 17, 1759 to
December 30, 1760

Armand Francis Lucier

HERITAGE BOOKS
2007

HERITAGE BOOKS
AN IMPRINT OF HERITAGE BOOKS, INC.

Books, CDs, and more—Worldwide

For our listing of thousands of titles see our website
at
www.HeritageBooks.com

Published 2007 by
HERITAGE BOOKS, INC.
Publishing Division
65 East Main Street
Westminster, Maryland 21157-5026

Copyright © 1999 Armand Francis Lucier

Maps: "Sketch of the Cherokee Country," from George Bancroft's *History of the United States*, 1852; and "British Colonies and Northern New France, 1750-1760" from *Montcalm and Wolfe* by Francis Parkman, © Little, Brown and Company, Boston, 1897.

All rights reserved. No part of this book may be reproduced or transmitted in any form or by any means, electronic or mechanical, including photocopying, recording or by any information storage and retrieval system without written permission from the author, except for the inclusion of brief quotations in a review.

International Standard Book Number: 978-0-7884-1378-3

CONTENTS

FOREWORD..v
MAPS..vi, vii
CONTRIBUTORS..viii

September 1759..1
October 1759...13
November 1759..47
December 1759..71

January 1760...93
February 1760..99
March 1760..123
April 1760..133
May 1760..141
June 1760...155
July 1760...175
August 1760...203
September 1760..219
October 1760..249
November 1760...259
December 1760...271

Index...299

FOREWORD

Volume IV of the French and Indian War Abstracts begins with the Boston dateline of September 17, 1759, and concludes with the Charlestown, South Carolina, dateline of December 30, 1760.

This is the final phase of events that led to the capitulation of Canada to the British and provincial forces. Also found in this book are accounts of other actions from the frontier forts, outposts and settlements, and many reports relating to the so-called Cherokee War.

This volume reveals the roles that the different Governors, Majesty's Councils and Houses of Representatives played in procuring for the field generals the soldiers, provisions and other necessities that contributed to the reduction of Canada.

All articles are presented here as they were originally published, with no alterations to spelling, composition or capitalization, except where it was thought necessary for clarity and understanding.

                                    Armand Francis Lucier.

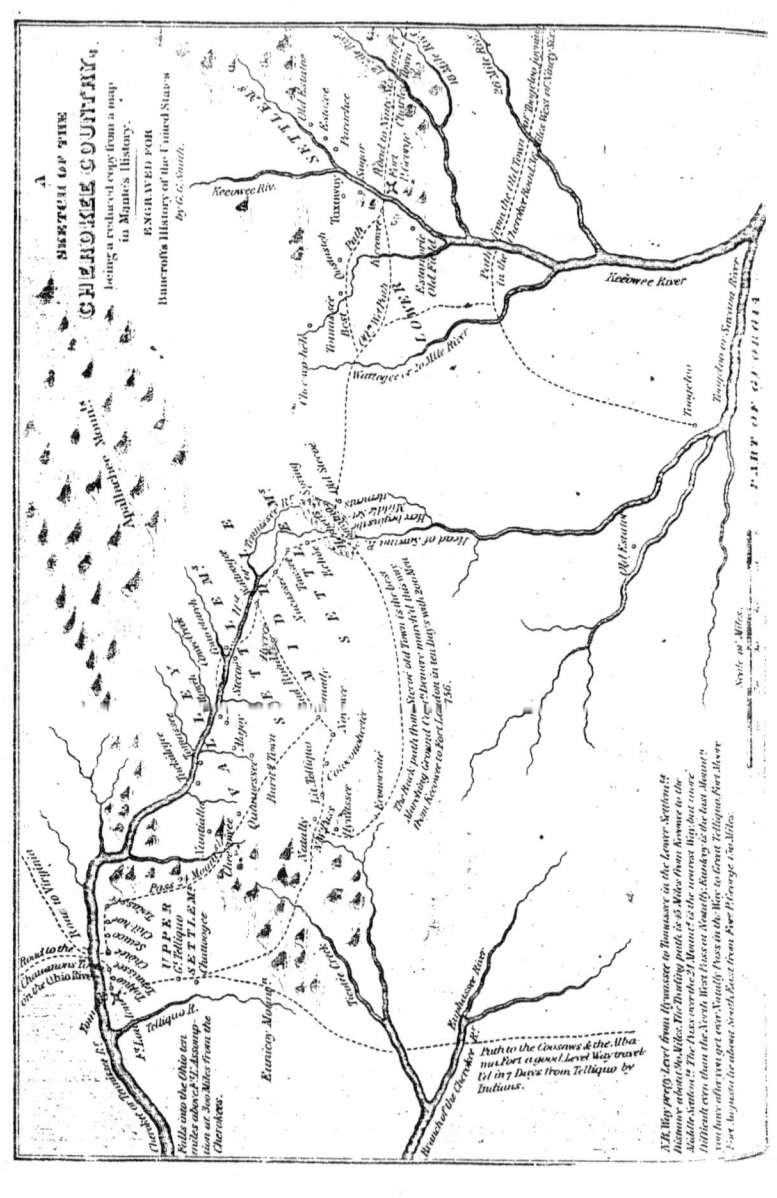

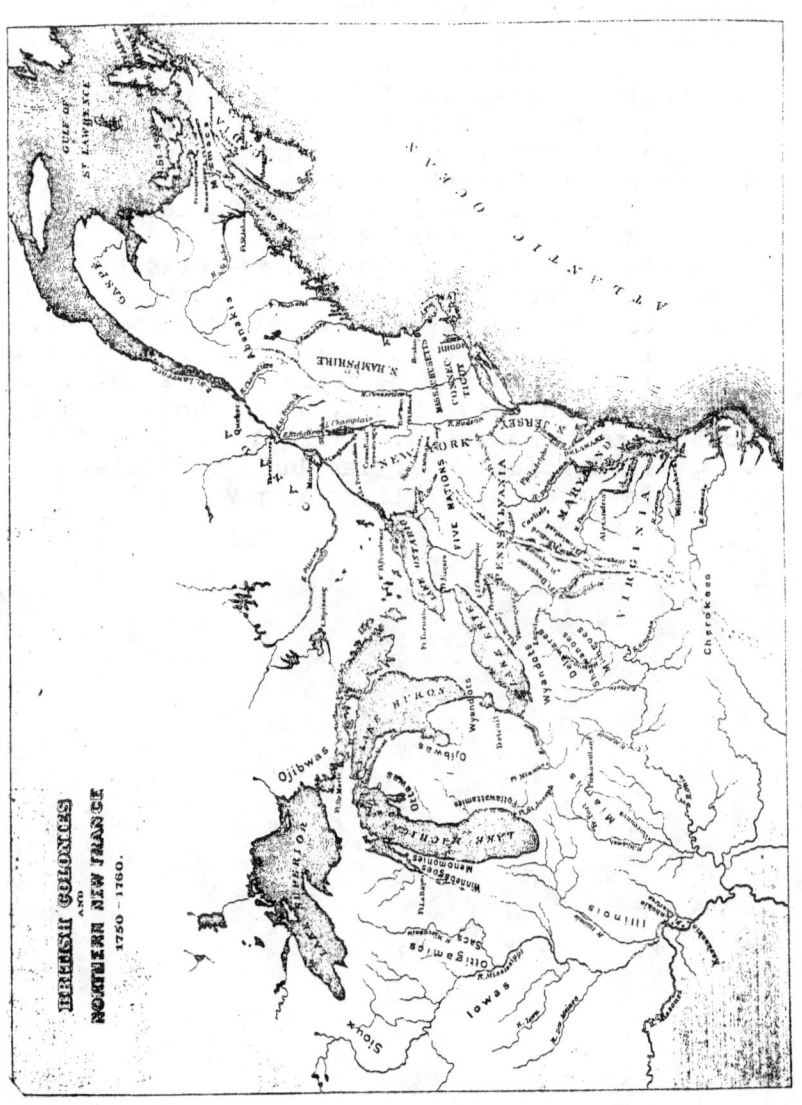

CONTRIBUTORS

Boston Gazette. Boston Massachusetts.
The Boston Evening Post. Boston Massachusetts.
Connecticut Gazette. New-Haven Connecticut.
Gentlemen's Magazine. London England.
Halifax Gazette. Halifax Nova-Scotia.
Maryland Gazette. Annapolis Maryland.
New-Hampshire Gazette. Portsmouth New-Hampshire.
New-London Summery. New-London Connecticut.
London Gazette. London England.
New-York Gazette [Weyman's] New-York, New-York.
New-York Mercury. New-York, New-York.
North-Carolina Gazette, New Bern North Carolina.
Pennsylvania Gazette. Philadelphia Pennsylvania.
Pennsylvania Journal. Philadelphia Pennsylvania.
Providence Gazette. Providence, Rhode-Island.
South Carolina Gazette. Charlestown So. Carolina.
Virginia Centinel, Williamsburg Virginia.
Virginia Gazette. Williamsburg Virginia.

SEPTEMBER 1759

BOSTON Sept. 17. By the most authentic Accounts from time to time relating to the Strength and Destination of the Enemy's Forces it appears ―――― That Gen. Wolfe id opposed by three Quarters of the Forces in Canada ―――― That on the Side of Owego, there is no Fortress but that of La Galette (which is of but little Strength) to oppose the Army of Brigadier Gage on their Passage to Montreal, where there is now only a number of old Men, Women and Children. That the troops which are at and near St. John's are those which retired from Ticonderoga and Crown-Point upon the Advance of our Grand Army under Gen. Amherst. ―――― That the French Naval Forces on Lake Champlain is at present inconsiderable, a Vessel of 10 Guns being Commodore; but a Vessel of greater Force was a Building. ―――― So that it appears that the Fate of Canada has and does depend, under Providence, either upon the advance of our Grand Army, an Army at present with as much Health, Spirit and Unity as ever was known ―――― or the proceedure of Gen. Gage's Army and our Indians, towards Montreal, which must make such a Diversion in Favour of General Wolfe, as would more than probably give him the Opportunity of reducing Quebeck, and all Country around. ―――― We have been for some Weeks impatiently expecting to hear of one or other of the Army moving which if practicable, and not beyond the general Plan, will doubtless be the Case ―――― Which this good News arriving, the Betts will be six to one that Canada will be reduced this Year; to the Intentional Honours of His Majesty's Ministry, Generals and Troops; the universal joy of all North America; and the whole British Empire.

By the Courier who arrived last Thursday from

Albany, we learn, that Lieut. Fletcher with 10 Men, and one Hopkins, Serjeant Major of the Rangers with 7 Men, went from Crown Point on a Scout, and had got within a little Way of St. Joseph's when they separated, after agreeing where to meet at a certain Time; but a Party of the Enemy being out, discovered Fletcher and his Men surrounded them, and made them all Prisoners; ―――― That Hopkin's Party, discovering the Enemy they all separated: however after some Hours, Hopkins with four others got together when they discover'd the Enemy's Encampment on an Island about 8 Miles this Side of St. John's where they saw their Motions, and observ'd three Men coming down to the Water, who were gone to fish, and no sooner had they begun, then Hopkins with his Men run into the Water, about Breast high, and bro't them off, notwithstanding their hallowing, which alarm'd the Enemy, who were seen to be thick on the Ramparts of the Fort, they being within Gunshot, but the Enemy did not Fire for fear of killing their own Men: ―――― These Prisoners say, that the French are 4000 strong on this Island, and have 100 Canoes there, well planted, where they design to make a Stand; they also inform of Lieut. Fletcher and his Party being taken, who gave the French Intelligence of Hopkins, and that a party was out in order to Way-lay him, but luckily he did not leave his Whaleboats where he determined to meet Fletcher, and by that Means escaped for he had scarcely put off before the Enemy appear'd and fired upon him but did no Damage; one of the Men that separated, had got back again to Crown-Point, but the other two were still missing: And, that the Enemy had lately launched a large Vessel of Force, in order to attack ours on the Lake.

BOSTON Sept. 17. Extract from a Letter from the Commanding Officer at Annapolis Royal Dated August 27th 1759.

"We have plenty of Live Stock here, as the famous Monsieur Benufalen's Party seems to be employ'd in supplying us with live Cattle; having taken from them since we have been here upwards of 100 Head: No longer ago than a fortnight about 50 or 60 of the French pass'd a short

Distance by the Fort, with a large Drove of Cattle, they came to the Water side, and challeng'd us to give them Battle which was immediately accepted, we drove them off, took two Firelocks, a Number of Blankets, Coats, Jackets, &c. and thirty odd Head of Bullocks, and returned safe next Day; Had a fine Auction, and the Plunder will amount to at least 1500 Pounds old Tenor."

Extract of a Letter from the same Place, Dated August 28.

"On the 4th Instant, four of our Men, being Indians, went down the River without Leave, in a large Float to get Wood, and the Enemy came upon 'em, and took or kill'd three, one made his Escape and got into the Fort bur was wounded. ——— On the 5th Major Tapley with one Hundred Men was detach'd in pursuit of 'em, but return'd on the 7th without seeing the Enemy. ——— The Names of the Indians killed or taken, are Solomon, Ned, Pilot Sowomoog, and James Horn; one Joseph David, wounded, but got into the Fort.

N. B. Captain Mayhew had the Command of the Party of the 60 Men, who took the Cattle from the French, as they were driving them from Cape Sables."

Last Wednesday came to town by Land from Saco, several Persons who arrived there on Saturday se'nnight from the Bay of Fundy, where they had been to view some of the Lots of Land, granted by his Majesty to those of his Subjects who may incline to settle in Nova Scotia. ——— By them we have an Account. That our Provincial Troops at the several Garrisons at Annapolis-Royal, Chiegnecto, St. John's, &c. were still in good Health. ——— That Capt. Curtis being sent out with a Party up St. John's River, espy'd a Canoe with two Frenchmen therein, who endeavoured to escape, but were fired upon, both wounded and taken. Capt. Curtis brought one of them (the other dying of his Wounds) to Lieutenant-Colonel Arbuthnot, who commanded at Fort Frederick: The Prisoner inform'd him, that he had a Family which would submit to the English, if they could have Protection: Accordingly, after his Wounds were healed. Col. Arbuthnot, with 130 of the Troops in Whaleboats, set out with him but found no People where they landed; there were 20 small Houses, which they burnt, and taking out the Bedding and some of the Furniture: They then proceeded almost as far as St. Ann's when going into a Creek they saw three Vessels: a large Sloop or Schooner, and two small Schooners, which were those taken a Year ago, and have been there ever since. They brought off the two schooners, after loading them with Stores and rigging belonging to the large Vessel, which could not be got off, as there was not Water enough to float her: ——— Our Informant could not tell who the Vessels belong'd to: but heard the small ones formerly belong'd to Casco-Bay; One of them is gone to Halifax. ——— Colonel Frye has sent out a large Party from Fort Cumberland by Land to Pequot de Jaque, and the Monckton Schooner is gone to assist them.

Wednesday last arrived here Capt. Paul in a Sloop that came our with the Fleet from the River St. Lawrence which arrived here last Week under Convoy of the Diana: This Sloop put into Old York to repair some Damage she sustained when at Anchor near the Isle of Orleans, by Lightning: The Lightning came down the Spindle, cut the Iron Withe in two, and split off about on third of the Mast to the Keelson: the Deck was covered with the Splinters from the Mast; one Man was struck down, but recovered; that the Thunder was so severe that it shook some of the Oakem out of the Seams of the Vessel: This happened the latter end of July last.

Extract of a Letter from Crown-Point.

"As to the Situation of this Place, it is in Summer very agreeable, but I dare say, it will be excessive cold in Winter. ——— The soil is pretty good, and the French had some few Settlements round it: ——— The Fort which is Building is nigh where the old one was; it is to be a regular Pentagon, with three out-works, sufficient to contain 1000 Men in Winter, and more in Case of Necessity: ——— Our moving depends on General Wolfe's Success. One of our Indians and one of Roger's Rangers are gone by land to General Wolfe for which the Indian is to have 100 Guineas. The Road to No. 4. Will be good for our New-England Forces to go home; as also to supply the Fort with fresh Provisions, it being not above 60 or 70 Miles from hence."

Saturday last an Express returned from Crown-Point whither he had been sent with Dispatches for the General, upon the first News being received from Quebeck by Capt. Morton, on Monday the 3d Inst. at which Place he arrived the Saturday following, and left again the next Day; the other Express with the more favourable News bro't by the Diana Frigate, which arrived here the next Day after Capt. Morton, had not got up to Crown-Point when this Express came from thence. —— By him we learn, That General Amherst with his Army still remain there, busily employed in finishing the fine Fort erected in that Place: That the Army has been healthy, that only one Man of the six Regiments of Regulars had died a natural Death since they left Albany; that the Provincials were also pretty healthy, but not so much so as the Regulars; —— That the Brig launch'd there the first Inst. had got her Guns on board, and was nearly rigged; and that they were going to build another Sloop there immediately, which was to be finished in 12 or 14 Days, and to carry 16 Guns; —— That the French had 5 Vessels of Force on the Lake, viz. one of 16 Guns, one of 14, one of 10, and two of 8 Guns; and 'twas said the General intended shortly to push forward at all Event.

Extract of a Letter at Crown-Point, Dated, September 7th 1759.

"I have nothing now at present to offer, save that a small Party of our Rangers have brought in 3 French Prisoners from the other End of the Lake; they are Soldiers, and German by birth; very stupid, Ignorant, starved Fellows, and bring no Intelligence that can be depended upon: However, they say, that for a long Time they have heard nothing from Quebeck, till the Day before they were taken, a Report came from Montreal, that the Siege was raised and the English gone; but that gains no Credit here, as we know such Reports are most commonly spread about in Canada when Things go worst with them.

—— General Wolfe and Admiral Saunder's long Silence surprizes us all very much. —— Our Scout is not yet returned from Quebec. Yesterday about Dusk, there were three of the Enemy's Battoes discovered about 8 Miles off. —— A large Brigantine that will carry 22 Guns is launch'd at Ticonderoga, a small sloop and a Reddoe, or floating Battery, 6 small Reddoes, or Prows, and one large Piece of Cannon each, are ready: —— A Party is gone to try to burn some of the Enemy's Sloops. —— General Amherst is going on with Improvements of all kinds here. —— All that we hear from Lake Champlain is, that there were preparing to visit Cadaraqui and La Galette, and perhaps Montreal: —— The unfortunate Accident of General Prideaux's Death has much retarded our operations in that Part of the World. —— as to the Army here, I can with truth assure you that it is the quietest, soberest, most labourious and industrious, (as well as hitherto) the most healthy Camp I ever saw, or heard, or read of, —— If General Amherst's Plan, with regard to Crown-Point, is adhered to and finished, this will in 2 or 3 Years become the cheapest, fastest, and most Comfortable Garrison in the King's Dominions, it is about Lat. 44. and the Climate very good, centrical to every part of the British Colonies from Kenebeck to Delaware River, and in Time there will be three or four different Communications open betwixt it and the Settlements, and one from the Lake by a short cut to Lake Ontario, as well as a small Settlement projected from hence to the head of Wood-Creek, which will not only supply the different Forts with Provisions, but succour them in case of need, till the Country gathers: —— There is a great deal of good Land in the Neighbourhood, and the Climate more moist, and not so subject to Parching Droughts as on the Sea Coast, and is entirely well Wooded and watered. —— from the Serjeant who took the last three Prisoners, as well as from the Prisoners themselves, we learn, that the French have fortified a little Island about 90 Miles from hence, and 15 Miles this Side of Fort St. Johns called L'Isle de Noix, or Nut, and have made it very strong with Fascine Batteries and 70 Pieces of Cannon: This Isle will be more troublesome to reduce, as it cannot be regularly approached, the Channel on each Side is very narrow, and both Shores (for a great Way inland) This new Fortification is owing to the Enemy getting in a Fleet this Year, otherwise they had no Cannon to spare, but they have now got enough of them, as also Officers, Sailors, Sails, Rigging, &c. for their Sloops on the Lakes, and I am persuaded, that had they not got any Supply from old France this Year, we should have been in quick possession of Canada long before now."

In the New-Hampshire Gazette of last Friday is the following Paragraph. "We hear from Newbury that a Gentleman there has a Letter from Louisbourg dated the 26th or 28th of last month, giving Account that two Vessels had just arrived at Louibourg from the Fleet, and reports, that General Wolfe was actually in possession of the upper City: which we hope will prove true."

CHARLESTOWN S. Carolina Sept. 19. Letters from Augusta, dated the 20th of August say, That the Creeks in general are very much dissatisfied with peace said to be concluded between us and the Chactaws: And that the French had got some Friend Indians in the Creeks, during the treaty with Mr. Atkin, to kill a Chactaw and throw the body in the river, thereby hoping to raise a misunderstanding; but that when the Chactaws discovered the murder, they Immediately Declared it was committed as the instigation of the French who, after a while, should suffer for it. These circumstances seem to prove the friendly disposition of the Chactaws to be genuine.

Other advices from Augusta are, that a greater Number of the Cherokees that ever appeared before in those woods, have for six weeks past, been hovering about among the Creeks on both sides of the Savannah river, at no great distance from the Settlements; and that they had sent a talk to Governor Ellis calculated to make them free from evil intentions, yet in a while not the most promising; and desiring he would meet them at Broad-River, to hear what they had further to say, And that a Runner from the Young Twin, dispatched from the Cherokee country was said to have arrived in the Coweta's town, on the same day our express advised the traders of his conspiracy.

Extract of a Letter dated Savannah, Aug. 26.

"Some letters have been received from the Creek nations, that they are many more from Augusta, all of which represent the temper of those Indians to be very bad." When the news of our glorious success in North America reached them, we hope to receive different Accounts. It is said, that the French troops at Venango, before General Pridioux invested the Fort at Niagara, had made themselves so sure of succeeding in an Expedition in recovering Pittsburgh, that they proposed afterwards to make themselves masters of our forts in the Cherokees: But as they have been grossly deceived by General Johnson's success in reducing Niagara, and defeating their party, 'tis probable this turn in the affairs may have great influence on the Cherokee; who in all likelihood, have been puffed up with promises of the extraordinary matters, by the French.

Sept. 15. On Monday last a Runner arrived in Town, with Dispatches from King Hagler of the Catawba's, to his Excellency the Governor, They were for some Ammunition and other Presents, which have been ordered them; and to ask that a Fort may be built in their Nation, for the protection of their Wives and Children while they go out to War. ——— Sixty of the Catawba Warriors under Capt. Jo---ny, are gone to join General Stanwix's Army at Pittsburgh. ——— The Runner set out upon his return on Wednesday. ——— As no Express are not yet come from either of the other Forts in the Cherokee Country; we are to suppose that nothing has gone amiss there since the Young Twin left Keowee. Private Letters on the 3d Instant do not mention one Word of any Supplies being stopp'd from going to Fort Loudoun.

Williamsburg Sept. 21. Extract of a Letter from a Gentleman at New-York, dated Sept. 14.

"Mons. Morin, who is mentioned in the Papers,

says that 12 Days before he was taken at Niagara, he was in Pittsburgh Fort, a whole Day, in Disguise, drest and painted as a Friend Indian, treated well by the English, and shown every part of the Fort; he tells us where Gen. Stanwix was at the time, and how far off Col. Byrd was with the Virginia Forces; he mentions the weakest Part of the Fort, where he intended to Attack it soon after, and says he wanted no more than four Hours to be Master of it, had he not been called to assist Niagara. I hope this will be a Caution to the Commanders of our frontier Forts, hereafter to make stricter Enquiry and Examinations, before they shew their Weakness."

NEW-YORK Sept. 24. Extract of a Letter from Albany, dated Sept. 20.

Roger's Scout which went out the 23th inst. towards St. John's, soon fell in with 300 Enemy: He has taken and scalp'd 200 of them, but am afraid Major Rogers is either killed or wounded —— We have lost 3 Men, how many wounded I cannot say. The 18th a Party was sent from Crown Point to escort in the Prisoners.

NEW-YORK Sept. 24. Camp at Crown Point, Sept. 14, 1759.

"We are still here, great preparations for going on, but not yet ready. Many People begin to think we shall not go further this Year: in short, the General only knows whether we shall or not. The News from General Wolfe does not turn out so bad as was at first imagined, his loss was very small, chiefly owing to the Impetuosity of those that made the Attack. Gen. Amherst makes do doubt is in our Hands by this Time. Some of our Men of War and Troops have passed the Town and done a great deal of Damage. It is said, that if General Wolfe cannot take the Place this Fall he will winter with his Troops on the Isle of Orleans, 3 Miles from Quebeck, if so, he is sure of the whole Country; his scouting Party brought in 500 Head of horned Cattle, and beat the Canadian Parties every where, and have killed more Indians than has been done this War. ——

The French are in the utmost Distress, which we learn from all Hands. There has been a Flag of Truce here lately, their errand was about the Prisoners, and they made no secret of the Calamities of their Country. Montcalm'd Letters were dated the 30th of August, but does not say what Place he was at. The Officer of the Flag of Truce said our Batteries from the South Bank of the River has ruined Quebeck, and almost laid it to Ashes. Col. W-------n has had no Respects of Persons in his Bombardment; several Houses where the English Prisoners used to be kindly entertain'd, are now in Ruins. The two Officers and Indians that went from hence to Quebeck, are all taken, and the Scout that went to burn the Vessels are safely returned without doing any Thing, as they were discovered before Hand.

Rogers went out Yesterday with a large scout of 250 Men. Our Fort and Improvements are going on fast. We have had a great deal of rain lately which has made the Troops (especially the Provincials) a little sickly; but it's now very fine Weather and they are recovering ——— That all the News this Place affords, for the General keeps every Thing very secret."

BOSTON Sept. 24. The Courier from Albany informs us, That the Army remained at Crown-Point when the last Advices were received from thence and 'twas reported, That Lieut. Kennedy who was going with an Indian across the Country with dispatches to General Wolfe, was taken by the Enemy six Days after he set out.

BOSTON Sept. 24. Last Monday Evening arrived here Captain Roberts and Ford, both from the River St. Lawrence: ——— They left the Isle of Orleans about ten Days after the Diana Frigate: There are Letters by them dated at Point Levee the 21st of August; but we find none that gives any Particulars of the further Operations of the British Forces against Quebeck. ——— The best Account we can gather by these Vessels is, That another large Battery besides those we have mentioned already, have been erected against the City and played upon with such Success that all the Houses within Reach of the Shells and Shot were demolished: That the Enemy made no Sallies from their Entrenchments upon that Part of our Army which were at Mount Morancy:

but they had sent a considerable Body of Troops to endeavour to surrender General Murray, who, as we formerly mentioned, had landed above the City, who had repulsed them several Times, whereby he prevented their Design of cutting off the Communication he had with the other Parts of our Forces; and that he kept his Ground good, and had been joined by some Succours.

There was a talk, that two of the largest Ships were to go up against the Town, and a general Attack be made in about a Week. ——— That the Deserters from the Enemy, which came to our Camp, reported, that the French were allowanced to half a Pound of Meat per Day; and that it was Death in their Camp to mention Gen. Amherst's Name; By which 'tis probable the French had Intelligence of the Success of our Forces to the Westward: Just as the last Schooner was coming away, Admiral Saunders received Intelligence from the Shore, that a Party of our Men which were out discovered a Number of the Enemy Indians in a Barn at some Distance from the City, which they surrendered and took 10 Prisoners.

Extract of a Letter from the River St. Lawrence dated August 15, 1759.

"I wish I could inform you by this opportunity of the taking of Quebeck. The opinion of most here, is that it will require another campaign, except Gen. Amherst should join us, but at present cannot bear any account from him. ——— in the attempt on the enemy's entrenchments, some days ago, we lost about 400 killed and wounded. ——— The French are entrench'd up to the very nose, in all places they are likely to be attack'd; and as our men of war can be no service in covering our Troops, will probably make all our attacks on their deficient. ——— I imagine we shall sail from hence by the latter end of September; and, if we do not succeed, shall destroy the Country all the way we come down, which which is full of Houses, and very plentiful of Corn, &c. ——— We have killed a great many of enemy, and have taken 500 Prisoners: I reckon we have had about 700 killed and wounded. ——— We find Quebeck a much stronger place then we Expected; however, we have often set the town on fire and in short, it is at present only a heap of ruin."

PHILADELPHIA Sept. 27. We hear from Pittsburgh that on the 7th Instant, His Excellency General Stanwix held a Council with the Indians there, who all seemed to be firmly attached to the English Interest. That there were among the Indians eighty Tawa's. That more Indians were daily expected, they coming from all Quarters to make Peace: And that our People had begun to Build a Fort at that Place, which when finished, will be very large, and exceeding strong.

On the 21st of last Month a Waggoner was killed and scalped at Pittsburgh.

OCTOBER 1759

BOSTON Oct. 1. By the Courier which came in last Saturday from Albany, we have Accounts, That the Enemy have four Vessels on Lake Champlain, and that they have appeared near Otter River: That the French have drove Pickets in the Water from both Shores near the Isle of Noix, and placed a floating Battery betwixt, in the Eastern Channel. By means hereof the Enemy are at present superior on the Lake, but by the Works carrying on, it is hoped we shall soon be an overmatch for them there. ——— That Every Thing is carried on with the utmost Vigour and Spirit, but the late heavy Rains which have fallen about the Camp have retarded our Works, that our People however, continue Healthy.

We also hear from Albany, that Major Rogers was gone out on a Scout with 250 Men, and that two Days after he set off one Captain Williams of the Regulars, who went out with Rogers's Party, by some Accident, his Gun went off and tore his Hand and Arm to such a Manner that he with 4 or 5 Men return'd back to Crown-Point, which was the last Account they had received from Rogers, when the Courier left Albany, which was last Tuesday so that we imagine they can be no truth in the Account under the New-York Head, of Rogers's having taken and scalped 200 of the Enemy.

NEW-YORK Oct. 1. Extract of a Letter from Albany September 27, 1759.

The following is part of a Letter from Crown-Point by this Days Post, "A Party of Mohawks just bring the News of the rebuilding of Fort Frontenac being destroyed, and the surrender of La Galette, wherein 'tis said were a considerable Number of English Prisoners. The Party has a Colour and Stand with them, and came thro' the Woods, Rogers had not joined them. Capt. William of the Royal, and a few more were wounded, in stepping over some Logs by the Pieces going off but slightly.

CHARLESTOWN S. CAROLINA Oct. 3. On Sunday Evening an Express arrived in 4 Days from the Cherokees, with dispatches for his Excellency, from the commanding officers at Fort Loudoun and Prince George. We hear that the Upper Cherokees have absolutely stopt the communication to Fort Loudoun, and have killed and scalped two of the soldiers of that garrison, and other white Men. The passes are strongly guarded by different parties of Indians. All the traders in the nation (except one, who is killed) are arrived at Fort Prince George. The Little Carpenter has been out with a party some time, said to be gone against the French. The Judge's Friend, another head man, always taken for a stanch friend to the English, it is said is at the bottom of the present disturbance; he has come down to Keowee and demanded the ammunition that was so prudently ordered to be stopt there, but received a flat denial.

Substance of Capt. Stuart's Letter to the People on the Frontiers, dated at Keowee, 25th of September.

"Affairs in this Nation are as bad as can be; traders are all come down, and under the protection of our forts, and a man dares lie out of it, several parties of the enemy are come down upon the back settlements and some of them are come your way. Make the best use of this Intelligence, without spreading the panic too far. Be upon your guard, collect yourselves into bodies, and stand like men. The Keowee Indians seem to be our last Friends as yet, God knows how long."

A list of the towns, &c. of the Cherokee Indians, put into our hands, makes the number of gun-men in the whole nation, not to exceed 2000; some say they are 2500, others more. The nine upper towns, where Fort Loudoun is situated, are said to be there about 500 gun-men.

We hear that the independent and provincial companies have orders to hold themselves in readiness to march at an hour's warning, and that similar orders have been sent to the militia of the back settlements.

PHILADELPHIA Oct. 4. Extract of a letter from Pittsburgh, Sept. 13, 1759.

"The Enemy, attentive to their own Security, gave us no Disturbance; they are employed in forming a large Post at Detroit. ——— The Indians sit quiet, smoking their Pipes, with an Ear turned this Way. ——— Some say, that no Indians about the Lakes will give any Disturbance, except the Chipaway. ——— Our Communication is entirely free, and our convoys came to us with the greatest Safety."

On Saturday last arrived in this City three Mohawk Indians from Pittsburgh, to which Part they were dispatched by Sir William Johnson, with the News of the Reduction of Niagara. They say that wherever they came till they got to Pittsburgh, the Western Indians were fled. They received some presents from the Government which they were well pleased.

CHARLESTOWN S. Carolina Oct. 6. Altho' Letters from the Cherokees to the 10th of Sept. afforded us great hopes, that every thing would soon be quiet again in the nation, yet we have very different and very disagreeable accounts from thence, by an express which arrived here last Sunday from Fort Loudoun and Prince George. The accounts they bring, are, that the upper Cherokees have begun to commit open acts of hostility against us, by killing and scalping 2 soldiers belonging to the garrison of Fort Loudoun, and one William Veal, a trader of Chilhowee; by attempting to drive off a stock of 70 head of cattle from Fort Loudoun, which however was prevented by Capt. Demere who had them drove into the fort, and killed and salted, but it was feared they would not keep; and by placing parties at all the passes on the communication between Fort Prince George & Loudoun, which are many and difficult. ——— That all traders had notice from some Indians who were averse to the measures taken by the nation, of the danger they were in, who thereupon left all their stores and goods, and were secretly escorted to Keowee, where they arrived the 24th ult. and remain under the protection of the fort. ——— that it was not certainly known whether the middle Cherokees were concerned; but there was no doubt that the upper had come into the scheme of the lower, and made the stopping of the ammunition at Keowee the pretence. ——— That four large parties of indians from Cullasatche and other towns were gone out (according to all appearances) but as the commanding officer at Keowee had sent notice thereof to the settlers about long-Canes, Ninety Six, Saluda, &c. 'tis hoped little mischief will be done in those parts, altho' they are much exposed. ——— the man who brought the dispatches found it difficult to avoid the enemy; one who set off before him was fired at and was wounded, but got back to the fort.

We hear that our excellent Governor is determined to go in person to the Cherokees, as well to humble our persidious enemy, and to reestablish the peace, security, and prosperity of the province, which none have ever appeared to have more sincerely at Heart; and we hear, that a great number of gentlemen will attend his Excellency as volunteers.

We have no advice of the Creeks intending to join the Cherokee: their headmen deny strongly having any concern in the present trouble: but confess themselves not ignorant of the Cherokees bad disposition.

Letters from Georgia, dated the 4th Inst. advise, that Togulki (Malachi's son) with a young Cherokee fellow the Lieutenant with 6 warriors, and Scrawney, with 4 head warriors, besides attendants, Women and Children (in all 47 indians) from the Coweta's, one of the most frenchised towns in the Creek nation where arrived within a few miles of Savannah, on a visit to Governor Ellis, in consequence of an invitation his Excellency had given them; and that it was still expected the Mortar and the Gun Merchant, with other Creeks of great note would soon follow.

BOSTON Oct. 8. By Capt. Hewes from the River St. Lawrence, we have the pleasure to hear, That Ensign Hutchin, who was sent by General Amherst to General Wolfe, arrived at the Army on the 4th of Sept. He was, by the Governor's orders, escorted by Lieut, Howard, a Serjeant and four Men from Fort Western on Kennebeck River. This Mr. Howard is the Person who the Governor sent out last Year as a Surveyor with Capt. Nichols, to reconnoitre the Road going to Chaudiere, of which he made a Survey.

The above mentioned Capt. Hewes came out from the River in Company with several other Vessels bound here; but he was latest from our Camp at Point Levee; and says, that General Wolfe's Army decamped from Mount-Morancy, and landed at Point-Levee, without the loss of one Man: ——— That as the Inhabitants of the villages would not comply with General Wolfe's proposals in his Manifesto, four large Parties were sent out to destroy the Country: two of them proceeded by Land, the other two Parties down the River by Water: That while they lay at Isle of Madame saw two large Villages on Fire: That Rangers make great Havock thro' the Country: ——— That a Party has gone in a Man of War to the Straights of Belle Isle to destroy a Village there: ——— That thro' the Enemy's Obstinacy the whole Country was almost laid waste. ——— That a general Joy was diffused thro' the Army and Fleet on the News of General Amherst's Success at Crown-Point and Niagara, &c. ——— That when Ensign Hutchins, with Mr. Howard and the others who went with him thro' the Eastern Country to General Wolfe, arrived, they were sent aboard one of the Men of War to refresh themselves, having been much tired and fatigued, and their Clothes, Skin and Flesh pretty much torn by the Shrubs and Bushes they were obliged to pass thro' ——— We also learn, That General Wolfe has erected another Battery on Point Levee, to play in the Remains of the City.

Extract of a Letter from Point Levee Sept. 1.

"Besides the Southerland, Capt. Rouse and 3 Frigates, there have been 11 other Vessels great and small, gone above the Town: ——— We have had Amherst's Regiment and one Battalion of the Royal Americans up there under the Command of General Murray; the former Regiments is returned and have destroyed a Magazine and small Village;

but have suffered considerably: Our People have got all their Cannon from Mount-Morancy Camp, and the quitting that Post this Day: It is said that the Troops are going above the Town, to destroy the Ships there. ——— Our People have been so near as to see them; but they are haul'd over a shoal Place, that we cannot come at them with our Ships, so must destroy them by Land if we can: There is a Detachment of 500 Men sailed Yesterday down the River, to destroy all they can on the South Side as low as the Isle of bee; we have destroyed all the Houses and Barns for some Miles down the River on the North Side: We have burnt and destroyed a great Part of the Town. Our People have often Skirmished with the French, but of little Purpose: The French and Indians often turn Hogs and Sheep out to the edge of the Woods that our People may be drawn into a Snare, which they sometimes are killed. ——— Several Deserters have come to us at different Times; they all agree that the French have between 14 and 16,000 Men: Some Letters have been intercepted by us giving an Account of Niagara being in our Possession: One Letter mention'd that 10 lb. of Bread sells for a Pistole; and complain of great Hardships."

Extract of a Letter from Point Levee Sept. 4.

"Our Batteries are full playing upon the City of Quebeck, and it seems to be beat to Pieces. ——— Gen. Murray hath been 45 Miles above the Town, and has destroyed a considerable Magazine and a vast Quantity of Cattle of the Enemy's and we have now Reinforcement gone above, both of Shipping and Troops, which will enable them to destroy all their Shipping and Settlements; so that upon the whole we shall have them in very miserable Circumstances, and doubt not but should the War Continue another Year, we shall make an easy Conquest. ——— Yesterday General Wolfe finished decamping on Morancy, and is now encamped on Point Levee." ———

Sept 4. Since I have finished my Letter we have News from General Amherst: And as it is said he is within a Week's March of us, it has diffused an universal Joy throughout the whole Camp: Scarce any doubting that we shall make a finishing stroke this Season."

Extract of a Letter from Quebeck-Road Sept. 6.

"General Wolfe, with the Body of the Army is gone up the River, either to bring the French to a Battle or lay waste the open Country, and make a Diversion in favor of General Amherst. There is no Word of the Fleet moving. ——— More Ships, every fair Wind pass the Town, with very little Damage: some trading Vessels follow the Army that way."

We have undoubted Accounts from the River, that Brigadier Murray with 800 Men, has destroyed a large French Magazine, about 50 Miles above Quebeck wherein was contained all the Equipage of Mons. Montcalm, Vandreuil and Levy, and besides the Powder, a publick Stores it also contained the Church-Plate, and the most valuable effects of the principal Officers and Merchants of Quebeck, and also Field Equipage for the three Regiments, without the loss of a single Man, tho' oppos'd by Mons. Levy with 4000: The Fire was kindled with silk Stockings, Waistcoats, &c. the General not allowing the Soldiers to make any Plunder. ———

Twelve hundred Men are going to burn and destroy the South Shore. ——— All the Houses, &c. are burnt between Cape Torment and Montmorancy: and expected the Isle of Orleans would fare the same Fate.

Thursday last Ensign Hutchin arrived here in Capt. Jones, in 5 Days from Halifax, accompanied with Major Stobo who some Time ago made his Escape from Quebec, where he had been a long while Prisoner, as has been mentioned in some former Paper. ——— Mr. Hutchin informs us in general. That August last, in Company with Mr. Howard and two others, was Dispatched for Gen. Wolfe, which he delivered at the Camp at Point Levee the 3d of September, being 17 Days in travelling across the Country; in their Way they saw several Scouts of the Enemy, but pass'd them undiscovered: ——— That they were near the Village Chaudiere, which he says is a fine Settlement, that they saw and heard the Enemy threshing their Grain, and that it is a very plentiful Country: ——— That they took two Men and a

Woman about half Way from Chaudiere to St. Lawrence River, by whom they got Intelligence as to the situation of our Army, and of the way to get to them: —— That they had no Provisions for four Days before they got in and were near starved, and near tired out with rubbing thro' the Brush, &c. which tore their Cloaths to pieces, but not their Flesh: —— That had it not been for the Intelligence gain'd by the Prisoners above mentioned, whom they afterwards releas'd, they should have been oblig'd to deliver themselves up to the first Party they met with: —— That the News of General Amherst's Success againt Ticonderoga and Crown-Point was receive with universal Joy throughout the Fleet and Army; and that they were taken proper care of and well Cloath'd immediately upon their arrival.

That he left Quebeck in Capt. Haynes from this Place the 8th of September, and was taken on the 30th off Point Anglois, by a French Privateer Sloop of four swivel Guns and 50 Men, who all doubled arm'd, and fired a Volley of their small Arms into Capt. Haynes, and kill'd the Man at the Helm, a young Man named Barns, belonging to Plymouth: that they had on board an English Captain, who they had before taken, and who they fired upwards of 300 Small Arms at them before they struck: that the Enemy rob'b him and the other People on board of every thing they had, not even sparing him his Commission; but that he threw overboard General Wolfe's Answer to General Amherst's Letters after he struck.

And on Friday last Ensign Hutchins set out from hence in order to join General Amherst at Crown-Point.

Extract of a Letter from Albany, dated on September 20th 1759.

"The Intelligence we receive from Crown-Point concerning Major Roger's bringing in 200 Scalps and Prisoners, proves not to be well founded, tho' 'tis said the Account was wrote by a Regular Officer at Crown-Point: However, this may be depended on as Fact, that the Major is gone out on a Scout with a large Party, which our accounts mostly fix at 500 picked Men, and we make no

Scruples of judging, that the conduct will be such as to perpetuate the Character which has been so justly given him being a Brave Man notwithstanding any Thing wrote from Crown-Point with a view to depreciate it. —— General Gage goes on very briskly in rebuilding and enlarging Fort Ontario at Oswago, and in strengthning the Lines, which extend from the River Quite to the Lake; the whole of which when compleated, will be capable of making as good a Defence as any Place in North-America. We have an armed Vessel on Lake Ontario and another to carry 20 Guns in building. The 20 Pieces of Cannon taken off the New-York Battery, and said to be intended for Crown-Point, are sent to Oswego.

"About a Week ago was brought into this Place (Albany) by a Party of Soldiers, a High German, who was a Deserter from one of the Royal American Battalions. He was employed as a Spy, by the French, and dressed and painted like an Indian, but was discovered by one of General Gage's Parties and sent here to receive a Reward justly due to his Merit, but has since made his Escape from the centry by jumping over the Breastwork of the Fort, when accompanied to ease himself, and is not since retaken. The Centry is confin'd on the Occasion.

"This German Spy had before attempted to make his Escape in the very same Manner from Fort Stanwix (in his Way down) but the Centry, one of the New-England Provincial Troops, tho' unarmed, jump'd over the Ramparts after him and overtook him in about half a Mile's running, when giving his foot a trip, and at the same Time overtaking him with his fist on the back of the Neck, it brought the fellow to the Ground, and the brave New-England man fell on and belaboured in such a manner with his fists only, that he soon brought the German to a Temper of peaceably going back to the Fort. On their way back the met with a Guard coming to assist, tho' as it turned out there was no Occasion for them. This Action was the more brave in the New-England man, for as much as the German was a very able, lusty Fellow, far beyond the other in that Case.

"Our further Advices from Oswego, are, That Lieut. Backhouse, of the Light Infantry, with a Party, had been reconnoitre Caderaque and Oswegatche, and found both Places Deserted by the Enemy; on his Return he discovered two Enemy's arm'd Vessels, it is said, in a Creek not far from Oswego, and reported the same to General Gage; upon which the General immediately sent off 280 Volunteers to attempt to take or destroy them, and just as this Account came away, a great Firing was heard, so that, at least, there has been an Engagement, but whether in our Favour or not, Time must yet discover."

Last Week several French Neutrals were put under Confinement here, being strongly suspected of holding a Correspondence with Quebec.

BOSTON Oct. 8. Extract from Crown-Point dated September 20, 1759.

"I Hereby sent you an Account of some of our present Proceedings here. ——— Crown-Point is almost an Island, composed by Lake Champlain about 11 Miles round, all clear Land and as good a Soil as I ever saw, and a great many Houses, on it, but none inhabited since the Commencement of the War. ——— The old Fort is of no Strength at all: ——— It will be a Place of Strength before we have done with it, worthy to be called Crown-point. We are making an Addition of four Forts that Place, and each of them as strong as Ticonderoga Fort is, ——— We have built a large Brig, of 22 Carriage Guns and 18 Swivels; she is 200 Tons and carries 120 Men, and it is to cruize upon Lake Champlain. ——— We have also built a Vessel which we call a Floating Castle: which mounts ten 24 Pounders, and two 13 inch Mortars; is about 300 Tons, and finish'd as strong as Wood and Iron can maker her; and contriv's so that 'tis impossible for the Enemy to board her; she row's with 40 oars on each Side, and has two large Masts, with square Sails and turning rigging; so that in short no Ship can lay along Side her. ——— Here are likewise 5 Row Gallies, which mount 18 pounders, each of them one ; the Gun is placed fore and aft and fires out the Head; they row with 14 Oars on each side carry 30 Men, and can fight and go well: The Experiment was tried this Year, on July 13th, when a Party was sent consisting of 300 of our Army, and one of these Row-Gallies along with a Party commanded by Major Campbell of the old Highlanders; when on the same Day were met by a Party of 900 French, at a Place called the Narrows, on an Island on the Lake. ------ The French on our Approach, were glad to see so small a Party of us there, not expecting such a Thing as an 18 Pound Cannon in our small Fleet, came out to receive us, and immediately kill'd 3, Rangers and 2 Indians, and wounded several more in the Boats: But to their great surprize the 18 pounder set to work; and in less than a Quarter of an Hour they were all running away, faster than they came up: In the Affair the Enemy lost three of their Battoes, and all the Hands killed or drowned. ------ This was the first Experiment try'd with a Row-Galley. ------ Major Rogers is gone out with 207 Men, towards Montreal; but is not return'd as yet; and what Success he may have, is yet unknown."

BOSTON Oct. 8. Wednesday last the Great and General Court or Assembly of the Province met at the Court-House, being the Day they were last prorogued to by Proclamation, when His Excellency the Governor was pleas'd to make the following Speech to both Houses, viz.

Gentlemen of the Council and House of Representatives,

By the very important and interesting Events with which it hath pleased God to succeed His Majesty's Arms, we see the British Empire again rising in America; and by the wise and prudent Conduct under which they still continue to act, we may hope, if we persevere to the End for which we took up Arms, to see it so established as that we may no more fear the Power or Treachery of the Enemy in Canada. ------ As I most heartily congratulate you on these Events; so I encourage you to remain steadfast in these hopes, and to act under this Spirit and Resolution in all that may be required of you for this End. ------ By General Amherst's Letters to me you will see that the immediate Service requires of you. ------ It is with great Pleasure I can acquaint you that the Parliament of Great-Britain have unable His Majesty to recompence His Colonies for their Service according as the active Vigour and strenuous Effects of the respective Provinces shall appear to merit.

Amongst the many happy Events of this Year, there are none in which the People of this province will partake, with more sincere Satisfaction, than in seeing the Royal Heir to the Protestant Succession arrived to full Age; and upon this, I do most heartily congratulate you.

The Estimate of the current Service lye before you; and I have directed the Treasurer to lay before you the State of the Supplies for these current Services, and for the Payment of the Troops in the general Service: As your own Sense of the Service, has always indured you to make suitable Provisions for these; so I am sure your Sense of the Benefit, as well as Honor, that the Province derives from the very high Credit of it's Treasury, will lead you to make Good any Fund that may require your present Consideration.

Upon my Building the Fort at Penobscot, I did, at your request, dismiss the Garrison at Brunswick, I have now directed the Dismission of the Garrison at Pemaquid; From the same Desire of saving every Thing I can to the People amidst their many heavy Burdens, I have directed the Scouting Parties at the Lodgments on the Western Frontiers to be dismissed, as that Part of the Country is now entirely cover'd by the Operations of the Army in those Parts. And I should hope as the Measures taken in the Eastern Part shall produce the Effect, I may be able to dismiss still more in that Quarter. But in the mean while you will remember that as the Enemy's Home is destroyed, they must seek their Sustanence Abroad; and that Winter is the Season in which they have made the most destructive inroads both on our Eastern and Western Frontiers from Canada.

Gentlemen of the Council and House of Representatives.

I have directed the Secretary to lay before all Papers as will require your Consideration.

The State in which insolvent Debtors find themselves after having surrended their Persons and discovered their Effects to the Creditors, upon the late Act of the Relief of Debtors and their Creditors deserve your Attention; And you may depend upon my Assistance in any Remedy which you can apply for their Relief consistent with equal Justice to all their Creditors both in England and Here; and consistent with His Majesty's declared Will in the Disallowance already made.

The Act for providing Quarters for His Majesty's Troops and Recruiting Parties within this Province, being temporary, is expired; and will, as you will observe from some of the Papers laid before you, require your Consideration.

October 3d 1759.   T. Pownall.

NEW-YORK Oct. 8. Yesterday 100 of Montgomery's Regiment of Highlanders came to Town from the Ohio, and we hear are going to the Northward to join their Regiment.

PHILADELPHIA Oct. 11. Extract of a Letter from Pittsburgh, Sept 25, 1759.

"It is now near a Month since the Army has been employed in erecting a most formidable Fortification; such a one as will, to latest Posterity, secure the British Empire on the Ohio. There is no need to enumerate the Abilities of the chief Engineer, nor the Spirit shewn by the Troops, executing this important Task; the fort will soon be a lasting Monument of both. —— Upon the General's Arrival, about 400 Indians, different Nations, came to confirm the peace with the English; particularly the Towas, and Wyandotts, who inhabit about the Fort D'Etroit; these confessed the Errors they had been led into by Perfidy of the french; shewed the deepest Contrition for their past Conduct; and promised not only to remain fast Friends to the English, but to assist us in distressing of the common Enemy, whenever we should call on them, to do it. And all the Nations that have been at Variance with the English, said they, would deliver up what Prisoners they had in their Hands to the General at a grand Meeting that is to be held in about three Weeks. And as soon as the Congress was ended, the Head of each Nation presented the Calumet of Peace to the General, and shewed every other Token of Sincerity that could be expected, which their Surrender of the Prisoners will confirm. In this, as in every Thing that can secure the lasting Peace and Happiness of these Colonies, the General is indefatigable."

BOSTON Oct. 15. As ten Men were cutting Wood at about 12 Miles from Halifax, and a Mile and a half from Fort Sackville, a Number of Indians fired upon them and kill'd 2 and wounded 2 more, the others escaped: They belong'd to Captain Bourne's Company of Provincials. A Party was sent in pursuit of the Enemy, but did not overtake them.

Extract of a Letter from a Provincial Officer dated at Fort-Frederick at the River St. John's in Nova Scotia, September 16th, 1759.

"The 5th of the Month, Col. Arburthnot, with a Command of 9 Commissioned Officers (two of which belong'd to Col. Hoar's) and 82 Men, under Officers and Privates, set out for a Place about 160 Miles from this Fort. ——— The third Day after we were out, I was ordered to advance with a Party of 26 Men, with the Ensign of our Company, (Capt. Parker's) when we were got at some Distance from the main Body, a Number of the Enemy fired upon us; and, after a Fire of about a Quarter of an Hour, the Body came up and drove the Enemy back: We took some of their Packs; but none of the Enemy. ——— I received a Wound in my Back, but no where else, tho' 2 Balls touch'd me. ——— Six Men were Wounded, all belonging to Capt. Parker's Company, except one. ——— We brought off our Dead and Wounded, and returned to Fort Frederick the 11th Instant. ——— The Wounded are all like to recover, excepting Leonard Cummings of Litchfield, who we judge to be near his End. ——— Kendal of Dunstable is Wounded: William Shelding of Reading, a Corporal is kill'd: The rest of the Dead and Wounded belong'd to Col. Clap's Regiment, except one from Newbury ——— Our Officer and Soldiers are healthy, and a good agreement still continues among us."

By a Courier from Albany, we learn that the Stores, &c. were putting on board the Vessels in Lake Champlain, and 4000 of the Troops, in Boats, were to set out for St. John's as last Thursday, under the cover of the arm'd Brig and Sloop, so that in our next we hope to give our Readers an Account of their being gone. ——— That the latest and best Accounts they had from Oswego and Niagara, were, That the Western Indians were continually coming in and suing for Peace, and that they were also bringing in great Quantities of Furrs, &c. ——— The Courier also informs' that he met Capt. Schomberg at Sheffield, last Tuesday and that he propos'd to be at Albany that Night and at Crown Point the Thursday following.

Extract of a Letter from Crown Point Sept. 28.

"The Army is chiefly in good Health, except the New-Jersey Regiment, who are very sickly, Capt. Ogden, of the said Regiment is gone with Maj. Rogers toward St. John's; he has nine of his Men with him, and commands the Provincials. Our Fort is driving on with all speed, and will be a fine one. Tuesday Night last arrived here 70 odd Head of fat Cattle, from No. 4. They are a choice Parcel, and very welcomed to the Army. No. 4 is 78 Miles from Crown Point and marked every Mile on the Road. We are in a pleasant Place but withall is of Clay and cold soil, and seems unhealthy to our People; the Regulars have the Health much better than the Provincials. As to the Animals of the Country, there are not many Deers, but abundance of Bears, and as for Fowls, there seems to be but a few of any sort. The Lake yields Fish of divers Kind and Plenty."

BOSTON Oct. 15. By His Excellency Thomas Pownall Esq; Captain-General and Governor in Chief, in and over His Majesty's Province of Massachusetts-Bay in New-England, and Vice Admiral of the same &c.

A PROCLAMATION

It having pleased Almighty God, to give the most remarkable Success to His Majesty's Arms this Year in America, more particularly in the reduction of Quebeck (the Capital of Canada) and the adjacent Country:

I have therefore thought fit, with the Advice of His majesty's Council to issue this Proclamation; appointing Thursday the Twenty-fifth Day of October Instant, to be observed as a Day of Publick Thanksgiving throughout the Province, to commemorate these distinguishing Instances of the Divine Goodness ------ Hereby recommending it to Ministers and People to unite in their respective Churches and Congregations, in rendering to Almighty God their grateful Praises for these undeserved Favours; and in presenting their humble Prayers and Supplications for His most gracious Majesty King George, the Prince of Wales, and the rest of the Royal Family; and for the Continuance of the Divine Blessing upon His Majesty's Government and upon his Arms.

Given at the Council-Chamber in Boston, the Thirteenth Day of October, 1759 in the Thirty-third Year of the Reign of our Sovereign Lord George the Second by the Grace of God, of Great Britain, France and Ireland, King, defender of our Faith &c.

By His Excellency's Command
   A. Oliver, Secr.   T. Pownall.
      God Save the King.

BOSTON Oct. 15. Quebeck Surrenders.

On Friday last arrived here the Capts. Atwood and Harvey from the River St. Lawrence, but last from Louisbourg in 8 Days, and bring the glorious News of the Reduction of the City of Quebeck. From accounts of which important Affair we refer our Readers to the following Deposition of Capt. Atwood, and Extracts of Letters from Gentlemen of undoubted Credit and Veracity.

John Atwood, of the Schooner Betsey, Testifieth and saith, That on the 13th of September he sailed from Point Orleans; that on the same Day he heard a great Firing of Cannon, and three Days after his arrival at Louisbourg, one Capt. Weston, (belonging to Plymoth) arrived there from the Army and Navy, informing, and as otherwise heard, that General Wolfe having landed on the 13th of September (first mentioned) above Quebeck, was attacked by Monsieur Montcalm, with the main Body of the French Army; that the

Action lasted but 15 Minutes only; the English sustain'd three Fires before they return'd any; that the first Fire they made, broke the French Horse and bro't on a general Confusion among them, they retir'd or rather fled, and the English pursu'd them to their Trenches, and immediately drove them out and pursu'd them to the Walls of Quebeck. ——

That General Wolfe was kill'd after forcing the Trenches: The English then retreated to proper Distance, and raised a Battery of 16 or 18 Guns against it, which being finish in 3 Days, General Townsend sent in a Message to the French demanding the Surrender of the City, which they did very soon, but upon what Terms he cannot say —— That it was said we lost 4 or 500 Men in the Action, and the French 1500 killed and taken.

Capt. Atwood further added, That Mons. Montcalm and the second in Command were killed: and General Monchton wounded in the Lungs.

Letter from His Majesty Governor Whitmore to His Excellency the Governor.

Sir,

A Vessel has this Minute arrived from the River St. Lawrence, who has brought a Letter from Capt. Bray of his Majesty's Ship Princess Amelia, as follows, dated Isle of Orleans, September 19, 1759.

"I have only Time to acquaint you that the Garrison of Quebeck capitulated Yesterday to his Britannick Majesty's Troops, and English Colours wave triumphant on the Walls; I would write you the Particulars could the Vessel wait; Montcalm is dead, and the second in command kill'd, the third wounded and taken Prisoner, the fourth Kill'd the Day of Battle, their loss said to be 1500 killed and wounded, ours 5 or 600.

"General Wolfe is killed, General Monckton is shot thro' the Lungs, but in a fair Way of doing well; Col. Carlton lost an Ear, and shot in the Head; Maj. Barry lost his Nose, the Ball in his Head; Maj. Spitall wounded; all of these are doubtful Cases: Capt. Milbanks kill'd and I hear young Prescott: We have about 40 Officers kill'd and wounded, but cannot learn their Names."

I congratulate you on this signal Success of his Majesty's Army, an am,

>Sir your most obedient, humble Servant.

Louisbourg Oct. 1, 1759.   Edw. Whitmore.

Extract of a Letter from Louisbourg, Oct. 1.

"About 5 o'Clock this Afternoon, came in a Vessel from Quebeck in 11 Days passage, and brings the Account that Quebeck is in the Hands of the English. ——— General Wolfe with about 4000 Men landed above the Town, and on the 13th ult. the Troops came out of their Trenches, it is said 19000 and engaged him in Battle: The English beat them and pursued them to the Walls of the City, kill'd wounded and took Prisoners 1500. General Wolfe was kill'd in Battle, two Musket Balls were shot into his Body, and one in his Wrist; of the English it is said 600 are among the killed, wounded and taken. ———

Montcalm was wounded in Battle and died soon after, the next taking in Command was slain upon the spot, the third in Command was badly wounded, and the fourth was killed. ——— General Monckton wounded in the Lungs, but in a fair way of recovery. After pursuing the Enemy into the City, the English cast up the Batteries against the Town, and then, sent in to the French, and informed them what Batteries they had prepared, and if they would not immediately surrender themselves and the City, they would storm the Place and put all to the Sword; upon this the French sent out a Blank Charte, and our Troops to Possession the 17th of September, ——— This is Glorious News, but the loss of brave General Wolfe is some Allay to the Joy of Victory. ——— Two Vessels arrived here last Week with Orders from Adm. Saunders to carry some of the Provincial Troops from hence to Boston, and last Night Orders came out here that some part of them should hold themselves in readiness to embark at an Hours warning but since the above News arrived, there is a stoppage till we have more particular Account from the River."

Extract of a Letter from Louisbourg, Oct. 2.

"Capt. Harvey's being detain'd gives me the agreeable Opportunity to acquaint you, that yesterday a Vessel arrived here from the River, and brings the very important Mews of the Surrender of the City of Quebeck, the best account I am able to collect is, That on the 13th Day of September, Gen. Wolfe with his Army of Prussians, attacked the French Lines, and after a very hot Dispute for the space of about 20 Minutes drove the French from their Lines, and into the City. In this furious attack we had killed and wounded about 500, among the killed is the never to be forgotten General Wolfe, who it is said led on his Troops in Person. ——— The French had killed and wounded 1500; of the killed Gen. Montcalm is one, also Mr. Levy, the second in Command. ——— General Monckton is dangerously wounded. ——— Our Troops immediately erected their Batteries, and on the 16th summoned the City to surrender. ——— The French having lost the Gog and Magog, thought them to surrender on the 17th. ——— The Terms of capitulation, we are impatient to know. ——— A Packet is hourly expected, when we expect further Particulars. This may depended on as fact, as a Number of Letters from Gentlemen in the Army mentions the same in substance with the above. ——— I heartily congratulate you on the important Event."

Extract of a Letter from the same Date.

"I Must now congratulate you on the Success of our Arms, ——— Quebeck is taken, tho' with the loss of the valiant General Wolfe; it happened on the 17th of last Month. It seems General Wolfe crossed the River with his little Army of about 4000 strong; ——— within two Hours after Montcalm attack'd him with 10000 or 12000 Men. Our brave General received his three first fires, not a Man of our offer'd to fire till they were within reach of their Bayonets, then gave their Fire, and rushed on them: We kill'd 1500 Privates, and 200 Officers on the Spot, which oblig'd the rest to run, but we followed them so close that we took 200 of them Prisoners at their Sally-Ports. We have lost about 40 Officers, 200 Men, and about 400 are wounded. ——— They say Gen. Wolfe received three shot in his Body, and one thro' his Wrist, but liv'd long enough to ask how Affairs went on, and being answered we had gained a compleat Victory, replied, I die in Peace, and so expired in a few Minutes after. Capt. Colman is mortally wounded."

NEW-YORK Oct. 15. By the Skipper of an Albany Sloop that left that Place since the Post, we are informed, that they had received an Account there from Crown-Point, of four Deserters coming in there from St. John's who informs, that General Wolfe was in Possession of Quebeck.

Yesterday 2 hundred of Montgomery's Regiment of Highlanders, came to Town from the Ohio, and we hear are going Northward to join their Regiment.

NEW-YORK Oct. 15. Extract of a Letter from Crown-Point dated October 7, 1759.

"The Men in general work very hard at this Fort and which is most pleasing, all keep their Health extremely well, considering what they suffer. ——— This Fort & will be the finest in America when finished, ——— I hope it will be finish'd this Year. ——— There are three small Forts building, one by the Grenadiers, one by the Light Infantry of the Regulars, and the other by Gage's Light Infantry. ——— These small Forts are built upon Hills that partly command the large Fort; and are now almost finish'd. ——— I don't know whether I shall be able to write to you again, as the Fate of War is precarious, and we are just ready to set off on the Expedition down Lake Champlain; having received Orders to hold ourselves in readiness at an Hour's Notice: ——— We have a large Reddoe that carries six 24 pounders, a large Sloop that carries twelve 6 pounders and two 13 inch Mortars, and four Row-Gallies, carrying each one 24 pounder and a Howt. ——— Our Battoes are all newly clean'd and fitted with Masts and Sails: which I am afraid will cause some of them to go to the bottom; especially as this Lake is not like Lake George, for the Water in it rise sometimes as high almost as in the main Ocean; and it is so wide for 80 Miles, that you cannot discern the opposite Shore from either Side. ——— We are very busy putting our Provisions,

Cannon, &c. on board. ——— The Artificers and sick are to left behind. ——— The say some provincials are to go with us; whether they will or not, I cannot tell: but the Regulars that are to go, are as follows, viz. Royal Highlanders, 435: Prideaux's, 377: Montgomery's, 540, exclusive of 600 Grenadiers, 600 Light Infantry of the Regulars; Gage's Light Infantry, of the Rangers, and some few Indians. ——— such preparations we have made for the Expedition, as you cannot conceive. ——— The Regulars, I do assure you, keep their Health past Expectation; but I can't say it is quite so well with the Provincials; I wish I could, for they are brave Men when in Health and an Honour to their King and Country. ——— You need not write to me till you hear of our return."

Last Week a Gentleman came to Town from Crown Point, and by him we learn, that Gen. Amherst went off from there on Thursday the 11th ult. with 4500 Men, and a Train of Artillery, in which were two Mortars in order to penetrate the Enemy Country by Way of Lake Champlain. ——— The British Forces on the Lake went down at the same Time; viz. a Brig mounting 18 Carriage Guns, and many Swivels; a Sloop mounting 16 Guns, and the like Number of Swivels; a large Reddoe, carrying six 24 pounders, and some small Craft, on board which were two Howitzers. ——— The Troops that went off consisted of 2500 Regulars, 1500 Light Infantry and Rangers, and 400 of the Train of Artillery, &c. ———

NEW-YORK Oct. 15. A Proclamation, issued by the Hon. James De Lancey, Esq; Lieut-Governor of New-York, recommending it to the Inhabitants to return to their Settlements along Hudson's River, above Albany, as they may now abide there in safety to their Persons, Families, and Estates, it being now effectually covered and Secured from the Ravages of the Enemy: And that as his Excellency Major General Amherst, had assured him, that the Fortress erecting at Crown Point shall be so far Finished before the Troops go into Winter Quarters, as to answer the purpose of covering and protecting that Country; has also at his desire made known, that those who shall now chuse to go and settle between Lake George and Fort Edward, will there find three several Spots of cleared Ground, capable of continuing twenty four Families, on which will be left standing for their Convenience, that Wooden Huts and Coverings of the Troops that have been posted there since the beginning of the Campaign; and also promises his Majesty's Grant thereof to any Persons who shall apply for the same, on Condition of immediate Settlement thereof, in the form of Township; with a sufficient Quantity of Wood-Land adjoining for that Purpose.

BOSTON October 19. In Council Oct. 19, 1759.

Ordered That the Select-Men of several Towns where there are any of the late French Inhabitants of Nova Scotia now residing, do within Thirty Days, return into the Secretary's Office upon Oath, perfect Lists of the Names, Ages and Circumstances of all such, and the Capacity for Labour according to their best Judgement; And that if the Select-Men of any such Town shall neglect to return Lists as aforesaid, no Account of Charges which they shall hereafter bring on Account of such French People be allowed.

And Further Ordered, That the Resolution be published in the several Boston News Papers; and that it be likewise printed separately, and Copies thereof delivered to the several Members of the General Court, sent down from Conference.

                                        A. Oliver Secr.

In the House of Representatives, October 19.
Read and Concured,   S. White Speaker.
Consented to   T. Pownall.
Copy Attest. A. Oliver.

CHARLESTOWN S. Carolina Oct. 20. A Deposition of John Reid, a person inlisted in the service of the Hon. Edmund Atkin, Esq; his Majesty's agent and superintendent of the Southern Indians, taken at Augusta the 5th Inst. says, That on Friday the 28th of Sept. last when the Hon. Mr. Atkin was giving his grand talk to the Creek Indians at Tuckabatchee town, he the said Mr. Atkin was struck on the head with a hatchet by an Indian fellow of the Cassitah town, called Tobacco eater; which blow, he the deponent, believed was designed to have killed the said Mr. Atkin, but, by a sudden turn thereof, it only wounded him on the head and arm. That the said Indian fellow was secured and tied by the other Indians. That the matter above related happened about 6 o'clock in the evening of the said Friday the 28th of September last; and as to the same night, he, this deponent, was sent off by the said Atkin, to the lower towns, to give notice of what happened, and to prevent the white people there from being alarmed by other more imperfect accounts of the said matter. That he the deponent, being so near Augusta at the lower towns, thought it necessary to come down and give the same information, to prevent the Inhabitants being alarmed by some false account of the matter.

Our other advices from Augusta, are, that one Molton, a half breed, was the fellow that seized the Tobacco eater, when he struck Mr. Atkin, and was wounded in struggling to take the Hatchet from the assassin; that the first blow Mr. Atkin received only stunned him and fell's him to the ground; when the villain made another stroke, which wounded him in the arm, and a third, which fell on Mr. Waggonfield the agent's secretary, who is said to be dangerously wounded: that all the stores of the lower towns were deserted, as soon as the traders there heard what had happened: and one of the traders. Mr. Elchiner, who packed up and took his skins with him, had not been heard of since.

CHARLESTOWN S. Carolina Oct. 20. The arrival of 55 Cherokees within a mile of town. The names of the headmen among them (17 in number) are, Ocunnastota, the great warrior; Kettagusta his brother, and Tony, another warrior, all of Chote; the Spring warrior, of Great-Telrtihi of Toquo; Motoi and old Ceasar, of Chatuga; Scoliloski, the second man of Little Tellico; Cilina-ka, the black-dog, or Hywassee; Woahatchee, of Cousachee, of the Sugar-Town; the King, the old head-warrior, Oulasta, the beloved man, Oucatah old Hop's son in law, and Yahoulah, a warrior of Estatoe; Tiftoe, the 3d man, and Oconi-ker the wolf of Keowee. ───── on Thursday they were all admitted to a conference with the Governor in the council-chamber: ——— Yesterday they had another; and they are next to receive a talk from his excellency.

BOSTON Oct. 22. The Northampton Post Rider who came to Town this Morning, informs us, that he saw three Gentlemen at Deerfield, who came from Crown-Point by the Way of No. 4. and informed him that General Amherst had cross'd the Lake and landed safe at St. John's without any Opposition, and there entrench'd.

Yesterday Morning arrived Capt. Furlong in 16 Days from Quebeck: and by a Gentleman who came Passenger we hear the following authentic Account of the Battle fought on the Plains of Abraham, near the City of Quebeck, on the 13th of Sept. last, between the Generals Wolfe an Montcalm, and also of the surrender of that City to his Britannick Majesty's Arms, viz.

General Wolfe finding that within could invite the Enemy to give him Battle while he remained at Montmorancy, retired from thence the 11th of Sept. and resolved to endeavour to effect a Landing on the Back of the Town: to make sure of this it was absolutely necessary to surprize them; he therefore prevailed on the Admiral to send up above the Town some Transports, and a large Number of Boats, all of which got safe by, notwithstanding the Enemy's constant Fire upon them from all their Batteries, which were compos'd of above 130 Pieces of Cannon, from 6 to 42 Pounders, the latter fired hot Shots. ——— Gen. Wolfe march'd his Army from Point Levy to the River Etchmin, and embark'd them on board the Transports; on the 12th he gave orders for the Army to be in readiness to land the next Morning before Day Light, under the Heights of Abraham, and accordingly he landed, and immediately attacked and routed the Enemy taking Possession of a Battery of 4 24 Pounders and one 13 inch Mortar, with but an inconsiderable Loss: We then took Post on the Plains of Abraham, wither Mons. Montcalm (on hearing that we had landed, for he did not at all expect us) hasten'd with his whole Army to give us Battle. About nine o'Clock we observed

the Enemy marching down towards us in three
Columns; at ten they formed the line of Battle,
which was at least six deep, having their Flanks
cover'd by a thick Wood on each Side, into which
they threw above 1000 Canadians & Indians, who
gall'd us much; the Regulars then advanced very
briskly up to us, and gave us their first Fire
at about 50 Yards Distance, which we did not
return, & it was Gen. Wolfe's express Orders
not to fire till they came within 20 Yards of
us: ⎯⎯⎯ They continued firing by Platoons,
advancing in a very regular Manner, till they
came close up to us, and there the Action became
general. ⎯⎯⎯ In about 15 Minutes the Enemy
gave Way on all Sides, when a terrible slaughter ensued, we pursued them to the Walls of the
Town, regardless of an excessive heavy fire from
their Batteries, and gained a complete Victory:
⎯⎯⎯ At 4 in the Afternoon Mons. Bocanville
appear'd with 1500 Foot and 200 Horse on the
great Road that leads form Montreal to Quebeck,
marching towards a Post on the Plains, occupied
by a body of our Light Infantry; and immediately noticed of which Brigadier Gen. Burton, with
the 35th and 48th Regiments, march'd to the Left
to receive him, but he no sooner perceived our
Dispositions made to engage him, that he faced
the Right about and made a most precipitate Retreat: At Ten at Night we surprized the Guards
and took Possession of their Grand Hospital
wherein we found between 12 and 1500 sick and
wounded. ⎯⎯⎯

  The Troops lay on their Arms all Night, and on
the 14th in the Morning, we secured the Bridge
of Boats they had over Charles River, and made
ourselves Masters of all their Posts that were
or might be of any Consequence, leading to the
Town; and at Night we broke Ground at 100 Yards
from the Walls, where we had every Thing preparing for erecting a Battery, in order to make
a Breach and Storm, but were prevented by their
beating a Parley, and sending out a Flag of
Truce with the Articles of Capitulation, and in
a few Hours we made Possession of the City,
where we found 250 Pieces of Cannon, a Number
of Mortars from 9 to 15 Inches, Field Pieces,

Hawitzers, Royals, &c. with a large Quantity of Artillery Stores.

The Day after the Engagement the Enemy abandoned Beauport, leaving behind the about 80 Pieces of Cannon and 3 Mortars having first set Fire to all their floating Batteries, and blown up their Magazine of Powder for supplying them and the Troops that were on that Side.

The poor Remains of the French Army with about 10,000 Canadians have retired to Jaques Quartiers, under the Command of Mons. Levy, but the Canadians are deserting him in great Numbers every Day, and coming in to surrender themselves: ———— Mons. Vaudreuil stole out of Town during the Battle and escaped. ———— The French in the Town and about us are starving for want of Provisions, for which it is reasonable to imagine the whole must shortly surrender, even at Discretion; we have sent up to Trois Riviers for 5 Frigates and 11 Sails of Transports, which arrived here last Spring from France and which the Enemy have deserted upon hearing of the surrender of the Town: ———— The Enemy lost in the Engagement, Lieut. General Montcalm, two Brigadier Generals, one Colonel, two Lieut. Colonels, and at least 1500 Officers and Men killed and taken Prisoners; amongst the Prisoners are 38 Officers: ———— On our Side was kill'd the brave and never to be forgotten Gen. Wolfe, with 9 Officers, 4 Subalterns, and 44 Privates. Wounded Brigadier General Monckton, Col. Carlton, Quarter Master General, Maj. Barry, Adj. General, and 50 other Officers, with 26 Serjeants, and 557 Rank and File: This Action is the most glorious, as the Enemy at least were 12,000 strong, besides 500 Horses; we were about 4,500 some of us did not engage.

Brigadier Murray is appointed Governor of the Town, and the whole Army left to garrison it, Brig. Gen. Burton commands in the Lower Town, with the 48th Regiment, and Detachments from the several others; Brigadier Townshend is gone Home in the Fleet to England, and Brigadier Monckton intends for the Continent.

Capt. Furlong informs, That the Garrison of Quebeck, which consisted of 4,000, were embarked aboard Transports, and lay ready to sail for England when he came away: ——— That about 8000 of the Inhabitants, Men, Women and Children, had come in to Point Levee, and taken Oath of Allegiance got Possession of their Estates, and were employed in gathering in the Harvest: ——— That Mons. Montcalm was kill'd on Horseback in the Engagement, and his Body taken and buried in the City, and not carried on board Admiral Saunders as had been reported: ——— That General Wolfe's Body was sent Home in the Leestaffe, in which also went Lieut. Col. Hale and a Packet containing the Particulars of the Conquest of that important Place.

BOSTON Oct. 22. A Letter from Albany, Dated September 30, 1759.

"A Gentleman lately from Crown-Point, whose Veracity may be depended on, gave me the following Relation which I send you: ——— About three Weeks ago a Serjeant and six Men were sent on a Scout towards St. John's; he conceal'd himself in the Bushes two or three Days near the Fort, in order to make a Prisoner, but without Success; at length he observed three Soldiers go in to swim in the Lake, close by four armed Vessels; he immediately stripp'd himself and went into swim likewise, his Party lying concealed: He swam along till he came to the three Soldiers, when he enter'd into a familiar Discourse with them in French, which the Serjeant spoke fluently; among the rest that he told them, he said, that where he enter'd to swim, there was such a prodigious Number of Fish that he could hardly get along for them: the three Soldiers extremely anxious to be shewn the Place, which the Serjeant undertook, and swam along with them to the Place where the Men lay in Ambush, when they rush'd out upon the poor Frenchmen and made them all three Prisoners, under the Muzzles of the Guns of the Enemy. When the Serjeant brought the Prisoners to General Amherst, the General was exceedingly pleased with the Affair, and told the Serjeant, he was obliged to him for catching such Fish, and that he had fish'd to a very good Purpose."

Extract of a Letter from Albany, October 15.

"Yesterday an Express arrived here from Oswego, with the agreeable News that Capt. Lawtridge had taken three Prisoners near Montreal, who declare that Quebeck was taken the 18th of September: —— That Mons. Vaudreuil is retreated and makes a stand between Quebeck and Montreal, and that it was Mons. Ramesay that surrendered the City; the above they declare to be Fact.
—— But our Armies are gone forward, both to the Westward and the Northward, and hope soon to hear all this Country to be English; its said Gen. Amherst have given the sole Command of the Troops at Oswego to William Johnson."

NEW-YORK Oct. 22. Tuesday last the General Assembly met here; and Thursday by Recommendation of his Honour our Governor, adjoined themselves till the Third Day of December next, having first Voted for the Continuance of our Forces in the Pay of the Province for some Time to come, and as an Encouragement, allowed them Waistcoats, Stockings, Shoes, &c.

BOSTON Oct. 29. A List of the Killed and the Wounded of the British Troops at the Plains of Abraham, near Quebec, the 13th of September 1759.

Killed, General Wolfe, Wounded Brig. Monckton; Col. Carlton, Quarter-Master-General; Major Barry, Adjutant-General; Capt. Smith, Aid de Camp; Brigade Major Spittal.

Amherst's Regiment.

Killed Two Privates, Wounded Lieuts. Maxwell senior and junior, Skeen and Ross, 5 Serjeants, and 52 Rank and File.

Bragg's Regiment.

Kiled, Lieut. Cooper, 3 Serjeants, and 5 Privates. Wounded Capt. Curry, Span, and Millbank; Lieuts. Evans and Ruxton; Ensign Fairfax and Edgerson; 4 Serjeants, 1 Drummer, and 89 Rank and File.

Otway's

Killed. Lieut. Mason, and 6 Privates, Wounded Capt. Mausfell and Gardner; Lieut. Gore, Allen, Marturin, and Cockburn. 1 Serjeant, and 28 Rank and File.

Webb's

Wounded 3 Privates.

KENNEDY"S

Killed, 3 Privates. Wounded Ensign Jones, 2 Serjeants, 2 Drummers, and 26 Rank and File.

Anstruther's

Killed, Ensign Tottingham, 1 Serjeant and 8 Privates, Wounded Capt. Bird; Lieuts. Kemple and Grant; Ensign Dainty, 3 Serjeants and 80 Rank and File.

Monckton's

Killed 5 Privates, Wounded Capt. Holland, Lieut. Calder, Jeffries and Shaw; Ensign Camaron, and Steel, 2 Serjeants, 1 Drummer and 80 Rank and File.

Lawrence's

Wounded 2 Privates.

Fraser's

Killed Capt. Ross, Lieuts. McNeal and McDonald, 1 Serjeant, and 14 Privates, Wounded Capts. McDonald and Frazer, Lieut, Mc. Daniel, Archibald Campbell, Alexander Campbell, John Douglas, Alexander Frazer, sen. Ensigns McKensey, Malcomb Fraser and Gregorson, 7 Serjeants and 132 Rank and File.

Whitmore's Grenadiers.

Killed. Lieut. Jones and 3 Privates, Wounded 26 Rank and File.

Hopson's Grenadiers.

Killed 1 Private.

Warburton's Grenadiers.

Wounded Capt. Cosnan; Lieut, Pinforn & Nevin.

The following is said to be the Disposition of the British Army the Day of the Engagement.

1600 under Major Scott and Capt. Gorham, ravaging the Country.

1500 encamped on the Isle of Orleans.

2000 encamped on Point Levy, under Colonel Burton.

5000 under General Wolfe, Townsend, & Mockton, 12 Miles above Quebec.

Montcalm's Army, 'tis said, consisted of above 10000 Men, and his Situation so advantageous, that he often said 100000 Veterans could not force his Trenches.

But alas for thee Montcalm, and the Troops! tho' happy for Quebec, and his Inhabitants! That not only thy Body was not Invulnerable; but also the Entrenchments not impregnable against one Twentieth Part of the Number of Troops, who were animated not by a French, but by a far more noble Spirit, viz. A British. May that Country enjoy Liberty, to which they have hitherto been Strangers.

 The French Prisoners say, that Mons. Montcalm was almost sure of success before he attacked our Troops; telling his Men, Wolfe was but a young Officer, and he would soon Chastise him. ———— Montcalm was killed on Horseback in the Engagement, and his Body taken and Buried in the City. ———— General Wolfe was shot as he was charging his Men to keep down, being squartted, till the Enemy gave three Vollies, and was mortally wounded by the Canadians; but being satisfi'd that the Enemy were fleeing before him, he quietly submitted to Death ———— A Death in such a Manner, and in such a Cause, rather to envied than Pitied! ———— It is said most of the Indians have left the French Army. ———— That the Batteries at Quebec are surprizingly strong the Walls of the Town being near 150 feet thick.

 Extract from Oswego, dated October 8, 1759.

 "This Evening about 6 o'clock, returned from a Scout of 15 Days, Capt, Lotteridge, with 14 Onondago Indians, bringing 2 Scalps and 3 Prisoners, by whom we have the following Account: That on the 18th of September, Quebec surrendered to Brigadier Townshend. The three Prisoners, on separate Examinations, unanimously declared: That two Canadian Officers came express to Monsieur La Corne, at La Galette; the first; to acquaint him, that on the 16th of September, General Wolfe had attacked Montcalm's Retrenchments in three Columns; and after a bloody Engagement had forced them: That Montcalm was killed; and the Regiment of La Sarre (who were Montcalm's Favorite) only five Men had escaped: That Wolfe and Monckton were both killed: and that Monsier De Ramsay, the Kings Lieutenant at Quebec, surrendered the Town to our Army, on the 18th of September, with 600 Prisoners. ———— That Monsieur Levey, being at Montreal when he heard of Quebec's Capitulation muster'd all the Burghers and Peasants he could and marched down with an Intent to support, and

and return to the Charge, the Remaining of Montcalm's defeated Army: But he was happily met in the Way by Col. Murray's Party, and most Handsomely drubb'd with great loss. ——— They add, that Vaudreuil and Levy, are at River Jaque Quartier, half Way betwixt Trois Riviere an Quebec; that almost all the Canadians are run away to their Farms, in order, if possible, to secure some Harvest."

Extract of a Letter from Crown-Point Oct. 16.

"This is the Thirty-fourth Day since Major Rogers went out on a Scout, and we have heard from him but once since, and 'tis said he is not expected sooner than the 24th of this Month; a Party has been sent out to meet him with Provisions at the Head of Connecticut River, where he is expected to be at a certain Day: ——— General Amherst set out the 11th Inst. with a Party of between 4 and 500 Men, in order to pay a Visit to the Enemy at Nut Island: An Officer has returned from him, by whom we learn that three French Vessels are pinn'd in Otter Creek, which its hoped are in our Possession before this Time, as its impossible for them to get out, the Wind blowing hard at North. ——— Four Captains of the Ranging Companies have been missing for a considerable Time past, and 'tis feared are all either kill'd ar taken, viz. Burbank, Tute, and the two Jacob's."

Last Thursday Afternoon the Express returned here from Crown-Point, whither he was sent from hence with the Advice of the Surrender of Quebeck: By him we learn, that he left Crown-Point the 18th Inst. in the Evening, and further informs, that Brigadier Ruggles commanding there, and that that our Men in general were hearty, and still employed in building the new Fort. ——— That just before he came away, a Whale Boat from General Amherst arrived there with an Account, that the Troops which had sail'd from thence, were arrived at the Island called the Three Brothers in Lake Champlain, about 40 Miles from Crown-Point, where they had been detained by contrary Winds; but that on the 18th Instant they proceeded forward; but where designed, the General kept in his own Breast; tho' it was

generally thought for St. John's and so on. ——
That on Tuesday Morning before Captain Loring with the armed Vessel discovered and Pursued three Enemy's Vessels, being armed Sloops, two of which the Enemy run into a Creek and scuttled them, and went off leaving the Guns on board, which our People took out from afterwards; The other Vessel was taken, and being Man'd join'd our Fleet. Thursday fell in sight of another of the Enemy's Vessels, a Schooner, which they went in pursuit of; and, 'tis said, this Schooner, and a Ship, if launch'd, were the only Vessels of Force the French have on the Lake.

We hear that Capt. Russel in a Schooner from this Place bound up to Quebec with Cattle, &c. was lately cast away near the Isle of Lebeck, in the River St. Lawrence: Vessel and Cargo lost.

Thursday last was observed as a Day of Publick Thanksgiving, when the several Churches and Congregations united in their Praises to Almighty God, for the late successes of His Majesty's Arms, more especially against Quebeck the Capital of Canada, agreeable to his Excellency's Proclamation issued on the 13th Instant.

Saturday last two Deserters from St. John's taken up near No. 4. one of them named Thomas Shiennit, and was a Serjeant in the Battalion of Bern, which was stationed at Quebeck, but himself with a Detachment of said Battalion was order'd some Time ago to St. John's.

The other is named John Istor, and says he is a Native of Genoas, and a Protestant, and came over to Canada about 4 Years and a half ago with a new raised Company in which he was a Serjeant: They report, they left St. John's the 22d of September at which Place there was 2500 Men, who were working upon an Entrenchment there, under the Command of Mons. Borklamare: ——
That at about 6 Leagues Distance from St. John's the French had an advanced Post upon the Meadows of Boileau, and Nut Island, guarded by about 1000 Men: —— That they had but about 40 Pieces of Cannon in all, from 6 to 12 and 18 Pounders, at St. John's: —— That they had 7 Barks upon the Lake mounting from 6 to 8 Guns: ——

Thursday had been very well supply'd with Provisions and that the 3500 Men at the afore said Posts 900 were Regulars, the rest Canadians, and that at Montreal there were no Troops at all.

Istor says, That he was at General Braddock's Fight, and at that wherein Major Grant was defeated, and has been all along upon the Ohio, and the Parts adjacent, and had arrived at St. John's but 7 Days before he deserted.

Shiennit also says, That he was at Fort DuQuesne at the Time when General Forbes came near it, on which they blew up the Fort, and sent down the Cannon, 14 in Number, six 6 Pounders to Orleans, and the other eight to Fort Cherokee; most of the latter were 4 Pounders: This is an Indian Fort, and has Barracks for 40 or 50 Men, is made of Logs and has four Battalions: ——— Shiennit was also at the action before the Fort at Niagara and escaped after they retreated to Presque Isle, from thence the People belonging to the several Parts of Louisiana dispers'd to their respective Posts: ——— That he was in Company with 350 others came across Lake Erie and Huron, cross'd the Carrying Place for 30 Miles, and came into the River St. Lawrence opposite to La Galette, by the Little River Miamie, and arrived at Montreal about the beginning of September: ——— That he was at Montreal 3 Days, and that there were no Troops at that Place, no Works made, nor Guns mounted; there was some Guns, but no Carriages.

BOSTON Oct. 29. Monday last being the anniversary of His Majesty's Coronation Day, the same was observed by the firing of Guns at Castle William, and the Batteries at Noon, as usual on this Occasion; and on board the Diana at One o'Clock: His Excellency the Governor's Troops of Horse Guards under the Command of the Honourable Colonel Royall were muster'd upon the Occasion, and went thro' Exercises, &c. upon the Common to the acceptance of his Excellency of which he stood to Review them; They then escorted his Excellency to the Royal Exchange Tavern in King Street, where was a Handsome Diner provided by the Officers of the Guards for the

Entertainment of his Excellency the Governor, His Honour the Lieutenant Governor, a Number of of Civil and Military Officers, and other Gentlemen of Distinction, which shared in Drinking his Majesty's, the Royal Family, Mr. Pitt, the brave Officers who were at the Reduction of Quebeck, and other Loyal Toasts.

NEW-YORK Oct. 29. Last Saturday Evening, in firing the Minute Guns at the Funeral of Mr. Marston, late City Merchant, A Man on board a Sloop, in loading one of them, was blown to pieces; occasioned it is tho't by the Gun not being well spong'd.

Yesterday arrived here a Schooner from South Carolina in 16 Days, She met with very bad Weather in her Passage especially on the Coast, and on Saturday Afternoon as she lay at the Hook, in firing a three Pounder for a Pilot, the Gun burst, and terribly wounded two of the Men and the Captain slightly, before doing considerable Damage to the Vessel.

NOVEMBER 1759

CHARLESTOWN S. Carolina Nov. 1. The last Letters from Fort Loudoun are dated the 3d ult. had advice, that a party of Cherokee Indians had stopped the path over the four and twenty mountains, and likewise that of Telliquo, that the women that use to come to the fort, were forbid to go thither again on pain of death, and that they were continually scouts, in search of white People's tracts: that Capt. Demere, however, at last found an opportunity to send for Ocunnastota with 2 or 3 other headmen to the fort, who accordingly came: when the great warrior came, he asked him, why the Cherokees killed the white People, and had so suddenly declared war? told them, he was better provided with ammunition and provisions than they imagined; and assured them, that the Carolina, Virginia and other Provinces, would not suffer their insults and cruelties to go unpunished: Ocunnastota answered, that the town of Chote, Tenesse, Toquo, and Timothy, were not guilty of any of the outrages complained of, that they were committed by young people who would give ear to no admonitions, and persuaded themselves that the English designed to destroy them all, and make slaves of their wives and children; the French having told them, "that when the English had once erected a fort in their nation and made some settlements they would with hold ammunition from them, and extirpate all the men;" and those Indians had lately great offers from the french fort, for Englishmen's scalps, and promises of large supplies of ammunition, &c. That Captain Demere assured him we had no such design; but had disposition of the lower nation; and offer'd to convince him of the contrary, whenever he wound fix a time and go down to Koenee: That upon this the great warrior came down to fort Prince George, and too with him by the way of several other headmen. ⸺ When he arrived there, he applied for ammunition and was refused it; upon which he resolved (being first assur'd that he should come and return in safety) to join the deputies he found coming to the governor from the lower towns. Since they left Keowee, we are informed that nothing has happened amiss in the lower nation, and that the Indians are likely to remain quiet while this gang is in power.

   Charleston S. Carolina Nov. 1. On Monday the 21st ult. ended the conference with the Cherokees. On the first day of these conferences, Thursday the 18th, Ocunnastota, the Great Warrior of Chote, upon the Indians being acquainted, that the Governor was ready to hear what they had to say, told his Excellency, "That They were not come to give a talk or make proposals to him; that hearing he had sent a letter to the nation they expected to receive a talk from him." The Governor ordered the interpreters to acquaint them, "That it was true, he had sent a letter to their nation, upon receiving the copy of a talk sent by John Vann to Governor Ellis of Georgia, said to be delivered by Woahatchee in the name of the upper, middle and lower towns 'desiring the said Governor of Georgia to interpose his good officers in accommodating matters between the Cherokees and the government, and declaring their intentions to be peaceable,' ⸺ not to invite them hither, but to inform them that he was ready to hear what they had to say." The great warrior upon this told his excellency, "That he was then unprepared; that his hands were bare, and he brought no tokens; but that he would give a talk next day." The Governor agreed to receive it. Friday the 19th, the indians met the governor again, in the council-chamber. The great warrior and three others spoke. The substance of their talk, was, "That they were sent by Old Hop to make the path straight to brighten the chain, and to accommodate differences: they confessed, that outrages had been committed by their nation, but (as usual) alledged, that their young men were the authors, and pretended, that they had been provoked to commit them, by the irregularities of some of the white people at the fort: then they desired, that all that was past might be now forgot; but did not offer skins at the governor's feet, and offered strings of white beads, which his excellency permitted them to lay dawn, but would not receive. Then they had finished their talk, the governor ordered them to be acquainted, that he would consider it, and give them notice to attend, in the council-chamber: when there, the governor told them, "That altho' the great warrior and the other indians of the upper nation then present, pretended to be deputed to come to him, he knew they were not, and that they only came in consequence of their being refused ammunition at Keowee; that he had advices then in his hand, received the night before, that since they came away, a large party was gone out from Settico, one of the upper towns, to fall on the settlements on Broad-River; and that a soldier from fort Prince-George, who was sent out to drive some cattle had been stopp'd by the indians of Conasatchee, who took his horse by the bridle, led into the middle of the town, pulled his hat off his head, and cut it to pieces with a tomahawk, and bid him go and say, it was war; that therefore they had no right to be protected, according to the talk he had sent up to their nation; that altho' those of the lowest nation were deputed, yet, as there had been a party from thence afterwards; who fired at an express coming down to him, they also were not entitled to protection, nevertheless, as they said they should be so. His excellency then enumerated the other outrages and murders the people of their nation had committed; acquainting them, 'that the people of this province, determined no longer to bear their insults, were in arms; that he himself was going, with a great many of his warriors, to their nation, to demand satisfaction; that it, when he arrives there, the satisfaction he should ask, was given, it would be peace, the path would be open again, and the trade restor'd; but if they refuse to give it, he would take it.' The governor concluded by telling them, 'that they should return home with him and his warriors, and they should be safe, only by going with them, and advising them not to expose themselves by straggling out of the direct road, where he would not answer for their safty.'

CHARLESTOWN S. Carolina Nov. 1. We can with confidence assure our readers that 1500 men, draughted for the militia of this province, are to be employed on an expedition to procure satisfaction for the repeated outrages committed on, and insults offered to, his Majesty's subjects, by the perfidious Cherokees, the general assembly having resolved to provide pay for the people that shall be employed, and other necessaries for that service; and we have reason to believe, from the steps taken previous to the Meeting of our representatives, as well as from some advices, received since, that the most part, if not the whole, of that force, is actually assembled, and repairing to the general rondezvous at the Congarees. The Governor will command this army in person, and will be accompanied by the captain of the artillery company with several others of that useful corps, and many young gentlemen of fortune, as volunteers.

On Wednesday last arrived an express from Augusta, with letters from the Hon. Edmond Atkin, esq; disparched thither by an Indian called Rogguery, dated at Tuckabatchee's the 2d inst. ¿he letters, we are, told barely mention the affair that befel that gentleman, as it relates in Reid's affidavit; and neither mentions what satisfaction, nor whether any, had been offered to be given for the outrage committed upon his Majesty's agent; neither is any mention made about Waggonfield his secretary, being wounded, nor any more particulars of affairs in the Chactaw nation than we have already given.

Letters from Augusta on the 15th, gives us no information in those particulars where Mr. Atkin has left us in the dark. Some apprehend dangerous consequences to follow the attempt on that gentleman's life; others treat it as an effect of a private pique the Tobacco-Eater had against him.

By express which arrived here yesterday from North Carolina, we have advice, that Governor Dodd has sent orders for making draughts from all the northern regiments of militia in his province to act against the Cherokees if necessary; and that he was sending ammunition to those regiments, and taking every other measure proper in the present juncture.

CHARLESTOWN S. Carolina Nov. 1. On Friday the 26th ult. at 10 o'Clock his Excellency the Governor as commander and chief of the Army, set out from his house, on an expedition to repel the invasion of and humble the Cherokees, accompanied by the hon. brigadier general Bull and Col. Howarth, and attended by several of the officers appointed for the expedition, and makes the best of his way to the general rondeznous at the Congerees, where he expects to find at least 1000 of the militia ready to proceed with him to the Cherokees.

According to calculations made by several gentlemen, it is computed, that the expedition to the Cherokees cannot cost this province less than 20,000 pounds sterling, or 140,000 pounds currency.

BOSTON Nov. 5. By Courier from Albany, who came in last Saturday, we learn, that General Amherst, with the Troops that set off from Crown-Point on the 11th ult, for St. John's after they had proceeded down the Lake, were obliged by Reason of the Severity of the Weather, to encamp for 5 Days on a small Island there: ——— And that the General finding the Weather beginning to grow still worse, and the Men so chill'd and Frost bitten, as to render some of them unfit for Duty tho't most prudent to return back to Crown-Point, where he arrived the 21st ult.

We also learn, that there has been no Account received at Crown-Point from Major Rogers since he set out from thence, altho' he has been gone so long a Time, with a Party of 300 Men: so that the Report published in last thursday's Paper said to come by the Way of No. 4 on his destroying the Town of St. Francois between Quebec and

Montreal, and his losing 100 Men in the Attempt is without foundation.

Extract of a Letter from Crown-Point Oct. 22. "Our Army under General Amherst returnned here Yesterday in the Battoes, the high contrary Winds, and in general bad Weather they had all the Time they were absent, which was likely to continue, prevented their proceeding down the Lake more than 60 Miles: Our Navy (which the General left behind on the lake) however took one of the French Sloops, and chased two others into a Cove, from whence they could not get out, when the Frenchmen sunk them both, and fled" but our Sailors are endeavouring to get them up: We have had three touches of Frost here; ant it has been stormy a whole Week from the N. E. Our Forts, Bloch-Houses and Roads, are surprizing when we consider the time they were done in."

BOSTON Nov. 9. His Excellency General Amherst having made Provisions for the Subsistence of the Men raised by the Government, and under his Command the last Campaign, at the Westward, upon their Return Home; All Taverners and others are hereby notified that they are not to supply any of the said Men on Account of the Government, as to Account for such Supplies will be allowed except in Case Sickness only.

A. Oliver, Secr.

WILLIAMSBURG Nov. 9. We are informed from Carr's Creek, in Augusta county, that on the 10th of last month, a party of the Indians with two Frenchmen, appeared in the neighbourhood, they murdered with shocking barbarity, ten persons, men, women and children, took 11 Prisoners, burnt six farms, killed the cattle, and carried off all the horses, loaded with the goods of the people killed or captivated. Capt. Christian, with a party of militia, being joined by an equal number of the frontier battalion from Fort Dunlop, under the command of Captain Fleming, went in pursuit of the enemy over the Alleghany mountains, and after several days march at last came up with them. It was intended to attack them in the night, but a musket being fired accidentally, which gave the enemy an oppertunity to escape. The party were, however, fortunate in recovering all the prisoners, horses and goods, and many things belonging to the Indians, which they had left in the flight. The French orders were found, dated at Scioto, by which it is believed the Indians were Shawanese. The loss sustained by the people on Carr's Creek is reckoned to be upward of 200 pounds.

CHARLESTOWN S. Carolina Nov. 10. The Man-Killer of Stickowee (otherwise called the Round-O) with his Indians, viz. 43 men, 5 women, and a child met his Excellency at a place called Boggy-Creek, where his Excellency received him in a very kind manner, took him by the hand and gave him a friendly talk; the Governor received one from him in the same stile. The Man-Killer assured his Excellency, "that the 15 Towns under him, were, to a man, friends to the English; that they had always shewn themselves so, and had never been concerned in any of the Murders and outrages with which other towns of were charged:" and added, "That he was willing to join the Governor in any thing he thought proper, for obtaining the satisfaction that his Excellency required."

BOSTON Nov. 12. Extract of a Letter from Col. Bagley to his Excellency the Governor, dated Louisbourg, Oct. 27, 1759.

"We have good Allowance of every specie, both in Quantity and Quality; good Quarters and a supply of fuel: The Governor is willing to do every Thing for us to make us comfortable: A good Harmony subsists among the Troops of every Rank. ——— Would beg leave to assure your Excellency, that Governor Whitmore, Lord Rollo, and the Gentlemen in the Garrison, treat us with every Respect; no Corps in the Garrison is more taken Notice of, nor better treated."

Since our last arrived here a number of Topsail Vessels chiefly belonging to this Place, having been employed as Transports up the River St. Lawrence. They left Quebec the 8th of October with a Number of other Vessels that had been employed in the same service, bound for Europe and several of the Ports on the Continent, under Convoy of the Scarborough, Capt. Stott, and in several of these Vessels are a Detachment of the Train of Artillery, which with Capt. McCloud's Company of the Train are to be stationed here this Winter: also about 140 Provincial Troops and Rangers: a Number of the Officers who were wounded in the Siege of Quebec are also come in these Vessels: In one of the Ships are the Seamen raised by the Province in the Spring, to serve on board his Majesty's Ships, who have been discharged agreeable to Adm. Saunder's Engagement: ——— The Louisbourg grenadiers were sent to that Place under convoy of the Pocupine Sloop of War, which after seeing them safe into Post proceeded home. ———

And on Saturday last arrived here the Fanny's Revenge, Capt. Blake, who left Quebec 10 Days after the above Vessels, in Company with Admiral Saunders, with General Townshend, as also all the other Men of War that were there, except one 70 Gun Ship and 4 Cats, who were to remain there till the 25th of October and two Frigates and a Sloop in one which Gen. Monckton, who had almost recovered his Wound, intended for New-York, the other two were to remain there for the Winter: That 5 Ships of the Line, under Commodore Lord Colville were to be stationed at Halifax, the others were to proceed to England: ——— That Gen. Murray commanded at Quebec and that all the regular effective Troops, which would amount to about 5500 Men, were to garrison that Place during the Winter: ——— That the Inhabitants of the Villages were daily bringing in their Arms, surrendering themselves, and taking the Oaths of Neutrality: That a great Number were also coming in from Mons. Boccanville's Encampment at Jaques Quartiers, about 3 Leagues above the City, which first consisted of 6000 Canadians, and 900 Regulars; but were now greatly reduced by their breaking off in such large Bodies, and it was tho't that all that broken army must very soon be dispersed or submit for want of necessities. ——— That provisions especially Bread, was very scarce among the Canadians; and the Inhabitants, being so poor, having little else than what they call their Paper Money to purchase Necessities of the English: ———

That General Vaudreuil had gone after Mons. Levy, to Montreal but with what Force is uncertain; —— That the French Frigates and Transports which were at a considerable Distance above the City, were not yet removed, nor were they like to be soon, the Enemy haven taken an Opportunity when the Freshets were high, to haul them over the Shoals where it is not possible for our Vessels to get at them. —— The British Ships before they left Quebec, took out all the Provisions, Powder, &c. which they could spare for the Garrison: And that the Number of French Soldiers and Marines shipp'd off from thence amounted about 900. ——

BOSTON Nov. 12. Saturday last his Excellency the Governor prorogued the Great and General Court to the 5th of December next. The Court being apprehensive that the detention of his Majesty's Troops at Quebec to garrison that conquest, would prevent those 2500 of our Provincial Troops which are Garrisoned at Louisbourg, and Nova Scotia, being relieved this Fall, had made no Provisions in their late Session for the Men's more comfortable Subsistence there, and for the Relief of such of the Families as might be in Necessitous Circumstances at home, and continued the Establishment for the Men's Wages during their stay there, They likewise lengthened out the Enlistment for the Ship King George now out on a Cruize.

Saturday Evening last arrived here the arm'd Ship Europa, in 12 Days from Louisbourg, having on board 150 of our Provincial Troops, draughted out of Col. Bagley's Regiment which has been station'd there; the remainder it's said are to remain in Garrison at that Place this Winter.

By the last Mail from Albany, which came in Yesterday, we learn, that the first Battalion of Highlanders were to Garrison Fort Edward during the Winter: That Col. Grant was to Command the Rivers there. That there was a Report at Springfield, that Major Rogers with his Party were return'd to NO. 4. after having destroy'd St. Francois, and killing near 500 Indians, Men Women and Children, with little or no loss to himself, but the particulars are not yet

Received.

We hear from Worcester, that on the 9th Inst. Capt. Paine, of Col. Ruggle's first Battalion, died there of Small-Pox, which he took at Albany, in his return from Crown-Point: And we hear that the Small-Pox is very brief in Albany.

NEW-YORK Nov. 12. Our last advices from Albany are, That most of the Provincials belonging to New-York were to be discharged on the 10th of this Month; that Lieut. Col. Ayres was to command at Niagara during the Winter, with the 44th Regiment: —— That Col. Haldiman with the 4th Battalion of Royal Americans, to command at Oswego. —— That the Fort at Crown-Point was not quite finished, but was in a sufficient Posture to make a great defence, should the French attempt to attack this Winter: and that General Amherst was building a Number of Barracks round about it. —— That the 55th Regiment (late Prideaux) now under the command of Col. Robinson, was to be quartered this Winter in New-Jersey: The Scotch Regiment (Light Infantry) commanded by Brig. Gen. Gage, to be quarter'd between New-York and Albany, along the North River. —— The 2d Battalion of the first Regiment of Foot (Royal Scotch, or Pontus Pilate's Guards) commanded by Lieut. Gen. St. Clair to be quartered in the City of New-York: and the 42d Regiment (Royal Highlanders) commanded by Lord John Murray on Long Island.

Extract of a Letter from Crown-Point Oct. 29.

"Capt. Loring is just arrived from his Cruize, having been down Lake Champlain as far as the Isle aux Noix, or Nut Island, with the Brig Duke of Cumberland, and the Sloop Boscawen. The Day after he sailed from this Place he fell in with a Topsail Schooner, which he gave Chase to, but the Frenchman not inclined to fight ran into shoal Water, where the Brig and Sloop could not follow him, and by this Means escaped: In the Afternoon of the same Day he gave Chase to three Sloops, which were discovered about 6 Leagues to Windward, but it growing calm, and Night coming on, the Sloops got into a Bay, and the French finding that they could not pass our Vessels in the night, and get down to St. John's, sunk two of their Sloops, and run the other ashore; this Capt. Loring got off, and he has brought her with him. Thus Mons. Delabtat's Squadron is entirely ruined."

BOSTON Nov. 14. The Co-partnership between Samuel Blodget and William Tatler, in supplying the Officers and Soldiers at Crown-Point, being disolved, and the Company's Accounts in the Hands of Samuel Blodget: --- These are to desire all Officers and others who are still indebted to them to make speedy Payments to said Mr. Blodget living a few Doors to the Northward of Mr. Church's Vendue, and next House to the late Decon Simpson's in Boston.

PHILADELPHIA Nov. 15. From Pittsburgh our advices, of the 28th of October, are as follows, viz. "That every Thing goes extremely well there: fine Weather; Plenty of Provisions, and the Works growing to Admiration, under the Direction of the indefatigable General. That on the 27th ult. the Treaty with the Indians were concluded, to the mutual Satisfaction of all Parties concerned: That they have engaged formally to deliver up the Prisoners; and one Nation alone gave the General 41 Sticks, being the Number of their Captives; and they promise that except those that may die, we shall see them all."

CHARLESTOWN South Carolina Nov. 17. Sunday last several Volunteers set out from hence, for the Army on the March to the Cherokee Country under Governor Littleton. Yesterday and to-Day many more have gone to join the said Army. Capt. Stuart, with his Detachment, arrived safe at Fort Loudon the 27th ult.

Our Letters from Gentlemen in the Army from the 5th to the 13th instant contains the following advices, viz. November 5th in the Night, two of Round O. otherwise called the Mankiller or Otacitte's Gang of Indians had disappeared, tho' they had been very kindly treated. ——— Nov. 6th two more of the same Gang went off privately; upon which the Governor ordered a Captain's Guard over the rest. The same Day the Express that arrived here the 2d from Virginia reached the Camp, but nothing had transpired of the contents of his Dispatches; 'twas said some

Troops were ordered to hold themselves in readiness to march from that Colony. ——— November 7th The Governor went to Otacitte's Camp, which was placed in the Middle of the Army's Encampment, took him by the Hand, & gave a friendly Talk; His Excellency told him, ——— "That he was glad to see them, hoped they had every Thing they wanted, as he had ordered they should; that his good will and Intentions towards them were the same now as before, and they should be kindly and well treated; that the Reason for his sending for them to encamp near him, was, that they might be at Hand whenever they had any Thing to say to let him know it, that he had placed a Guard round the Camp to prevent the common white People being troublesome to them; and that he was sorry to find that 4 of their People had gone off, as they might go to the Nation, misrepresent Matters, and make them believe that his and Ocunnastota's Parties were ill treated or in Danger."

Otacitte expressed much concern at the Misconduct of the 4 Indians who had gone off, promised to take Care that no more should go in the same Manner; and was pleased with the Talk His Excellency gave him; as a Proof of it, he proposed to send the Raven (one of the People and a Runner) with a good Talk to the middle Towns. This Day the Independents, Provincials, Artillery and about 70 Waggons arrived at the Congarees, with Ocunnastota's Gang of Cherokees: The rest of the Waggons had got up before: The two Parties of Indians gave a great shout at seeing one another, and seemed overjoyed: They were however encamped separately and a Captain's Guard placed over the Party, as had been over the other. The same Night the Raven with Mr. Alliott a Trader, were sent off with Otacitte' Talk, telling them "That he was well and plentifully supplied with every Thing he wanted for himself and those that were with him; and that he was coming to them Hand in Hand with his Elder Brother," The other with the Governor's acquainting them, "That he was very well knew they had been always steady in their Attachment to the English, and that he should make a proper

Distinction between them & those of their Countrymen who had spilt the blood of white People."
—— November 8th Col. Chevelette's Battalion marched for Saluda old Town: The rest of the Army could not proceed for want of a sufficient Number of Carriages for their Provisions. Nov. 9th a Company of 10 Men and Officers from Rock River, joined the Army: One of the Men reported, that 11 Families had been killed and scalped lately on the Frontiers of Virginia, by a Party of Indians supposed to be from Settoco. The same Day two Catawba's arrived in the Camp from Saluda old Town, with Advices. That 10 Chickesaw Head-Warriors were arrived there, and wanted to join the Army and receive the Governor's Commands. November 10, being his Majesty's Birthday, was celebrated by Order of the Governor; and the Day and Evening was spent in a manner suitable to the joyful Occasion. —— Nov. 11th Being Sunday, Divine Service was performed in the Camp, and attended with great Decency. This Day the Governor received by Express a very friendly Talk from the Little Carpenter, which his Excellency returned in the same Stile. —— Nov. 12th, Orders were given for the whole Army to be ready to decamp the next Morning at Day Light. —— Nov. 13th by 8 o'Clock all the Tents were struck, and by Ten the Army were in full March for Ninety-six, whence we expect to hear from them next.

Said Letters further acquaint us, that a peculiar Harmony prevails throughout the Army, and no Distinction was made between the Regulars and the Provincials and Militia; that thet continued to good Health, and high Spirits; that his Excellency constantly reviewed them twice a Day, was indefatigable assiduous in planning & prosecuting every Measure that could contribute to this Expedition on to a speedy and happy Conclusion; and that no General was ever more universally esteemed, nor more deservedly.

BOSTON Nov. 19. The Transports and Store Ships bound here from Quebec are now all arrived; In them came Col. Williamson, Commander of his Majesty's Royal Train of Artillery in North-America: Col. Scot. who commanded the Rangers,

&c. with the Ranging Companies, and 300 of additional raised by the Province, and sent up the River St. Lawrence, are returned, except about 100 Rangers, left under the Command of Captain Hazzen.

About 50 of the Provincial Troops (invalids) are also returned from Halifax: The Remainder of the several Regiments there, and the other parts of Nova Scotia are also to Winter there at their respective Posts.

BOSTON Nov. 19. We have just received the particulars of Major Rogers and his Party (consisting of 142 Men) destroying the Indian Town of St. Francis, and taken from the Major's own Mouth; but for want of Time and Room must defer publishing the whole till next Week, and shall only say, that the Night they arrived, the Indians were at a Great Dance: The Major entered the Town in the Evening alone, went thro' it, and was spoke to several Times by the Indians, but being dress'd in their Manner passed undiscovered: ——— The whole Party enter'd the Town about an Hour before Sunrise, when the Indians were all asleep, and killed great Numbers of them in their Beds, with their Swords, Bayonets, Tonahawks, &c. and afterward set fire to the Town, which was soon rendered to Ashes, together with great Numbers of the Enemy, as it was impossible for them to escape. Rogers's Men surrounding the whole Town. Some of the Indians took to the Water, but were there destroyed by a Party fix'd for that Purpose: ——— By the best Comparative they kill'd and burnt around 2 or 300 of the Enemy. ——— Major Rogers lost but one Man, a Stockbridge Indian; and had about six more slightly wounded; they brought off 9 Prisoners and retook 3 English Captures: The Town had Store of Riches, one Man found and brought off 170 Guineas, and another a Silver Image of 10 lb. Sterl. When our People enter'd the Town they saw between 6 or 700 English Scalps, moving in the Wind, which were fix'd on Poles, and fastened to the top of their Houses.

BOSTON Nov. 19. Extract of a Letter from South Carolina Oct. 1, 1959.

"The Indian War suspected by many, and regarded

by a few as chimerical, has at last proved an affair of the most serious consequence; unhappily I am too well warranted to assure you that the whole frontier Inhabitants between Savannah and Saludy Rivers, which indeed makes the best frontier of this Province, have left their Habitations and betaken themselves to Forts of their own construction, containing 30 or 40 men together: ——— This imminent Danger has broke up some Settlements of very great value, the Planters and Farmers having left their Plantations, and some of them their most valuable effects, in the Incursions and Ravages of the Barbarians."

Oct. 11th. Our News is more and more alarming: an Express arrived here Yesterday with an account that the Hon. Mr. Atkin, superintendent for Indian Affairs, was very near being killed in a full Assembly of the Creek Nation, receiving a stroke from one of them with a Tomahawk, which cut him down the side of his Face and Shoulder."

NEW-YORK Nov. 19. Saturday night arrived from Quebec, his Majesty's ship Fowey of 24 Guns. ——— On board her came passengers, brigadier general Monckton, major Spittal, and several other gentlemen of the Army: and Yesterday morning the General was saluted by a Discharge of 21 pieces of cannon from Fort George, and by all his Majesty's ships in the harbour; the Fowey had but 16 passengers from the Isle of Orleans.

PHILADELPHIA Nov. 22. All our late Letters from Georgia (except one) are full of Commendations of Governor Ellis's Conduct with regard to Indian Affairs in general but more particularly the Creeks that lately made his excellency a Visit at Savannah; they seem to think that he could offer almost any purpose with them. Although they came to Savannah in no very Promising Temper, they departed the 18th ult. in the best Humour imaginable, and made perfectly happy by the Distribution of considerable Presents to every individual according to his Rank. At the Conference they acknowledged that they have been privy to, and disposed to act a Part in the Cherokee Designs, rejoiced that they did not, and had been intended to make Mr. Ellis a Visit, promised to exert themselves in bringing their Nation to a good Humour, and in hindering their Countrymen form imposing, should there be a general Breach between the English and the Cherokees; they opened, without referto, all the Causes of their Discontent; complained in very bitter Terms of some Person's Conduct; earnestly wished his Majesty's Agent among them might be recalled; and expressed their Fears lest some Mischief should befal him. The outrage commited on Mr. Atkin was afterwards mentioned to them, in an under and deliberate Manner, which notwithstanding alarmed them very much; he agree, on having his Life was not in Danger, they seemed composed, but repeated their interest that he might be recalled. At parting with the Governor, warm professions passed on both sides.

PHILADELPHIA Nov. 22. We hear from Reading, that one Ebenezer Holbort, a Lad about 17 Years old, who was taken Captive by the Indians in the Winter of 1755, lately made his Escape from an Indian Town in Lake Erie, and came there about ten Days ago. He has learned the Delaware Language perfectly. The Indians, he says were exceedingly alarmed upon hearing that Sir William Johnson had beat the French and Indian Army, from Venango, before Niagara.

PHILADELPHIA Nov. 22. On Saturday last the Hon. James Hamilton, Esq; our governor, arrived here from New-York, He was met on the road and accompanied to town by a great number of the principal inhabitants of the place, when his commission was read at the court house, in the presence of a vast concourse of people, And yesterday his honour set out for New-Castle.

CHARLESTOWN SOUTH CAROLINA Nov. 23. Our advices from the army by express arrived on Saturday last, are that the runaway Cherokees, who left our Camp at the Congarees, have alarmed the whole Cherokee nation, so that they have sent runners to the different parts with painted tomahawks for immediate assistance, in particular for the Creeks; and that the prevailing sentiments of their councils, recommend to meet our army with their whole collected force 12 miles on this side of Keowee, at a place called Twelve-mile River, and there give battle.

Extract of a letter Dated Camp at Congarees, Novenber 25, 1759.

"The army is now about 1000 strong, including part of Col. Chevillette's regiment now at Saluda, which will join us there. We expect the first division that marched from Charlestown in three days, our number will then be about 1300; this force we look upon as no wise sufficient to give us that respectable figure we would chuse to appear in to the savages, orders are therefore sent out to draught 135 men from each of the four lower counties regiments, to be under the command of Major Benjamin Singletan, who has orders to follow us to Ninety six, where it is believed we will halt till this reinforcement comes up. The gentlemen here well wishers and friends to their country, are sensibly affected by these delays, they wish too, that things could be carried on, with a less sparing hand, and all seem to be more sorry for the difficulties his excellency has to encounter, than any experience themselves, but his spirit, assiduity and resolution, seem superior to every obstacle. The militia are not the best cloathed in the world, and none of them have any tents; they seem altogether unwilling to act under any officers but those of their own regiment, but we hope, tho' they are poor, they are still the same people with us, and that if we come to action, those who appear at present in the most unpromising light, will shew themselves not undeserving the regard shewn them by all.

Several expressed and messengers have arrived from the Cherokees, but no person is suffered to go thither, we learn the Indians are well apprised of our design, and if our advices are to be depended upon, very much afraid. We are very healthy, and have good stomachs, tho' our meat is not very fat, the fine air creates an appertite, —— the water is good."

A few days ago some public spirited Gentleman set on foot a Subscription to furnish the Money for the Service of the present expedition to the Cherokee nation (if it should be wanted) at the disposal of the Governor; and we hear 36,000 pounds are already subscribed.

BOSTON Nov. 26. By several Vessels who arrived here since our last, from Quebeck, we learn, That all the Ships of War and Transports employed in the late expedition were sailed from thence, except a Bomb and Fire, which haul'd up and unrigg'd and some small Vessels were employ'd in bringing Wood for the use of the Garrison there; which, 'Tis said, consisted of 6 or 700 Men, who were generally in good Health, and almost free from the Fluxes, which for some Time was brief among them, after the surrender of the City: That they had good provisions in the King's Stores for Twelve Months. That the French Inhabitants who had capitulated were put to great Difficulties in procuring the necessities of Life, as those must recently be more so, thereabout, who had not: —— That the remaining of the French Army continue encamped and entrench'd about 35 Miles from the City: but as the Winter was approaching 'twould be impossible to continue long in that Situation: Four of our People, going ashore from one of the Vessels bound here, 'tis said to hunt for Horses, were taken by a French Scout, and carried to their Camp, but were soon set at Liberty, and were come back.

BOSTON Nov. 26. From Number IV. The following Particulars relating to the Destruction of the Indian Town of St. Francois, by a Party of Rangers, under the command of Maj. Rogers, may be depended on for truth, as it was taken from those who were present in the Action.

Upon the 13th of Sept. Maj. Rogers marched from Crown-Point with about 200 men, and upon the 3d, of Oct. they came within sight of Ft. Francois, which the Major discovered from a tree, at about three miles distance, where he halted his detachment; consisting of 142 men, officers included, being reduced to that number by reason of some of the tired whom he sent back: — At eight in the Evening he, with two officers, went forward to recoonoitre the town, where he found the Indians in a high frolick dance; he went thro' the town, and was Spoken to several times by the Indians, but was not discovered, as he was dress'd like any one of them; having taken a satisfactory view of the place, and it's situation, he returned to his party at 2 o'clock; at half after three he marched his men to within 500 yards of the town, where he lighted them of their packs, and form'd them for the attack; at half an hour before sunrise he surprized the place while they were asleep, which was done with such expedition by our men, that the enemy did not have time to recover themselves, or to take up arms in their own defence for Rogers having devided his men into parties, and allotted each their station, they all fell on fell on at once, broke open their houses, shot some as they lay in bed, while others attempted to flee by back ways, were tomahawked, or run thro' with bayonets by our men who stood without, so that they were almost wholly destroyed, except some few who ran to the water, thinking to make their escape that way, but were pursued by about 40 of our men, who dispatched most of them likewise, by sinking both them and their boats; ——— A little after sunrise the parties set fire to all the houses, except three, which the Major kept as a reserve, because in them was plenty of corn, but the rest were entirely consumed, and many of the enemy who had concealed themselves therein, which our men learnt from the crying and shrieking of those miserable wretches, when they perceived their houses on fire, and themselves like to be made the fuel: The sword without, which prevented all escapes, and the fire within rendered their situation most unhappy, most miserable: ——— About seven in the morning the affair was over, in which they had killed some say 300, and some more, but by the lowest computation, there could not be fewer then 200 who were slain by the sword, by the fire and water: The party took about 20 prisoners, and retook 5 English captives that were among them; the prisoners, who were mostly superannuated they let go except 5, whom they brought off: ——— When Rogers paraded his men, he found he had Capt. Ogden badly wounded, being shot thro' the body, and 6 men slightly wounded, and one Stockbridge Indian killed. That hath Maj. Rogers, with little loss on his own side, almost wholly cut off one tribe and destroyed abundance of riches, it being extremely rich for a place of that bigness, having in it English goods, and vast quantities of wampum, and likewise considerable silver and gold, one ranger is said to bring off, 170 guineas, and another a silver image of ten pounds weight; but the hurry in which they set fire to their houses, could not give many an opportunity of bringing off more. ——— As soon as the Major had got his men together, he ordered them to load themselves with corn, out of those reserved stores, and while they were performing this, he examined the prisoners and captives; who gave the following intelligence, That a party of 300 French, and some Indians were above 4 miles below them, down the river: and that his boats were way-laid; and that three days before attaking the town, a party had gone up to waylay him at Wigwarm Martineques, expecting that he would fall upon that place: ——— Having received this intelligence, Rogers determined to return by Number IV. as being in opinion of all the best and safest way: They marched in a body for about ten days, when provisions becoming scarce, they were forced to separate near Memnphremagog lake; and having divided his men into small bodies, they determined to assemble at Ammonusuk river, a little above Coos: ——— Two days after, they parted, a body of the enemy came upon one of our parties commanded by Ensign Avery, and took 7 of his men prisoner, two of whom made their escape that night, and came to Rogers next morning; wherefore Avery with the remainder of his party joined the Major, and came with him as far as Coos, where he left his men, and he with Capt. Ogden came down upon a small raft to this place. There came with them one soldier and an Indian captive: Provisions have been dispatched up to their relief, which if arrived seasonably 'tis hoped they will all get in.

[The severe treatment which those Indians met with from Rogers and his party, if upon any occasion such usage can be justified, surely it might be here; for these St. Francois Indians, both in this and former wars, have been severest savages to the frontier settlements of the Massachusetts and New-Hampshire, than any other whatsoever; and have been guilty of more inhumanities, bloodshed and murdering, than perhaps any tribe on the continent: For proof of this, when our men entered the town they saw 6 or 700 English scalps waving in the wind, upon the tops of poles, which were stuck up on their houses and such like eminent places: ——— wherefore it seems they have now been punished for their cruelty, & that a just providence never design'd that those bloodthirsty heathen should go down to the grave in peace.]

BOSTON Nov. 26. By courier from Albany we have received an extract from the journal of Major Roger's last scout and his destroying the indian town of St. Francois, dated No. 4. Nov. 1st, and sign'd by the Major himself, which in substance is nearly the same as that was inserted before, except that the Major makes no mention of their bringing off any plunder: ——— That it was twenty-two days after they left Crown-Point before they came in sight of St. Francois: ——— That the two officers which went with him to reconnoitre the place, before he made the attack were Lieut. Turner and Ensign Avery: ——— that the prisoners he brought off with him were two Indian boys and three girls: ——— That half an hour after his arrival at No. 4. he dispatched a canoe with refreshments to Lieutenant Grant, who with some of his party he left at Cohorse intervals, and which he imagined would arrive to them in about 30 hours after; and, that he had also, sent off two other canoes with provisions to Ammonusuk river for the relief of the other parties left behind.

Extract of a Letter from Crown-Point Nov. 12.
"Last week a party of the enemy surprized a party of our men down this lake, who were on shore getting of Yards, &c. for the French vessels they were endeavouring to weigh, wounded 5 of them, and one is missing. ——— Sixteen of Maj. Rogers's party including 3 prisoners, and

one English captive, came in here about four days since, three more came in the Evening, and left two others about 5 miles off, and the Major is expected here every hour."

CHARLESTOWN South Carolina Nov. The Purport of a talk sent to his Excellency Governor Ellis, from one of the principal head-Kings, (evitopagola Mingo) of the Chactaw-nation Indians with a white wing, from the Mucculossa town, viz.

"I desire you would acquaint the Governor, in my behalf, as well as our nation, that we set out from our country, with a full resolution to see him, and beloved men, at the government seat & a sincere intention to make a firm treaty and peace with the English, that our nation might be once more happy in their friendship, and a well established trade with them; and that although, when he arrive at the nation of our brother Creeks, we were stopped by order of the great King George's beloved man Mr. Atkin, yet we are still resolved to see the Governor, and compleat the good work we have begun: Therefore we desire you will deliver this white wing to the Governor a token of our earnest and sincere intentions of a perpetual friendship with the English, which we hope will be accepted. When we come to see the Governor, we will make the path white and smooth, so that there will be nothing bad in the way, and never to be stained with blood any more. We have been blinded a long time by the French, against our own interest; but now our eyes are opened, and we are resolved to have a strong peace, and a trade with the English."

BOSTON Nov. 27. Province of Massachusetts-Bay.

Public Notice is hereby given, that the Great and General Court in this last Session made provisions for the Payment of two Months Wages in Part of the Wages due to such non-commission'd Officers and Soldiers who are now in his Majesty's Service, and in the Pay of this Province, at Louisbourg and Nova Scotia, and who have left Famalies in the Province that are Necessitous; ——— Provided those who have the care of such Famalies shall produce a Certificate from the Commanding-Officers of the Militia Company such non-commission'd Officers or Soldiers belong to, that such Soldiers in the Service Eastward, and that the Families of such Soldiers is necessitous.

It is desired, That when any such Militia Officer shall give Certificate of Consequence or said Order, said Certificate be explicit and conformable to the Order, that so there may be no Delay in affording the Relief proposed by the Court: And all Persons who may obtain such Certificates are desired to lodge them at the Secretary's Office.   Boston, 27th Nov. 1759.
                                    A. Oliver, Secr'y.

Last Friday arrived here Capt. Hatch from Quebec but last from Louisbourg in 11 days in whom came Passengers Miles Conyer and William Brockback, two Mates belonging to the Transport Ships Providence and Industry, Captain Castle and Burnard; and gives the following Account, that on the 24th ult. on their Passage from Quebec for London they were cast away on the Island of Aticosta upon which both crews took to their Boats, and soon after they put off to Sea they discovered several other ships ashore, but can give no Account who they were; after being in their Boat 48 Hours they discovered Captain Hatch's Schooner ashore on the Island of Macdonald which they assisted in getting off, and in her they proceeded to Louisbourg, where they left their Captains and the rest of the People well.

Yesterday a Vessel here in 6 Days from Louisbourg, by whom we learn that Captain Clement in a Sloop belonging to this Place, was lately taken coming down the River St. Lawrence, by a French Letter of Marque Ship from Old France for Quebec, with Provisions; but being informed the Place was in the hands of the English, they put away for the West Indies after having put 6 Men on board the Sloop with Orders to follow them, but soon after being seperated from the Ship in a hard Gale of Wind, the Frenchmen submitted themselves to be carried to Louisbourg, where they arrived before this Vessel came away.

Extract of a Letter from South Carolina, dated November 6, 1759.

"We have just received advice, that the Little

Carpenter (head of the Cherokees) who was abroad with a party during the whole disturbances, is come to fort Prince George, at Keowee, with four French scalps, and two Prisoners. ——— He declares his attachment to us, and his detestation of the cruelties of his people."

DECEMBER 1759

CHARLESTOWN SOUTH CAROLINA Dec. 1. It is pretty certain, that the small pox has lately raged with great violence among the Catawba Indians, and it has carried off near one half of that nation, by throwing themselves into the river as soon as they found themselves ill. This distemper has since appeared amongst the inhabitants at Charraws and Waterees, where many families are down; so that unless special care is taken it must soon spread thro' the whole country the consequence of which are much to be dreaded. The small-pox went almost thro' the province in 1636, when it made prodigious havoc, and has ever since been kept out of it, by the salutary laws enacted for that purpose.

PHILADELPHIA Dec 2. Extract of a Letter from Charlestown, South Carolina November 7, 1759.

Congerees, Nov. 3, 1759

"The Governor, on his arrival here, did not find the expected Number of Troops. The collected Force of the 3 Battalions (Cheveilette's, Powels's and Richardson's) does not exceed 800 Men, but he intends to lose no Time and will therefore, on the arrival of the Regulars and Provincials, with the Baggage, Waggons and Artillery, proceed to the Cherokees. Further Draughts to the Number of 300, are ordered to follow. We hope to be joined (according to Directions sent to that Purpose by his Excellency) by the North Carolina Forces at Keowee. It is said the Little Carpenter is returned from the Expedition he was upon, and had brought in some Scalps, and two French Prisoners."

Since our last an Officer of the second Battallion of the Pennsylvania Forces arrived here who left Montreal the eight of last Month. By him we are informed, that Major Grant, who was taken with his Corps, in September 1758, at Fort Duquesne, was return'd (upon exchange of Prisoners) with about 200 to Crown-Point. That in general they were well used by the French but that M. Chavegnier, who commanded at Venango did not treat them with the greatest Politeness, till he received a Letter from his Son, who was taken near Fort Henry, in Berks County in this Province, about two Years ago; in which Letter the young Gentleman told his Father, that he was most kindly used by the English, and hoped, in return, he would shew such as them as Providence ought deliver in his Hands, all the most genteelly treated by him: The Canadians were most dissatisfied under the French Yoke; but as they could not contrive their own Deliverance hoped the English would effect it from them early in the Spring.

CHARLESTOWN SOUTH CAROLINA Dec. 2. The Army is healthy and in high Spirits; but the Rifle-barrel Men continued to desert 10 and 12 at a Time. They arrived at Ninety-Six the 21st ult. where they were building a Fort, and were to move forward for Keowee as Yesterday.

BOSTON Dec. 3. The following is said to be a Copy of what the late General Wolfe delivered to his Army the Day before the battle. Dated on board the Southerland, September 12, 1759.

"The enemy's forces are now divided; great scarcity of provisions in their camp; universal discontent among the Canadians: and the second officer in command is gone to Montreal, or St. John's, which gives reason to think that general Amherst is advancing into the Colony.

A vigorous blow struct by the army at this juncture, may determine the fate of Canada. Our troops below are in readiness to join us; all the light infantry, artillery and tools, are embarked at Point Levy, and the troops will land where the French seem least to expect them. The first body that gets on shore are to march directly to the enemy, and drive them from any little post they may occupy. The officers must be careful that the succeeding bodies do not, by any mistake fire upon these that go before them. The battalions must form upon the upper ground, and be ready to charge whatever presents itself. When the artillery troops are landed, a Corps will be left to secure the landing place, while the rest march on, and endeavour to bring the French and Canadians to battle.

The officers and men will remember what their country expects from them; and what determined body of soldiers, inured to war, are capable of doing against five weak French battalions, mingled wit disorderly Peasantry.

The soldiers must be attentive and obedient to their officers, and resolute in the execution of their duty."

BOSTON Dec. 3. By a Letter from Nova Scotia we learn, That on the 12th of October the inhabitants of St. John's River, having heard of the surrender of Quebec, sent to Lieut. Col. Arbuthnot, who commands 250 Provincial Troops at Fort Frederick, "desiring to surrender themselves Prisoners at Discretion, whether he shall please to receive them as Prisoners of War, and so remove them of their Lands, or wether he would grant them leave to continue to the Canadians." Col. Arrbuthnot's Prudence did not permit him to trust them on any Terms he therefore went up the River, and in two Schooners bro't off with him 196 of these Inhabitants, and more we hear are coming in. ——— On the 3d of November, Pere Germain, the Jesuit Missionary both to the Inhabitants and Indians of those Parts, wrote to Col. Arbuthnot from St. Ann's desiring the same leave to continue to serve his Cure as is granted to the Priests of Canada; and that he had abandoned the Indians, and is willing to take Oath of Fidelity to the Britannic Majesty; but that if his continuance in those Parts be disagreeable to the English Government, he will, with Permission, retire to France; as he would by no means stay in the Country without Consent of the true Masters of it. ——— That as to his Character of Indian Missionary, he will employ his Power to reconcile the Indians of those Parts to the Government from which they are much estranged, at least will prevent their doing Mischief. ——— Lieut. Col. Arbuthnot has this Summer destroy'd several of the Villages, and taken and destroy'd several of their Vessels up the River. ——— And on the 18th of September had a smart Skirmish with some of the Inhabitants and Indians. ——— The Effects is the best Proof of the Services of the Officers and small Garrison Provincials ——— and we could not but think that the mention of these particulars is due to the Assiduity and Alertness with which they were perform'd; and we hope the Men will not disgrace these Services by an unsoldier-like Impatience for getting home before they can be duely relieved.

By the return of an Express from Crown-Point which place left last wednesday se'nnight, we learn That General Amherst was expected on the saturday following at Ticonderoga on his return to New-York. ——— That the regiment of the several provinces were on their return home; those of the province to come by way of No. 4. ——— That 242 English prisoners were brought to Crown-Point by a flag of truce, in order to exchange for as many French ones, who were at Albany on their way from New-York: That the three French vessels taken and weighed by Commodore Loring, were bro't under the Fort it Ticonderoga, where they, with the English vessels were secured, by being enclosed large picquets: The English garrison which consisted of about 2000 men, were healthy, and well stored with provisions: The accounts which they had there from the enemy, were, that they were in great want of provisions in Canada (our informant saw Major Grant taken at the Ohio) Capt. Kennedy, Lieut. Fletcher, and a number of other officers, taken by the enemy at defferent times, from four years ago until within two months ago.

NEW-YORK Dec. 3. Among the Prisoners lately arrived at Crown Point, from Canada are Major Grant, taken at Pittsburgh, Captain Kennedy, and many others. Some of the People are now here who were at Montreal when the News arrived there of the surrender of Quebec, and the Death of Monsieur Montcalm. They say that the French in general were prodigiously down-cast, and dreaded their own Indians more than the English; but most of the Canadians were in a great measure pleased with the Articles of Capitulation; but that Monsieurs Vadreuil intended to retake Quebec in the Winter by Storm, for which Purpose he gave Orders for 20,000 Pair of Snow Shoes to be immediately made.

CHARLESTOWN S. Carolina Dec. 8. Our last advice from the army on their march to the Cherokee nation, from the 19th to the 28th ult. inclusive, are as follows. ——— Nov. 19th. upward of 400 provincial arms were delivered out to the militia and regulars. Presents were also distributed amongst the Chickesaws, and more promised them when the expedition should be over. All the waggons got up. Orders issued to march forward the next day. Many of the people fell sick. ——— Nov. 20th. Decamped from Seluda old town, and at noon march'd, the morning being taken up in distributing ammunition. At 3 P. M. halted at half-way swamp. The army the consisted of about 1400 gunmen above 100 waggons, besides carts and pack horses. The Chickesaws staid behind to send off the women and children. Sickness and desertion increase. ——— Nov. 21st. at 9 A. M. marched for Ninety six; arrived and encamped there at 2 P. M. after crossing two creeks. All the baggage and provisions got up. The Chickesaws also joined the camp. Here they found Chenallotochee, brother of Tiftoe (one of Oconnastota's party under guard) he pretended to be hunting in these parts, and that hearing of the governor's approach, he came to see his excellency; being told that the governor would see and talk to him at another time, he went out to fetch in his party, and promised to return next day. ——— Nov. 22d. the ground was reconnoitred for a proper place to build a magazine and stockade fort, to secure ammunition and provisions, and to retreat is necessary; to save time, expence and trouble, Mr. Gonedy's Barn was fixed for a store house, and it was resolved to stokade it in. Chenallotochee returned to the camp with his party: The governor admitted him into his presence; asked, what he came about, and what he had to say? he answered, that he was hunting, and desired to see his brother; whereupon, after being told that his excellency had

said to the rest of the Indians in his former talks, and that he might either continue to hunt with his party where he was, or go home to his nation and tell what he saw and heard, he was soon dismissed. with leave to see his brother Tiftie, and the rest of Occactota's party, that they were well: when he saw them, he seemed pleased to find that nothing more had befallen them than confinement; and told Tiftoe, "that the 4 Indians who had deserted from the Congarees, had carried bad talks into the nation, and reported, that they were all made slaves; that the Indiand who went from town, had given a good talk, but he had heard that the Raven had also carried a bad one, which had put the the whole nation in a ferment: Tiftoe told him. "that they had all been well and kindly used since they have been with the army; and blamed the run-aways for being abrid'd of liberty:" he told them farther, "that those of his countrymen who were concerned in killing the English must be delivered to the governor." Chenallotochee then said, he was willing to accompany his excellency, and act with him in getting satisfaction; and desired to be permitted to stay in the camp all night: this the governor did not think proper (for notwithstanding his fair speechs, is was suspected he came only to see the strength of the army, and to converse with his countrymen, to discover whether it would be prudent or advisable to oppose the army's passage over 12 mile river, as had been designed) and he was ordered to depart immediately; which he did at 4 P. M. when orders came Tiftoe was talking to him about delivering up the murderers: telling who they were, and who were proper persons to seize them. Maj. Bond arrived this day with his Volunteers. Great plenty in the camp; that defection continues. Sickness also continues, but no Mortality. ——
Nov. 23. Mr. Elliot returned from the nation; left Keowee the day before, and Fort Louwdoun the 15th, all well in both those garrisons: he saw the Little Carpenter, who appeared a good deal concerned at the vigorous measures this government was pursuing, professed much

friendship for the English, and said, if the
Governor would permit him he would meet his Excellency at Keowee: Elliot represented the middle towns as peaceable and well disposed; many
of the upper and some of the lower, the same,
a good deal terrified; but said, that the towns
who had been concerned in the murders, who might
make up about 500 men, remained refractory, and
made preparations for a war. This day some of
Col. Richardson's men joined him from the borders
of Noth-Carolina, and reported, that Maj. Waddel
was to have set out from Fort Dobbs with 900 men
on the 20th; for which report there does not
however seem to be any foundation. The army be-
ween 13 and 1400 strong. An account was received
that Chenallotochee was gone to Keowee and said
he would give a good talk. ——— Nov. 24th.,
Capt. Dugeon, the Engineer, laid out a ground
for the stockade; the Pioneers, volunteers,
servants, &c. open the ditches for planting the
puncheons. Elliot was sent off express, 'twas
thought to give permission to the Little Carpenter to meet the Governor at Keowee; whither
the middle towns people has already agreed to
come, though they expressed an aversion to being
joined to those of the upper and lower towns
(who they say are bad) they should not be distinguished, but be treated as one people. ———
Nov. 25th. Nothing remarkable happened. Continued to work on the stockade. ——— 26th. two
runners arrived in the camp from the nation,
with an English flag and brought a talk and a
large quanties of wampum; and express arrive at
the same time from Keowee, intimating, that
these runners were only spies, and came to converse with their countrymen under pretence of
seeing the governor; his excellency would not
see them, but ordered that they should immediately depart and go home. Letters from Kenowee
said, that the army having so many headmen of
the nation in custody, had puzzled the Indians
very much, and that it was the only thing that
had prevented their doing more mischief, an of
committing farther acts of open hostility. From
certain orders issued on this day, it was thought
the governor had received intelligence of some

scouting parties being about, to observe the motions of the army. Nov. 27. the banquette to the stockade was finished, and the gates put up. Some volunteers from Fort-Royal joined the army. An express arrived from Virginia. Meazels, purgings and pleuritic complaints rather increased than abatted. ——— Nov. 28th. the whole army was reviewed, except the Indian guards, and rangers, and found considerably short of the returns; there were 1299 effective men. Orders were given to march to which every man is to be under arms an hour before day, and so continue, till sun-rise, to prevent a surprize, that being always the time when Indians made their attacks. A garrison was to be left at Fort Nintysix which is 90 feet square, has sheds on one side of the store-house for the men, and will be a great service to the inhabitamts of these parts in all times of alarm. And Major Singleton was ordered to join the army by long marches, with 200 men of the new draughts.

CHARLESTOWN South Carolina Dec. 8. In a Letter from Augusta, dated 24th ult. it is said.

"That the whole Chactaw Nation of Indians are now in the British Interest, except about 100 whom the French employed and paid as rangers. That the Superintendent still remainsd at Oakfuskees; and the Mortar of the Aokaboys, with 18 warriors, is gone to join the Cherokees.

BOSTON Dec. 10. A Journal of the Expedition up the River St. Lawrence; containing a true and particular Account of the Transactions of the Fleet and Army, from the Time of their Embarkation at Louisbourg till after the Surrender of Quebec.

On the 1st of June 1759, we embarked on board the transports at Louisbourg, bound on the expedition to Canada. ——— The 4th day we set full sail for the river St. Lawrence, which we made on the 9th, and were till the 16th before we got into it. For about 40 Leagues up the river, the dept of the water 100 fanthoms. The 19th day we came into 17 fantom water; and on the 23d we join'd with Dorell, who with 7 sail of line, and some frigates lay as guard to protect the river, at the Isle of Coudre. ———

this island pleasantly situated, lies partly, high, and was very well peopled before we came up: ——— And passing this island about a league off we anchor'd, and two of our boats went in shore and was attack'd by a small party of Canadians and Indians, and were obliged to retreat to their ships.

The 25th, we made the out end of Orleans, and on the 27th Landed on it without the loss of a man. ——— A small party of the rangers were almost surrounded by a large party of Indians; but the rangers rush'd thro' them with the loss of only one man, what the damage to the enemy sustained is uncertain.

The 29th, the French sent down five fire ships among our fleet; but did no damage. The same day we march'd 6 miles under the command of Col. Carlton, and encamped that same night in sight of the French army, and likewise in sight of the town. ——— Gen. Monckton's brigade and a party of rangers landed on the south side; we had a small attack, by which we had 3 kill'd 2 wounded and 4 taken prisoners.

July 1st, the enemy came against our detachment on the south side of the river with floating batteries; but our shipping soon drove them off. The same day the Louisbourg grenadiers went a foraging: we had two kill'd and scalp'd belonging to the 22d regiment.

The 5th, a barge was sent between the island and the main land, to sound the dept of water; the French fir'd four cannon shot at her, and came down on a large bar of sand, from whence they fir'd small arms; also five canoes came down the river, full of Indians who took the barge, made one man prisoner and wounded another. On the same day their floating batteries attack'd our shipping; but were soon obliged to quit their firing. ——— Gen. Monckton open'd a small battery upon the south side, but lost not a man.

The 8th, we landed om Quebec shore, without any interception, and marched up the river about 2 miles, when the Louisbourg grenadiers were ordered out to get fascines, they scarce sat down to take a small refreshment, and detach'd a small party of rangers to guard the skirts of the woods, before a large party of Indians surrounded them, kill'd and scalp'd thirteen, and wounded the captain-lieutenant and 9 privates; they likewise kill'd and wounded 14 Royal Americans, wounded 2 of the 22d and one of the 40th regiment, we got only 3 prisoners, and kill'd two of the savages.

The third day our shipping was drove off by the enemy shells. ——— We got only some few prisoners, till the 12th day, when the French built a battery against us, but had not time to mount any guns on it, for we soon demolish'd it with our said pieces and hawitzers. The 14th day their floating batteries came out after our boats but soon drove them back again, ——— the 17th, we set the town on fire, about 12 o'clock which continued burning all that day.

On the 17th we went out a fascining, and to make oars, with a small party to cover us, ——— 5 were kill'd, of which 4 were scalp'd, and we were oblig'd to quit the wood directly; the Indians came up very near, and kill'd and scalp'd one man close by us; the grenadiers of the 45th regiment, fir'd upon them, and kill'd one, but the Indians carried him off; we had 5 killed and 3 wounded; but our people returning up on them, made them fly so fast that they were oblig'd to leave their match coats, with several other things behind them; but could not get one of the prisoners. A deserter came to us, from whom we got some account of their forces, which, however imperfect, gave us some encouragement.

The 19th, the deserters went out with the light infantry, to show them a place to cross the falls; the Indians fir'd on them, but hurt none: likewise the same night some of the shipping pass'd the town and one run ashore on the south side of the river.

The 19th day the floating batteries came out to attack out shipping round the harbour; but our batteries on the land side drove them off, so that the shipping received but two shot.

The 21st, all the grenadiers cross'd over to the island of Orleans, the Indians attack'd us very smartly as we were marching to the water side. ——— The same day the enemy open'd two batteries on us, which raked our camps. Our troops with seamen, stormed a battery on the south side, spiked the cannon, broke the mortars, broke into their magazine, took all the powder, and threw their shot and shells into the water.

The 22d, set the town on fire, which burnt all day: some of the shipping attempting to pass the town, but the enemy fir'd so hot at them, they were oblig'd to turn back.

The 23d, 300 provincials landed on the island of Orleans, which was some reinforcement.

The 25th, the Louisbourg battalion and three more companies of grenadiers, with 3 companies of light infantry, went round the island of Orleans.

The 27th, they arrived again at the camp; and received the news that our forces on Montmorancy side had been attack'd the day before, and had got the better of the enemy, in which, 'twas said they had 300 kill'd. Our loss was 5 officers and 32 privates, 12 of whom were kill'd the rest of them wounded. The same day went to get the plunder which was discover'd on the march round the island, consisting chiefly of wearing apparel and some cash: The same night the French sent down five fire-floats, which were tow'd ashore by the men of war's boats, where burnt without doing our shipping any damage.

The 29th, Otway's, Hopson's Whitmore's and Warburton's grenadiers went on board two transport ships, the rest in flat bottom boats, with full intent to land on a part of the French shore; so as by that means we might come at the town: the first push we made on the 31st of July with 13 companies of grenadiers, supported by 5000 battalion-men; as soon as we landed we fixed our bayonets, and beat the grenadier's march, and so advanced on; during all this time their cannon play'd very briskly on us; but the small arms in their trenches, lay cool till they were sure of their mark; they then pour'd their smart shot like showers of hail, which caus'd our brave grenadiers to fall very fast: the

General saw that our attempts were in vain, retreated to his boats again: the number of the kill'd and wounded that day was about 400 men; ——— in our retreat we burnt the two ships, which we had ran ashore on that side to cover our landing.

The 3d of August, a party of Capt. Dank's rangers went from the island of Orleans to Quebec side, a little down the river; they were attacked by a party of French, and was smartly engag'd for the space of half an hour; but the rangers put them to flight, kill several and took one prisoner: the rangers lost one lieut. who died of his wounds, and two or three privates. They got a good deal of plunder.

The 4th, the French made an attempt to cross the falls, but our Havits and cohorns obliged them to retreat without accomplishing any thing.

The 8th, two centinels being at the falls, they took an Indian and brought him prisoner to the General who sent him on board the Admiral. At 12 o'clock at night we threw a carcass and one shell on the enemy's battery of nine guns, which blew up their magazine, platform, and burnt with such violence that some of the garrison were obliged to get into boats to save themselves from the flames. The 9th day we set the town on fire, being the third time.

On the 10th the French sent down sort of a floating battery; one of the ships's boats being sent out to see what it was, and just as the seamen were going to get on it, it blew up and kill'd one midshipman and wounded 4 sailors. ——— The same day about thirty sailors went a plundering on the south side of the river, but were surprized by a party of Indians and drove off, with the loss of the plunder.

The 11th, there was an engagement between our scouting parties and the Indians; our people drove them off; we had several killed and wounded.

The 12th, we had account of Gen. Murray's going to land above the town; he made an attempt to land twice, and was beat off, he made the third attempt and landed on the south shore with the loss of about 100 killed and wounded. The same day we had an account from the enemy, that Gen. Amherst's army was in such a bad condition that they were obliged to turn back again.

On the 13th we had an account by a deserter from the enemy, that they were in great want of provisions, and that a body of French and Indians were come over the falls, the same side our army was on, had with them four days provisions, and were there still.

The 15th, Capt. Gorham returned from an incursion, in which service were employ'd under his command, 150 rangers, a detachment from the different regiments, highlanders, marines, &c. amounting in all to about 300 an arm'd vessel, three transports, with a lieutenant and seamen of the navy to attend him; of which expedition they gave the following account: ―――― "That on the 4th of August they proceeded down to St. Paul's Bay, where was a parish containing about 200 men, who had been very active in distressing our boats and shipping. ―――― At 3 o'clock in the morning, Capt. Gorham landed, and forced two of their guards, of 20 men each, who fired smartly for some time; but that in two hours he drove them all from their covering in the woods, and clear'd the village, which they afterwards burnt, it consisted of about 50 fine houses and barns, destroyed most of their cattle, &c. ―――― That in this they had one man killed and six wounded, who were carried off. ―――― That from thence they proceeded to Mal Bay, ten leagues to the eastward on the same side, where they destroyed another very pretty parish, drove off the inhabitants and stock without any loss; after which they made a decent on the south shore, opposite the Isle of Coudre, destroying part of the parish of St. Ann's and St. Roan, where were many handsome houses with good farms, and loaded the vessels with cattle, and then returned from their expedition."

The same day a party of highlanders came to the island of Orleans from Gen. Monckton' encampment, in order to destroy all the canada side. The same day our people set one of the enemy's floating batteries on fire; ―――― and in the night Gen. Monckton set the town on fire, (being the fourth time) and the flame raged so violently, that 'twas imagined the whole city would have been reduced.

The 18th, the enemy have a bomb from the town which killed one of our men and wounded 6 more.

On the 20th, the Louisbourg grenadiers began their march down the main land of Quebec, in order to burn and destroy all the houses on that side.

On the 24th, they were attack'd by a party of French, who had a priest for their commander; but our party kill'd and scalp'd 31 of them, and likewise the priest, their commander; they did our people no damage. The three companies of Louisbourg grenadiers halted about four miles down the river, at a church called the Guardian Angel, where they were ordered to fortify themselves till further orders, our people had several small parties in houses, and the remainder continued in the church.

The 25th, they began to destroy the country, burning houses cutting down their corn, &c. At night the Indians fired several scattering shot at the houses, which killed one highlander and wounded another; but they were soon repulsed by the heat of our firing: ———— It was said that the number of the enemy consisted of 800 Canadians and Indians. Sept. 1st, they set fire to the enemy's houses and fortifications, and then marched to join the grand army at Montmorancy.

The 26th of Aug. a Serjeant of the 35th regiment deserted across the falls, and tho' our people fir'd several shot at him, he got clear off to the country.

The 27th, some of the shipping went past the town, notwithstanding the enemy kept a constant firing of shot and shells at them, tho' without doing them much damage.

The 29th, five sail more pass'd the town, up the river, amidst the constant firing of the enemy; and on the 30th, four more of our vessels the town without receiving any considerable damage from the enemy's batteries ashore, tho' they kept up a very brisk fire upon them as they pass'd up.

Sept. 1st all the sick and wounded that were

on Montmorancy's side came over to the isle of Orleans; on the second instant, a large body of Wolfe's troops came over, with the Louisbourg grenadiers, and encamped that night on the same island.

The 3d day, all the army left Montmorancy's side, they set all the houses and fortifications on fire, and then embark'd in flat-bottom boats and come up above the fall; the French fir'd very brisk all the time on their passing, but did them no damage, they went over to Point Levee and encamped there.

The 4th, the Louisbourg grenadiers and the remainder of the army cross'd over to Point Levee from the isle of Orleans, and encamped there.
——— The same day four men came from General Amherst's army; they were 26 days in their journey, and inform'd us, that we were in possession of Ticonderoga and Crown-Point.

The 5th about 5 or 600 men march'd up the river, on Point Levee side, to go above the town, and carried one months provisions up in sloops, The same day one of the Royal Americans, who was taken prisoner by the French indians on the 31st of July, made his escape and came to the Porcupine sloop of war, which lay a little below the falls; he inform'd us, that there was but about 300 Indians with the enemy, that carried arms; but there was a great number of women and children, and that they were very scant provisions; likewise that he himself had been 48 hours without any thing to eat: he further said, that the enemy were very numerous in their entrenchments consisting of at least 14,000 men, of which 11,000 were Canadians and the rest regulars, the latter of whom were heartily tir'd with the siege.

The 6th, the schooner Terror of France, went above the town, in the middle of the day, as she pass'd the enemy kept up constant fire at her, and she receiv'd several shot in her sails, but lost none of her hands.

The whole army being at Point Levee side, the main body were order'd to get ready to march above the town, on the south side, and to take with them only one shirt and one pair of stockings besides what they had on: they marched up the river about 8 miles, and then embarked on board the men of war and transports that were up the river; the number that embarked was 3349 men, with a party of the train of artillery.

The 10th, the weather being very wet, and the troops very much crowded on board the men of war and transports, the General thought proper to land them on the south side again; which was a great decoy to the French: we then marched to the church of St. Nicholas, under the command of General Monckton, where we halted.

the next day we received intelligence of a small number of French and Indians, who were driving some cattle; we dispatched a party of 500 men, who took the cattle but the enemy got off.

The 12th, we received orders to embark on board the transports again, and to hold ourselves in readiness to land next morning at day light, under the heights of Abraham; accordingly we landed at the break of day, and immediately attack and routed a considerable body of the enemy and took possession of their battery of 24 pounders, and one 13 inch mortar, with but a very inconsiderable loss to our side. We then took post on the Plains of Abraham, whither M. Montcalm, (on hearing that we were landed, for he did not expect us) hasted with his whole army, consisting of cavalry as well as infantry, to give us battle; about 9 o'clock, we observed the enemy marching down towards us in three columns, at ten they formed their line of battle, which was at least six deep, having their flanks covered by a thick wood on each side, into which they threw above 1000 Canadians and Indians, who gail'd us much: We got two six pounders to fire against the enemy very soon, six more, besides two royal hawitzers, came up two by two, and fell into the service occasionally; whilst the enemy were making haste to attack before our artillery should be got up, as they dreaded our quick firing; accordingly their regulars then marched briskly up to us, and gave their first fire at about 50 yards distance, which we did not return, as it was Gen. Wolfe's express orders not to fire till they came within 20 yards of us: they continued firing by platoons, advancing in a very regular manner, till they came close up to us, and then the action became general: —— our artillery fired so briskly, seconded by the small arms from the regiments, who behaved with the greatest intrepidity, order, and regularity, with a chearfulness that foretold victory on our side, and in about 15 minutes they gave way, so that we fairly beat them in open field, drove them before us, part into Quebec, the rest ran precipitately cross St. Charles's river, over a bridge of boats, and some thro' the water.

The enemy lost in the engagement, Lieut. Gen. Montcalm, who had three wounds from our six pounders grape, of which he died next day; one Colonel, two Lieut. Colonels, and at least 1500 officers and men killed and wounded, and 200 taken prisoners at their very sally ports of which many were officers: —— We lost the brave Gen. Wolfe, who received three wounds, but had the satisfaction before his death to see his own plan so well executed, as to beat the enemy totally: he then said, "I thank God, now I shall die content," were his last words. Brigadier General Monckton; Col. Carlton, quarter-master-general; Major Barry, adjutant-general, and several other officers were wounded.

At four in the afternoon, Mons. Boucanville appeared in our rear, with about 1500 foot and 200 horse, upon which Brigadier Gen. Burton, with the 35th and 48th regiments march'd to the left to receive him, but he no sooner percieved our dispositions made to engage him, than he faced to the right about, and made a most precipitate retreat.

At ten o'clock at night we surprized their guard and took possession of their grand hospital, wherein we found between 12 and 1500 sick and wounded.

We remained the night on the field of battle, and on the 14th in the morning we secured the bridge of boats they had over the Charles river, and possessed ourselves of all the posts and avenues that were or might have been of any consequence leading to the town, and began to prepare for attacking the garrison in form, and got up for that purpose, twelve heavy 24 pounders; six heavy 12 pounders, some large mortars, and the 4 inch hawitzers, to play upon the town, and had been employed three days, intending to make a breach, and storm the city sword in hand, but were prevented by their beating a parley, and sent out a flag of truce with articles of capitulation, and the next day, being the 18th of September, the articles were signed, and we took possession of the city, where we found 180 pieces of cannon, from 2 to 36 pounders; a number of mortars from 9 to 15 inch, field peices, hawwirzers, royals, &c. with a large quantity of artillery stores, &c. &c.

The day after the engagement the enemy abandoned Beauport, leaving behind them about 50 pieces of cannon, and 4 mortars, having first set fire to all their floating batteries, and blown up their magazine of powder.

M. Vaudreuill, the governor-general of New-France, stole out of the city before the capitulation; leaving only about 600 men, under the command of Mons. Ramsay, by whom the capitulation was signed. The poor remains of the French regulars, with about 10,000 Canadians, retired to Jaques Quatiers under the command of M. Levy, but the Canadians deserted from him in great numbers, and came in to surrender themselves.

Sept. 19th, the French garrison were embarked on board transports: such of the inhabitants as would come in and take the oath of alligience were permitted to enjoy their estates.

Brigadier General Murray is governor of the town, and the siege from the first to last, 535 houses were burned down, amongst which is the whole eastern part of the lower town (save 6 or 8 houses) which make a very dismal appearance.

The enemy were above double our number by their confession besides their Indians, and were entrenched, had breast-works, fletches, redoubts, shore and floating batteries, &c. The enemy kept a diligent look-out, up St. Lawrence river, from thence to hinder and communication with Gen. Amherst, and had intercepted two officers and four Indians coming from him to us.

We burned and destroyed upward of 1400 fine farms houses; for we during the siege were masters of a great part of their country along the shore, and parties were almost continually kept out ravaging the country; so that 'tis tho't it will take them half a century to recover the damage.

NEW-YORK Dec. 10. We hear that his Excellency General Amherst, arrived at Albany, from Crown-Point, but last from Fort Edward, where he had been a little indisposed, on Saturday the first Instant, that he intended to embark for this Place in a Day or two; and that the three following Regiments might be expected hourly down.

The Second Battalion of the Royals to be quartered near in East-New Jersey; Colonel Montgomery's Highlanders to be quartered on Long Island; and the 55th in this city.

Mr. Vaudreuil, who escaped from Quebec immediately upon Montcalm's being defeated by Gen. Wolfe, was at Montreal when Major Grant left it, and more than once declared in Company, that at no other Hour, and no other spot of Ground, than those which the English Army avail themselves of, the destruction of the French could have been effected: and is short, that it was his Opinion no other General but Wolfe, could have succeeded in an expedition of so great Importance.

CHARLESTOWN South Carolina Dec. 15. There has been no advices received since our last that can be relied on, relative to our Army. Some Waggoners from Ninety-Six, report, that Yesterday sennight, it was affirmed there with some confidence, that it had passed Twelve-Mile River without Opposition from the Indians, and was within 6 Miles of Fort Prince George.

Some Gentleman arrived on Thursday Evening, by Land, from Philadelphia, passed thro' Williamsburg in Virginia 3 Weeks ago, the General Assembly of that Colony was then sitting. but no resolution was at that Time taken to send troops from thence to join the Army. The General Assembly of North-Carolina had made provisions for 300 Men, (50 Provincials and 250

Militia) to operate with our Forces, and Gov. Dobbs had accordingly given Orders for their marching; but there is reason to believe they will not reach Keowee till some time after the arrivals of our Troops at that Place.

We hear that Governor Ellis ordered the Magistrates at Augusta to use their best endeavours to prevail on more Chickesaws to go join Governor Littleton's Army; and that is endeavoring to prevail with a Party or two of young Creeks to do the same.

BOSTON Dec. 17. The English Prisoners who was exchanged this Fall by a Flag of Truce from Monsieur Vaudreiul at Montreal are returned to their respective Places. —— Capt. James Beach, one of those who was exchanged, is arrived here: He was taken about a year ago on his Passage from Bristol, by Capt. Delabroitz in a French Gun Ship, which was cast away in the River St. Lawrence. —— By him we learn, That when the British Fleet and Troops arrived before Quebec the English Prisoners who were Officers before (being 12 in Number) were removed from the City to Trois Riviere, where they tarried till the Day of the Battle was on the Plains of Abraham; when they were ordered for Montreal, but the success of our Forces was kept hid from them as well as the Inhabitants of Montreal, till a considerable time after: That about 800 of the Militia were sent from the French Army before Quebec surrendered, to gather in the Harvest, and send it to the Mills: That the Inhabitants Stock of Cattle and Grain were taken an account of, and two Third Part of the whole was appropriated for the King's use: That when they received the News in Montreal of the Death of Mons. Montcalm and the loss of Quebec, the French in general were prodigiously cast down, and dreaded that their own Indians more than the English; that the Canadians were pleased with the Articles of Capitulation: That Mons. Vaudreuil pleased them with the prospect of Peace early in the Spring; and, that it was needless for the Peasants to admit themselves to the English as they would enjoy their Possessions so soon again: While the Prisoners were at Montreal the French had Intelligence of Major Rogers destroying St. Francois, which they tho't to be a great enterprize; but just as a Flag of Truce was coming away they endeavoured to depreciate it, by reporting to the Prisoners that there not more than 40 Indians destroyed therein. —— it is said that the Island of St. John's is not strongly fortified, any more than Montreal; but that Nut-Island is made as strong as possible to make such a Pass. The Prisoners who were in Canada, are not all discharged, some are chusing to remain with the French, Tho' they must needs fare very hard, and others are among the Indians. ——

One of the instances of Kindness and Generosity of the brave British Troops after the taking of Quebec, has not been mentioned in the public papers which is, that when they had their allowance Provisions dealt out to them, on seeing the distressed Women, whose Husbands, Fathers and brethren, had been, and some were then inveterate Enemies, freely distributed half their Allowance to them, causing them to rejoice in receiving the Staff of Life from those who they had so great an aversion to. —— is it imagined that the Army in Germany under M. Contades, had that been victorious last Summer, would have behaved in like Manner to Hanover?

"But (said the late Gen. Wolfe) Britons breath higher Sentiments of Humanity, and liken to the merciful Dictates of the Christian Religion." which was verified in the brave Shoulders which he led on to Conquest, by their shewing more of the truly Christian majesty can pretend to.

CHARLESTOWN South Carolina Dec. 22. On the 9th instant our Army Commanded by his Excellency the Governor, arrived at Fort Prince George, opposite Keowee, the first Town in the Cherokee Nation, after a very fatiguing March of Ten Days: The same Evening 200 Men from Lieut. Col. Singleton's Corps joined the Army, and made it 1700 strong. The Small-Pox was at Keowee, but the Governor had taken all possible Precautions to prevent any communication with the Place, which is on the other Side of the River; and we make no doubt they will prove effectual. Six

Catawbas also joined the Army with the 200 Men above mentioned, but they had passes of Health from Justice Wyly at the Waterees. His Excellency had dismissed all the Cherokees that were along with him, except 38 Men of the greatest note, who remained with him in the Fort; these declare themselves perfectly satisfied to remain there in order to talk upon such Points as might be necessary for selecting an Accommodation: and the Little Carpenter, with other Headmen and Warriors, were on their Journey thither; so that it is likely that conferences between the Governor and the Heads of the Nation are by this Time begun.

BOSTON Dec. 31. Extract of a Letter from Fort Cumberland Nova Scotia, dated Dec. 7, 1759.

"We have a great number of French coming in which were formerly inhabitants of this Place: ―――― sixty have already come in, and in a month we expect we expect 160 more; and by the month of May next, there will be 1500 men, women and children; they would have come in this winter, but the creeks not being froze quite hard enough, and they having got a great many young children, prevents their travelling at present: ―――― they were in a starving condition, and we are obliged to supply them with provisions to keep them alive.

NEW-YORK Dec. 31. We hear that the Grenadiers and Light infantry of the Royal Scotch, and the Grenadiers and Light Infantry of the 55th Regiments are ordered to South -Carolina, to assist that Government in the Endeavours to bring under the Cherokee Indians; and that they are to embark this Week for that Place.

JANUARY 1760

PHILADELPHIA Jan. 2. From Pittsburgh we have advice, that our troops there are all well, and have plenty of provisions of all sort; that they are always a number of Indians at that place, who seem very friendly; and that there are extraordinary good barracks finished, sufficient to accommodate 800 men.

BOSTON Jan. 7. Province of Massachusetts-Bay, December. 28th, 1759.

By His Excellency Thomas Pownall, Esq; His Majesty's General and Commander and Chief of his Forces in North America, having received by the last Packet the King's intire Approbation of the signal Zeal and Spirit which the Officers and Soldiers have on all Occasions manifested for the Honor of His Majesty's Arms: And the General having acquainted His Excellency the Governor, that the Troops of this Province are included in the distinguishing Mark of the Royal Approbation.

The Troops of this Province are hereby informed of the same, not doubting that by the Continuance of their brave and good conduct they will still further recommend themselves to His Majesty's Favour.

By His Excellency's Command,

Wm. Brattle, Adj. General.

BOSTON Jan. 7. Daniel Jones at the Hat and Helmit, South-End Boston.

Notifies the Officers and Soldiers belonging to this Province, who have lately been discharged, that he will supply them with all sorts of English Goods suitable for the Season, which are just Imported, and to be sold at the lowest Rate. The Soldiers may be credited till their Muster-Rolls are made up, provided, they are recommended by their Officers, or such other

Person as may be depended.

NEW-YORK Jan. 7. The News of the reduction of Quebec, arrived in England the 17th of October last; when every demonstration of joy was expressed, that could flow from hearts affected by a laudable Zeal for the welfare of Britain, and for humbling a perfidious enemy: yet not unmindful amidst those general acclamations, of the national loss sustained by the death of general Wolfe, whose memory ought ever to be dear to Englishmen, so long as military accomplishments, courage and fidelity shall merit applause.

CHARLESTOWN South Carolina Jan. 8. Treaty of Peace and Friendship concluded by his excellency William-Henry-Littleton, Esq; Captain-General, and Commander in Chief of His Majesty's Province of South-Carolina, with Atakulla-Kulla (or Little Carpenter) Deputy of the whole Cherokee Nation and other Headmen and Warriors thereof, at Fort Prince-George, the 26th Day of December 1759.

(Publish by Authority,)

Article I.

There shall be a firm peace and friendship between all his Majesty's subjects of this province, and the nation of Indians called the Cherokees, and the said Cherokees shall preserve peace with all his Majesty's subjects, whatsoever.

II. The articles of friendship and commerce concluded by the lords commissions for trade and plantations, with the deputies of the Cherokee nation, by his Majesty's command, at Whitehall, the 1st day of September, 1730, shall be strictly observed for the time to come.

III. Whereas the Cherokee Indians have at sundry times and places, since the 19th of November, 1758, slain divers of his Majesty's good subjects of this province; and his excellency the governor having demanded, that satisfaction, should be given for the same, according to the tenor of the said articles of friendship and commerce above mentioned, in consequence whereof, two Cherokee Indians, of the number of those who have been guilty of perpetrating the said murders, having already been delivered up to be put to death, or otherwise disposed of as his excellency shall direct: It is hereby stipulated and agreed, that Twenty-Two other Cherokee Indians, guilty of the said murders, shall, as soon as possible after the conclusion of the present treaty, in like manner be deliverd up, to such persons as his excellency the governor, or commander and chief of this province, for the time being, shall appoint to receive them, to be put to death, or otherwise disposed of as the said governor or commander and chief shall direct.

IV. The Cherokees whose names are herein-after mentioned, viz. Chenohe, Ousanatah, Tallochama, Eallitahe, Quarrasattahe, Connasoratah, Katacroe, Otassite of Watago, Ousanolitah of Jore, Ousanolitah of Cowetche, Chifquatalone, Skiagusta of Stiquowee, Santoeste, Waohatch, Woeyah, Oucha, Christanah, Nicholche, Tony, Totaiah-hoi, Skaliloske, Chista, shall remain hostages for the due performance of the foregoing articles, in the custody of such as his excellency the governor shall please to nominate for that purpose; and whom any of the Cherokee Indians guilty of the said murders shall have delivered up. as is expressed in the said article, an equal number of the said hostages shall be forthwith set at liberty.

V. Immediately after the conclusion of this present treaty, the licenced traders from this government, and all persons employed by them, shall have leave from his excellency the governor, to return to their respective places of abode in the Cherokee nation, and to carry on their trade with the Cherokee Indians in the usual manner, according to law.

VI. During the continuance of the present war between his most sacred Majesty and the French king, if any Frenchman shall presume to come into the Cherokee nation, the Cherokees shall use their utmost endeavours to put him to death, as one of his Majesty's enemies; or if taken alive, they shall deliver him up to his excellency the governor, or the commander in chief of this province for the time being, to be disposed of as he shall directs. And if any person whatsoever, either white or Indian, shall at any time bring any messages from the French into Cherokee nation, or hold any discourse there in favour of the French, or tending to set the English or Cherokees at variance, and interrupt the peace and friendship so established by this present treaty, the Cherokees shall use their utmost endeavours to apprehend such person or persons, and detain him or them, until they shall be given notice thereof to his excellency the governor, or the cammander in chief of the province at the time being, and have received his directions therein.

Given under my hand and seal, at fort Prince George in the province of South-Carolina, this 26th day of December, 1759, and in the 33d year of his majesty's reign.

William Henry Lyttleton. (L. S.)

By his excellency's command Wn. Drayton, Secr.

We whose name are underwritten, do agree to all and every of these articles; and do engage ourselves and our nation, that the same shall well and faithfully performed.

In testimony whereof, we have, hereunto set our hands and seals, the day and year abovementioned.

Atakilla-kulla, (L. S.)	Oconostota, (L. S.)
Otassite, (L. S.)	Kettagusta, (L. S.)
Oconoeca, (L. S.)	Kilcannokeh, (L. S.)

Witnesses H. Hyrne, Adj. Gen.
Joseph Axson, William Foster.

Sworn Interpreters.
A True Copy   William Dratton, Secretary.

CHARLESTOWN S, Carolina Jan. 14. On Tuesday last the three Cherokees delivered up to the Governor in Consequence of the Treaty concluded between his Excellency and that Nation, on the 25th ult. and also Charles M. Gunningham, arrived in Town, under a strong Escort of Independents and Provincials.

And on Wednesday the Militia of this Town ceased doing Duty; being relieved by the said Independents and Provincials.

CHARLESTOWN S. Carolina Jan 19. The last account from Keowee, are that the small-pox has destroyed a great many of the Indians there, that those who remain alive and had not yet that distemper, were gone into the woods, where many of them must perish as the Catawbas did; and that another murderer called Scalp-Jack, of the town of Toxaway, had been delivered up to the commanding Officer of fort Prince George, in pursuance of the late treaty.

By a gentleman who left some of the Cherokee towns the 1st inst. we learn, that the Indians then behaved with the utmost humility, complaisance, and hospitality, and seemed as if they could not shew respect enough to the white people.

From Augusta, December 23, 1759. On Wednesday last, his Majesty's Agent and Superintendent of Indian Affairs, arrived here from Acksusky in the upper Creek nation accompanied by some of the traders, and some of the Creek Indians, having we hear, left the state of our affairs among the Creeks, Albahamas, Chicasaws, and the Chactaws on a most desirable footing at this juncture. He is now at fort Moore; and having been informed, when near the place, that Governor Lyttleton was marched to Keowee, his endeavouring to engage the men of his troops, whose time of service is now up, to go with him strait to the Cherokees, expecting that the famous Mortar of Ockehoy is now there, who was the bearer of his letters for accommodating the present differences between us and the Cherokees, and is to assist therein as the conditions of his reconciliation and favours: As he had the chief hand in beginning the present differences he is undoubtedly the fittest person to be employed to put an end to them, and perhaps the only man who can do it. At present the hands of the Creeks seem to be pretty well tied up from taking part openly with the Cherokees.

NEW-YORK Jan. 21. By Saturday's Post from Albany, we learn, That all was quiet and well at the several Fortresses of Crown-Point Ticonderoga, Fort William Henry, Oswego, and Niagara.

BOSTON Jan. 28. The Court taking into consideration the services of the 2500 men of this province troops, who were posted at Louisbourg, and at Halifax, and in the Bay of Fundy, had voted provisions of Four Pounds, as a reward to each man who continued in said service during the winter, and nine Pounds per man as bounty to each of these who shall enlist for another Campaign: and have further voted, as bounty for five thousand recruits more. Nine Pounds each man who shall enlist as aforesaid.

NEW-YORK Jan. 28. By several persons who come to town last week from Albany, we learn that all was quiet and well at the several fortresses of Niagara, Crown-Point, &c. ——— That several of the soldiers who were out on command there were very much frost bitten in the late extreme cold weather: ——— That there was very good sledding from Albany to Crown-Point: ——— That Maj. Rogers was returned from New-York, having left a young Indian Lad (one of the prisoners he bro't off from St. Francois) to be put to school to be instructed in English language: ——— That the two girls which he also bro't off: died lately with the small-pox at Albany: These children it is said, were relitive of Mrs. Williams, who was taken captive when in her infancy, and educated and married in Canada.

FEBRUARY 1760

BOSTON Feb. 4. The General Court in its present Session, have voted the following Encouragement and Bounties to those Soldiers who shall voluntarily inlist in his Majesty's Service for the total reduction of Canada.

A Bounty or Reward of Four Pounds to each of the private Men, and one Month's Pay to each Officer who remained in Garrison after the first Day of November last, and still continue there, over and above their established Wages; and that the Wages of all such Officers and Soldiers be continued according to the present Establishment, until the first Day of May next, or until the Time of their Discharge, in Case they should be discharg'd before the said first Day of May.

That a Bounty of Nine Pounds be given to each private Soldier and Non-Commission Officer now in the Service at Louisbourg, and the several Posts and Forts in Nova-Scotia, who shall inlist a-new for his Majesty's General Service; the Bounty to be paid in the Manner following. viz. Five Dollars at the Time of their inlisting, Five Dollars more, with with a Province Security of Six Pounds, at their passing Muster; this to be consider'd as over and above the Four Pounds Reward given as aforesaid.

That over and above the Number of Men who may thus inlist at Nova-Scotia, and Louisbourg, a Bounty of Nine Pounds and at the same time, as to those who shall inlist at either of the above said Places, to Five Thousand Men, including Officers, who shall inlist for said Service at any Time before the Fifteenth Day of March next, such Officers to be Inhabitants of this Province; the Privates and Non-Commission Officers only of said Five Thousand Men be intitled to the Bounty.

That the Inlistment for one Captain, two Lieutenants, and one Ensign, be the same at it was last Year, each Company consisting of a Hunfred Men including Officers. ——— That the Wages shall begin from the Date of their inlisting Orders; and that for every effective Man who they shall inlist, they be allowed and paid Three Shillings; but they are to be accountable for the Money they shall pay to any non-effective Man, who was so at the time of his inlistment.

And as to the Wages of the Men, that they shall be the same as they were last Year, viz. Thirty -five Shillings per Month, and they enter the Pay at the Time of their passing Muster.

That to each Man there be given when he shall begin the March, a Blanket, and such articles as were given the last Year, saving only, that such Blankets and Articles shall be given to the Men who shall inlist at Louisburg and Nova-Scotia at the Time when the other Men in Service at the several Posts there, shall be respectivly relieved.

That the Men shall not be held to continue in Service beyond the last Day of November next, and shall be discharged as much sooner as the Service will Admit.

BOSTON Feb 4. From the London Gazette Extraordinary. [Published by Authority]

Whitehall Oct. 16. Last Sunday morning arrived Lieutenant Percival, Commander of the Rodney Cutter, with the following letters from Major Gen. Wolfe, and Vice Admiral Sounders, to the Right Hon. Mr. Secretary Pitt.

Head Quarters at Montmorenci, in the River Saint Lawrence, Sept 2, 1759.

Sir,

I wish I could upon this occasion, have the honour of transmitting to you a more favorable account of the progress of his Majesty's arms; but the obsticles we have met with, in the operations of the campaign, are much greater than we had reason to expect, or could foresee; not so much from the numbers of the enemy (tho' superior to us) as for the natural strength of the country, which the Marquis de Montcalm seems wisely to depend on.

When I learned that succours of all kinds had been thrown into Quebec; that five battalions of regular troops, compleated from the best of the inhabitants of the country, and every Canadian that was able to bear arms, besides several nations of savages, had taken the field in a very advantageous situation; I could not flatter myself that I should be able to reduce the place. I sought however an occasion to attack their Army, knowing well, that with these troops I was able to fight, and hoping that a victory might disperse them.

We found they were encamped along the shore of Beaufort from the River St. Charles to the Falls of Montmorenci, and intrenched in every accessible part. The 27th of June we landed upon the Isle of Orleans; but receiving a message from the Admiral, that there was reason to think the enemy had artillery, and a force upon the Point of Levi, I detached Brigadier Monckton with four battalioms to drive them from thence. He passed the river the 29th at night and then march the next day to the point; he obliged the enemy's regulars to retire, and possessed himself of that post: The advanced parties upon this occasion had two or three skirmishes with the Canadians and Indians, with little loss on either side.

Colonel Carleton marched with a detachment to the Westermost point of the Isle of Orleans, from whence our operations were likely to begin.

It was absolutely necessary to possess there two points, and fortify them; because from either the one or the other the enemy might make it impossible for any ship to lie in the bason of Quebec, or even within two miles of it.

Batteries of cannon and mortars were erected with great dispatch to the Point of Levi, to bombard the town and magazines, and to injure the works and batteries: The enemy perceiving these works in some forwardness, passed the river with 1600 men to attack and destroy them. Unluckily they fell into confusion, fired upon one an other, and went back again; by which we lost an opportunity of defending this large detachment.

The Effect of their artillery has been so great (tho' across the river) that the Upper Town is considerably, and the Lower Town entirely destroyed.

The works for the security of a hospital and stores, on the Isle of Orleans being finished on the 9th of July at night, we passed the North Channel, and encamped neat the enemy's left, the river Montmoreci between us. The next morning Capt. Dank's company of Rangers posted in a wood to cover some workmen, were attacked and defeated by a body of Indians, and had so many killed and wounded as to be disable for the rest of the campaign: The enemy also suffered in this affair, and were in their turn driven off by the nearest troops.

The ground, to the eastward of the falls, seemed to be (as it realy is) higher than that on the enemy's side, as to command it in a manner which might be made useful to us. There is besides a ford below the falls, which they may be passed, for some hours in the latter part of the ebb and beginning of the flood tide; and I had hoped, that possible means might be found of passing the river above, for us to fight the Marquis de Montcalm, upon terms of less disadvantage than directly attacking his intrenchments. In reconnoiting the river Montmorenci, we found if fordable at a place about three miles up; but the opposite bank was intrenched, and so steep and woody that it was to no purpose to attempt a passage there. The Escort was twice attacked by the Indians, who were as often repulsed; but in these rencounters we had 40 (officers and men) killed and wounded.

The 18th of July, two men of war, 2 armed sloops and two transports with some troops on board, passed the town without any loss, and got into the upper river. This unable me to reconnoitre the country above where I found the same attention on the enemy's side and great difficulties on ours, arrising from the nature of the ground, and the obstacles to our communication with the fleet. But what I feared most, was if we should land between the town and the river Cape Rouge, the body first landed could not be reinforced before they were attacked by the enemy's whole army.

Notwithstanding these difficulties, I thought once of attempting it at St. Michaels, about three miles above the town: but perceiving that the enemy were jealous of the design, were preparing against it, and had actually bro't artillery and a mortar (which being so near to Quebec, they could increase as they pleased) to play upon the shipping; and, as it must have been many Hours before we could attack them, (even supposing a favourable night for the boats to pass by the town unhurt) it seemed so hazardous, that I thought it best to desist.

However, to divide the enemy's force, and to draw their attention as high up the river as possible, and to procure some Intelligence, I sent a detachment under the Command of Colonel Carleton, to land at the Point de Trempe, to attack whatever he might find there, bring off some prisoners, and the useful papers he could get. I had been informed that a number of the Inhabitants of Quebec, had retired to that place, and that probably we should find a magazine of provisions there.

The Colonel was fired upon by a body of Indians the moment he landed, but they were soon dispersed and driven into the woods: he searched for magazines, but to no purpose brought off some prisoners, and returned with little loss.

After this business I came back to Mountmorenci where I found that Brigadier Townshend had by a superior fire, prevented the French from erecting a battery on the bank of the river, from whence they intended to cannonade our camp. I now resolve to take the first opportunity which presents itself, of attacking the enemy, though posted to great advantage, and every where prepared to receive us.

As the men of war cannot (for want of a sufficient depth of water) come near enough to the enemy's intrenchments, to annoy them in the least, the admiral has prepared two transports (Drawing but little water) which upon occasion could be run aground, to favour a descent. With the help of these vessels, which I understood would be carried by the tide close to shore. I proposed to make myself master to a detached redoubt near the water's edge, and whose situation appeared to be out of a musket shot of the intrenchments upon the hill; If the enemy supported this detached part, it would necessarily bring an engagement, what we most wished for; and if not, I should have it in my power to examine their situation, so as to be able to determine where we could best attack them.

Preparations were accordingly made for an engagement. The 31st of July in the forenoon, the boats of the fleet were filled with grenadiers, and a part of the brigadier Monckton's brigade from the point of Levi: The two brigades under brigadier Townshend and Murray were ordered to be in readiness to pass the ford, when it should be thought necessary. To facilitate the passage of the corps, the admiral had placed the Centurion in the channel, so that she might check the fire of the lower battery which commanded the ford: This ship was of great use, and her fire was very judiciously directed. A great quantity of artillery was placed upon the eminence, so as to batter and enfilade the left of their intrenchments.

From the vessel which run a-ground, nearest in, I observed that the redoubt was too much commanded to be kept without very great loss; and the shore, as the arm'd ships could not be brought near enough to cover both with their artillery and musquetry, which I at first conceived they might. But as the enemy seemed in some confusion, and we were prepared for an action, I thought it proper time to make an attempt upon their intrenchments. Orders were sent to the brigadiers general to be ready with the corps under their command. Brigadier Monckton to land, and the Brigadiers Townshend and Murray to pass the ford, at the proper time of the tide, the signal was made, but in rowing towards the shore, many of the boats grounded upon a ledge that running off a considerable distance. This accident put us in some disorder, lost a great deal of time, and obliged me to send one officer to stop Brigadier Townshend's march, whom I then observed to be in motion. While the seamen were getting the boats off, the enemy fired a number of shell and shot, but did no considerable damage. And soon as this disorder could be set a little to the right and the boats were ranged in a proper manner, some of the officers of the navy went in with me, to find a better place to land: We took one flat bottomed boat with us to make the experiment, and as soon as we had insured a fit part of the shore, the troops were ordered to disembark, thinking it not yet late for the attempt.

The 13 companies of grenadiers, and 200 of the second Royal American battalion, got first on shore.

The grenadiers were ordered to form themselves into four distinct Bodies, and to begin the attack, supported by brigadier Monckton's corps, and were at hand to assist. But whether from the noise and hurry at landing or from some other cause, the grenadiers, instead of forming themselves as they were directed, ran impetuously towards the enemy's intrenchments in the utmost disorder and confusion, without waiting for the corps which were to sustain them, joined in the attack; brigadier Monckton was not landed, and brigadier Townshend was still at a considerable distance, though upon his march to join us in very great order. The grenadiers were checked by the enemy's first fire, and obliged to shelter themselves in or about the redoubt, which the French had abandoned upon their approach. In this situation they continued for some time, unable to form under so hot a fire, and having many gallant officers wounded, who (careless of their persons) had been solely intent upon their Duty. I seen the absolute necessity of calling them off, that they might form themselves behind brigadier Monckton's corps, which was now landed, and drove upon the beach, in extreem good order.

By this new accident and this second delay, it was near night, a sudden storm came on and the tide began to make; so that I thought it most adviseable not to persevere in so difficult an attack, lest (in case of a repulse) the retreat of brigadier Townshend's corps might be hazardous and uncertain.

Our artillery had a great effect upon the enemy's left, where brigadier Townshend and Murray were to have attacked; and it is probable, that if those accidents I have spoken of, had not happened, we should have penetrated there whilst our left and center (much remote from our artillery) must bore all the violence of their musquetry.

The French did not attempt to interrupt our march. Some of their savages came down to murder some wounded as could not be brought off, and to scalp the dead, as their custom is.

The place where the attack was intended, had the advantage over all others hereabout. Our artillery could be brought into use. The greatest part, or else the whole of the troops might act at once. And the retreat (in case of a repulse) was secure, at least for a certain time of the tide. Neither one or other of these advantages can any where else be found. The enemy were indeed posted upon a commanding eminence. The beach upon which the troops were drawn up, was in deep mud, with holes, and cuts by several gullies. The hill to be ascended, very steep, and not every where practicable. The enemy numerous in their intrenchments, and their fire hot. If the attack has succeeded our loss must certainly habe been great, and theirs inconsiderable, from the shelter which the neighbouring woods afforded them. The river St. Charles still remained to be passed, before the town was invested. In these circumstances I considered; but the desire to be in conformity to the King's intention, induced me to make this trial, persuaded that a victorious army has no difficulties.

The enemy have been fortifying ever since without so as to make a second attempt more dangerous.

Immediately after this check, I sent brigadier Murray above the town with 1200 men, directed him to assist Rear-Admiral Holmes in the destruction of the French ships, (if they could be got at) in order to open a communication with General Amherst. The brigadier was to seek every favourable opportunity of fighting some of the enemy's detachments provided he could do it upon tolerable terms, and to use all means in his power to provoke them to attack him. He made two different attempts to land upon the north shore, without success; but in the third was more fortunate. He landed unexpectedly at De Chambault and burnt a magazine there, in which were some provisions, some ammunition, and all the spare stores of cloathing, arms, and baggage, of there army.

Finding that their ships were not to be got at, a little prospect of bringing the enemy to a battle he reported his situation to me, and I ordered him to join the army.

The prisoners he took informed him, of the surrender of the fort Niagara; and we discovered by some letters, that the enemy has abandoned Carillon and Crown-Point, and were retired to the Isle Aux Noix; and that Gen. Amherst was making preparations to pass the Lake Champlain, to fall upon M. de Bourlamaque's corps, which consists of three battalions of foot, and many Canadians as make the whole amount to 3000 men.

The Admiral dispatched and mine would have gone 8 or 10 days sooner, if I had had been from writing by a fever. I found myself so ill, and am still so weak that I begged the general officers to consult together for the public utility. They are all in opinion, that (as more ships and provisions have now got above the town) they should try, by carrying up a corps of 4 or 5000 men (which is nearly the whole strength of the army, after the points of Levy and Orleans are left in a proper state of defence) to draw the enemy from their present situation, and bring them to an action. I have acquiesced in their proposal, and we are preparing to put it in execution.

The Admiral and I have examined the town with a view to a general assault; but, after consulting with the chief engineer, who is well acquainted with the interior parts of it, and, after viewing it with the utmost attention, we found, that tho' the batteries of the Lower Town might be easily silenced by the men of war, yet the business of an assault would be little advanced by that, since the few passages that lead from the Lower to the Upper Town, are carefully intrenched; and the upper batteries cannot be affected by the ships, which must receive considerable damage from them and from the mortars. The Admiral would readily join in this or in any other measure, for the public service; but I could not propose to him, on undertaking of so dangerous a nature, and promising so little success.

To the uncommon strength of the country, the enemy has added (for the defence of the river) a great number of floating batteries and boats. By the vigilance of these and the Indians round our different posts, it has been impossible to execute any thing by surprize. We have had almost daily skirmishes with these savages, in which they are generally defeated, but not without loss on our side.

By the list of disabled officers (many of whom are of rank) you may perceive, Sir, that the army is much weakened. By the nature of the river the most formidable part of this armament is deprived of the power of acting, yet we have almost the whole force of Canada to oppose. In this situation there is such a choice of difficulties, that I own myself at a loss how to determine. The affairs of Great Britain, I know, require the most vigorous measures; but then the courage of a handful of brave men should be exerted only when there is some hope of a favourable event. However, you may be assured, Sir, that the small part of the campaign which remains, shall be employed (as far as I am able) for the honour of his Majesty and the Interest of the Nation, in which I am sure of being well seconded by the Admiral and by the Generals. Happy if our effort here can contribute to the success of his Majesty's arms on any other part of America.

I have the honour to be, with the greatest repect, Sir, your most obedient, and most humble servant.   James Wolfe.

BOSTON Feb. 4. From the London Gazette Extraordinary.

Whitehall Oct. 17. Last Night Col. John Hale and Capt. James Douglas, late Commander of his Majesty's Ship the Aleide. arrived from Quebec with the following Letters to the Right Hon. Mr. Secretary Pitt.

Copy of a Letter from the Hon. General Monckton to the Right Hon. Mr. Pitt, dated River St. Lawrence, Camp on Point Levi, Sept. 15, 1759.

Sir,

I have the Pleasure to acquaint you, that, on the 13th Inst, his Majesty's Troops gained a very signal Victory over the French, a little above the Town of Quebec. General Wolfe, exerting himself on the Right of our Line, received a wound pretty early of which he died soon after, and I had myself the great Misfortune of receiving on my right Breast by a ball that went thro' Part of my Lungs (and which has been cut out under the Blade Bone of my Shoulder) just as the French were giving Way, which obliged me to quit the Field. I have therefore ordered General Townshend, who now commands the Battery before the Town (as which I am in Hopes he will be soon in Possession) to acquaint you with the particulars of that Day, and of the Operations carrying on.

I have the Honor to be &c.   Rob. Monckton.

P. S. His Majesty's Troops behaved with the greatest Steadiness and bravery.

As the Surgeons tell me that there is no Danger in my Wound, I am in Hopes that I shall be found able to join the Army before the Town.

Copy of a Letter from the Hon. Brigadier General Townshend, to Right Hon. Mr. Secretary Mr. Pitt, dated Sept. 20, 1759.

Sir,

I Have the Honour to acquaint you with the Success of his Majesty's Arms on the 13th Inst. in and Action with the French of the Heights to the Westward of this Town.

It being determined to carry the Operations above the Town, the Posts at Point Levi, and Isle d'Orlean being secure, the General marched, with the remainder of the Force, from Point Levi; the 5th and 6th, and embarked them in Transports, which had passed the Town for that

Purpose. On the 7th, 8th, and 9th, a Movement of the Ships was made up, by Admiral Holmes, in order to amuse the Enemy now posted along the North shore; but the Transports being extremely crowded, and the Weather very bad, the General tho't proper to canton half his Troops on the South Shore; where they were refreshed, and re-imbarked upon the 12th at one in the Morning. The Light-Infantry, commanded by Col. Howe, the Regiment of Bragg, Kennedy, Lascelles and Anstruther, with a Detachment of Highlanders, and the American Grenadiers, the whole being under the Command of Brigadier Monckton and Murray, were put into Flat-Bottom Boats, and after some movement of the Ships, made by Admiral Holmes to draw Attention of the Enemy above, the Boats fell down with the Tide, and landed on the North Shore, within a League of Cape Diamond, an hour before Day-break. The rapidity of the Tide of Ebb carried them a little below the intended Place of Attack, which obliged the Light-Infantry to scramble up a woody Precipice, in order to secure the Landing the Troops by dislodging a Captain's Post, which defended the small intrenched Path the Troops were to ascend. After a little Firing, the Light-Infantry gained the Top of the Precipice, and dispensed the Captains Post; by which Means the Troops, with a very little Loss from a few Canadians and Indians in the Wood, got up, and were immediately formed. The Boats, as they emptied, were sent back for the second Embarkation, which I Immediately made. Brig. Murray, who had been detached with Anstruther's Battalion to attack the 4 Gun Battery upon the Left, was recalled by the General, who now saw the french Army crossing the River St. Charles. General Wolfe thereupon began to form his Line, having Right covered by the Louisbourg Grenadiers; on Right of these again he afterwards brought Otway's; to the Left of the Grenadiers were Bragg's, Kennedy's, Lascelles's, Highlanders, and Anstruther's; the Right of this Body was commanded by Brigadier Monckton, and the Left by Brigadier Murray; his Rear and Left were protected by Col. Howe's Light Infantry, who was returned from the

Four Gun Battery before mentioned, which was soon abandoned to him. General Montcalm having collected the whole of his Forces from Beauport Side and advancing shewed his intentions to flank our Left, where I was immediately ordered with General Amherst's Battalion, which I Formed en Potence. My Numbers were soon after increased by the Arrival of two Battalions of Royal Americans; and Webb's was drawn up by the General as a Reserve, in right Subdivisions, with large Intervals. The Enemy lined the Bushes in their Front with 1500 Indians and Canadians, and I dare say had placed most of their best Marksmen there, who kept up a very galling, though irregular, fire, upon our whole Line, who bore it with the greatest Patience and good Order, reserving their Fire for the main Body now Advancing. This Fire of the Enemy was however checked by our Post in our Front which protected the forming of our Line. The Right of the Enemy was composed of half the Troops of the Colony, the Battalion of La Sarre, Languedoc, and the Remainder of their Canadians and Indians. Their Center was a Column, and formed by the Battalions of Bern and Guienne. Their Left was composed of the remainder of the Troops of the Colony, and the Battalions of Royal Roussillon. This was as near as I can guess, their Line of Battle. They brought up two Pieces of small Artillery against us, and we had been able to bring up but one Gun, which being admirably well served, galled their Column exceedingly. My Attention to the Left will not permit me to be very exact with regard to every Circumstance which passed on the Center, much less on the Right; but it is most certain, that the Enemy formed in good Order, and that their Attack was very brisk and animated on that Side. Our Troops reserved their Fire, till within forty Yards, which was so well continued, that the Enemy every where gave Way. It was then our General fell at the Head of Bragg's and the Louisbourg Grenadiers, advancing with their Bayonets: About the same Time Brigadier General Monckton received his Wound at the Head of Lascelles's. In the Front of the opposite Battalions fell also M. Montcalm, and his second in Command is since dead of his Wounds on board our Fleet. Part of the Enemy made a second faint Attack. Part took to some thick copse of Wood, and seemed to make a Stand. It was this Moment that each Corpse seemed in a Manner to exert itself, with a View to it own peculiar Character. The Grenadiers Bragg's and Lascelles's, pressed on with their Bayonets. Brigadier Murray advancing with the Troops under his Command briskly, compleated the route on this Side; when the Highlanders, supported by Anstruther's, took to their Broad Swords, and drove Part into Town, Part of the Works at their Bridge on the River St. Charles.

The Action Left and Rear, was not so severe, The Houses, into which the Light-Infantry were thrown, were well defended, being supported by Col. Howe, who taking Post with two Companies behind a small Corpse, and frequently sallying upon the Flanks of the Enemy, during their Attack, drove them often into Heaps, against the Front of which Body I advanced Platoons of Amherst's Regiment, which totally prevented the Right Wing from executing their first Intention Before this, one of the Royal American Battalions had been detached to preserve our Communication with our Boats, the other being sent to occupy the Ground which Brigadier Murray's Movements had left open. I remained with Amherst's to support this disposition, and to keep the Enemy's Right, and a Body of their Savages, which waited still more towards our Rear, opposite the Posts of our Light-Infantry, waiting for an opportunity to fall upon our Rear.

This Sir, was the Situation of Things, when I was told, in the Action that I commanded: I Immediately repaired to the Center, and finding the Pursuit had put Part of the Troops in disorder. I formed them as soon as possible. Scarce was this effected, when M. de Bougainville with his Corpse from Cape Rouge, of 2000 Men, appeared in our Rear. I advanced two Pieces of Artillery and two Battalions toward him; upon which he retired. You will not, I flatter myself, Blame me for not quitting such advantageous Ground, and risking the Fate of so decisive a Day, by seeking a fresh Enemy, posted perhaps in the very kind of Ground he cold wish for, viz. Woods and Swamps. We took a great Number of French Officers upon the Field of Battle, and one Piece of Cannon. Their Loss is computed to be about 1500 Men, which fell chiefly upon their Regulars. I have been employed, from the Day of Action to that of the Capitulation, in redoubling our Camp beyond Insult, in making a Road up the Precipice for our Cannon, in getting up the Artillery, prepairing the Batteries and cutting their Communications with the Country. The 17th, at Noon, before we had any Battery erected, or could have any for two or three Days, a Flag of Truce came out with a Proposal of Capitulation, which I sent back again to the Town, allowed them four Hours to capitulate, or no further treaty. The Admiral had at this Time, brought up his large Ships, as intending to attact the Town. The French Officer returned at Night with Terms of Capitulation, which, with the Admiral, were considered, agreed to, and signed at eight in the Morning, the 18th Inst. The Terms we granted, will I flatter myself, be approved of by his Majesty, considering the Enemy assembling at our Rear, and, what is far more formidable, the very wet and cold Season, which threatened our Troops with Sickness, and the Fleet with some Accident; it had made our Primary Road so bad, we could not bring up a Gun for some Time; add to this the Advantage of entering the Town, with the Walls in a defenceable State, and the being able to put a Garrison there, strong enough to prevent a surprize. These, I hope, will be deemed sufficient Consideration for granting them the Terms I have the Honour to transmit to you. The Inhabitants of th Country come into us fast, bringing in their Arms, and taking Oaths of Fidelity, until a general Peace determines their Situations.

By Defenders we learn, that the Enemy are reassembling what Troops they can, behind Cape Rougue; that M. de Levy is come down from Montreal Side to command them; Some say, he has brought two Battalions with him; If so, this blow has already assisted General Amherst. By other Deserters we learn, that M. de Bougainville, with 800 Men, and Provisions, was on his March to fling himself into the Town the 18th, the very Morning it capitulated, on which Day we had not compleated the Investiture of the Place, as they had broke the Bridge of Boats, and had Detrenchments in very strong Works on the other Side the River St. Charles.

I should not do justice to the Admiral, and the Naval Service, if neglected this Occasion to acknowledge how much we are indebted for our Success to the constant Assistance and Support received from them, and the perfect Harmony and Correspondence, which has prevailed thro' out all our operation, in the uncommon Difficulties with the Nature of this Country, in Particular, presents to Military Operations of a great extent, and which no Army can itself solely supply; the immense Labour in Artillery, Stores, and Provisions; the long Watching and Attendance in Boats; the Drawing upon Artillery by the Seamen, even in the Heat of Action; it is my Duty, short as my Command has been, to acknowledge, for the Time, how great a share the Navy has had in this successful Campaign. I have the Honour to be &c. Geo. Townshend.

BOSTON Feb. 4. We have advice from Charlestown, South Carolina, that a treaty of peace and friendship was concluded by his Excellency William Lyttleton, Esq; Captain General and Commander in chief of that province, with Atakullakulla (or the Little Carpenter) deputy of the whole Cherokee nation, and other headmen and warriors thereof, at Fort Prince Gearge, the 26th day of December last.

CHARLESTOWN S. Carolina Feb. 9. By an express from Ninety-six, with letters from Lieutenant Coytmore at Fort Prince George, we have the following advice, that since the conclusion of the late treaty at that place, about 30 of the cherokee warriors which had separated from a gang of 70 men of the same nation, had been to Mr. Elliott's house, (situated within a mile and a half of the fort) where they immediately butchered Mr. Elliott and ten others, and after plundering the store, carried off two captives. ──

That they had killed a soldier within 150 yards of the fort, and wounded another, who escaped into it; and had likewise killed nine white people in the other towns, some of which they cut up in quarters and stuck up upon poles. ——— That the Indians had a camp at about two miles distance all around fort Prince George, and scouts all the way down to Twelve-mile river to prevent any white man escaping out of the nation, or any intelligence going or coming from the fort. ——— That they had received intelligence that the whole Cherokee nation were arming against us, and that 500 of them were to invade our back settlements on horse-back (which is unusual among the Indians) in different parties; and as the whole of the Long Cane settlers, to the number of 150 souls, were moving off with their effects to go to Augusta, they were attacked by about 100 Cherokees on horse-back, they fought the Indians about half an hour, but were obliged to fly with the loss of 7 Waggons, and 40 of their People killed and taken, the rest got to Augusta. ——— Last Sunday another party of the enemy attacked a number of our people who were building a fort above 30 miles this side of Ninety-six; here our people defended themselves vigorously for 4 hours, beat off the Indians, and killed several of them. ——— Several parties of the Indians are said to be gone to Broad-river, and two towards the northern colonies, and some towards Georgia. ——— Fort Loudoun, it is reported, and we are afraid, is surprized and taken by the Indians; the garrison consisted of 200 men, under Capt. Demere; the Indians had also attempted to surprize fort Prince George, but mascarried in their design. ——— One of the white men killed at Elliott's was Mr. Axson, one of the sworn interpreters at the late treaty. Expresses have been sent to Gen. Amherst, for a body of his Majesty's troops to be sent hither and dispatches are sent to all the colonies by land and water.

BOSTON Feb. 11. We are credibly informed, that notwithstanding the many reports that have been spread some Time ago of Capt. Kennedy's being sent by Gen. Amherst with an Express to General

Wolfe, that it was not so, but that he was sent with a Flag of Truce to the Indian Town of St. Francis, with overtures of Peace, proposed to them by Gen. Amherst, and try to bring them over to English Interest: But they, contrary to all the Rules of War, (even the Savages themselves have heretofore held Flags of Truce sacred) immediately on his arrival, seized Capt. Kennedy, and the few others that were with him, and carried them Prisoners to Montreal: Intelligence of which afterwards coming to the General's Ears, he was so exasperated against them for there inhumanity, that he immediately propos'd the destruction of their Town to Major Rogers, who willingly undertook the Adventure; and the General gave him the choice of as many Men from the whole Army, as he should think requisite to take with him for the Purpose: ⸺ Accordingly he chose 250, and as many more to compleat his Number as was willing to go and be approv'd of by him. In his Way to the Indian Town, he went through a swamp of 50 Miles in Length, at least: and at Night, when he and his Party wanted to Rest, they were obliged to fell saplins, and lay them a-cross each other, in form of a Raft, and cover them over with boughs and Leaves to keep themselves from the Wet: ⸺ Several of his Party perished in this Swamp; and many tired before he came to it: So that when he got within the Sight of the Town, he had but 142 Men with him; with which he accomplish'd it. and there total overthrow. What do we owe to such a beneficial Man; and a Man of such an enterprizing Genius?

It is further said, That the Indians were so sensible that Major Rogers came against the Town of St. Francis on account of their detaining Lieut. Kennedy, that there were greatly exasperated with the French who had encouraged them thus to detain their Prisoners in View of a great Reward: This Behaviour of the French had given great Umbrage to some of their Tribes.

CHARLESTOWN S. Carolina Feb. 16. We are no longer in pain for the safety of Fort Loudoun and its garrison since the arrival of some dispatches from thence wednesday, from Capt. Paul

Demere, the commanding officer of that fort, to his excellency the governor; which were sent by a resolute negro called Abraham (belonging to Mr. Samuel Behg, a trader) who, being a good woodsman, undertook to bring them, upon a promise of his freedom as a reward. Private letters of good authority, brought by this negro, import that the Indians had made 20 attempts whatever, to the second inst. to possess themselves of that fort, yet the paths are every way-laid, and all communication cut off: That the garrison was healthy and in high spirits, and consisted of 180 Men, all determined to sell their lives dear whenever attacked; and plentifully supplied with every thing necessary (except flour) for four or five months: That they had heard of murders committed by the people of the lower towns, since which Captain Demere had constantly employed 50 men of his garrison to add to the strength of the fort. That all the towns of the upper nation were quiet except Settiquo, from whence, it was said, two parties had been sent out against Virginia: That Old-Hop of Cho'; was dead: That the Little-Carpenter and Great-Warrior of Chote still professed "much friendship for the English, that they were strangers to the intentions and outrages of the Lower Cherokees, and had refused to receive a Red Hatchet & scalp sent to them from thence." That Capt. Demere was however much on his guard, lest those men should be at last overborne by the current, or that prime consideration their personal safety; and that he had accordingly sent to Virginia for supplies and to solicit a reinforcement, the fort being nearer the colony than to this, and a better road: That Mr. Butler and Mr. Brannon, two traders supposed to have been murdered, had escaped from the Middle Towns, and were safe in fort Loudoun. A supply of hogs, being arrived there, just before the present disturbances happened, is confirmed. The abilities of the officers there are sufficiently known; so that we have not the least doubt of the garrison's being properly taken care of, especially as Capt. Demere is reckoned to have as much influence & interest with the Great Warrior of Chote, the

Little-Carpenter and other headmen of the upper Cherokees, as any other man whatever, if not more.

The last accounts from lieut. Coytmore, are of the 27th Instant, by the same express which brought the above intelligence; They import, that the Cherokees still continue to beset fort Prince George; that the hills about and in sight of it were full of Indians; that it was almost impracticable to give or receive intelligence; that many of the garrison were sickly, but that it was well supplied with firewood which was the only thing they stood in need off before; that the hostages for the observance of the late treaty, had been demanded to be released, but were still in custody; and that the number of Cherokees in arms, were about 800, and dispersed in parties from 12 to 40 men in each.

From Ninety-Six we learn, that on saturday the 3d instant, a party of the garrison there went out a scout, and surprized two stout young Cherokees, whom they brought prisoners to the fort: That about 40 Indians attacked that fort the next day firing upon it incessantly for two hours, but were bravely repulsed and had two of their gang killed.

Almost every day accounts are brought from different parts of the province, of the incursions of the Indians, of the murders and ravages committed by them, and of the desolation and desertion of the Back Settlements in consequence thereof. In many of them there is too much truth; most are very imperfect, and many absolutely false. There is no certainty of any Indians scalping parties having come 20 miles of the Congarees; neither that settlement nor Orangeburg are broken up; but the people are providing for the security of their families, by erecting three new stockade forts, the principal one at Beaver-Creek, which, we hope will effectually check the progress of the enemy in those parts till the inhabitants can be otherwise relieved.

Several expresses from Fort Moore and Augusta, bring advice, that the Cherokees have made incursions within 25 miles of those forts, on both the Carolina and Georgia side of the river. On the 3d instant one Davis, near Stephen's creek: removing to Augusta, with 23 women and children was way-laid and attacked by the Indians; he defended himself bravely as long as he could, and killed two of his assailants, but at last he was obliged to desert his helpless company in the hands of the enemy. The next day a party of militia went out in quest of the Indians and happening to fall upon the spot where Davis's action had been they thought it prudent to return without burying the cruelly mangled bodies they found there. On the 5th inst. another party went out, from Augusta, to sound the disposition of some Creek Indians at Little River; but were not returned the 7th. Several Creeks had warned white people to move from their settlements, saying, that the Cherokees would be with them at a certain day and hour. Many children have been found wandering the woods, of the that were attacked removing from Long Cane settlement; our man brought no less than 9 of them to Augusta, which he pick'd up in two different parties, some of them terribly cut with tomahawks and left for dead, and others scalp'd yet alive.

NEW-YORK Feb. 18. Part of a Letter from Albany, dated Feb. 11, 1760.

"Two Indians from Niagara, arrived here last night, with Letters importing, that every thing was quiet, and that the Indians, our new Allies, behave very discreetly. ⸻ These Indians say, That there is now a grand Congress at Onondaga, consisting of deputies from Ottowawa, the Chippawas, Misesaugus (we learn Jadiars) Huron, Caghuwago, Oswegatchee [situated between Frontenac and Montreal] the Six Nations, &c. and further add, that they expect the Result of those Deliberations, will soon be communicated to Sir William Johnson."

CHARLESTOWN S. Carolina Feb. 23. The whole province is now in arms; or arming, to repress the invasion of the perfiduous Cherokees. In those parts where the militia are most useful, strong parties alternately range the woods. ⸻ A reward of twenty five pounds is offered by the Government for every Cherokee scalp. ⸻ From fort Moore we learn, that a gang of 18 Cherokees, divided into 3 or 4 parties, on the 15th inst. way laid and killed Ulric Tobler, Esq; a Captain of the militia, wounded Mr. Calhoon, and two or three others in company escap'd unhurt. ——— About the same time two men were killed and were scalp'd near Germany's fort. ——— Gen. Stanwix, in consequence of the advices sent him, he detached the Virginia regiment commanded by Col. Byrd, from Pittsburgh to act against the Cherokees as occasion might require. ——— Only five or six people are yet killed by the Chrokees on the Georgia side of Savannah river. ——— That the loss of the Lone Cane settlers, who were attack'd by the Indians on the 1st inst. as they were removing with their wives and children to Augusta, amounted to 50 persons, chiefly women and children, with 13 loaded waggons and carts, and that the indians had butcher'd the dead bodies in a most inhumane manner.

BOSTON Feb. 25. From Halifax we have Advice, That the beginning of this Instant February arrived there two Schooners which had been sent by the Government to St. John's River in the Bay of Fundy, for the Inhabitants there. They were landed at Halifax, among them were the Jesuit Pere Germain, with some of the St. John's Indians.

BOSTON Feb. 25. Friday last an express returned here from Albany, by him we are informed that last Thursday se'nnight as Maj. Rogers with a party of his men and a number of Slays, with provisions and stores, were going from Ticonderoga to Crown Point, they were fired upon by a party of about 150 French and Indians, and 3 of his rangers killed, and 9 taken prisoner; several sleys were also taken by the enemy, and 2 or 3 horses killed, but, all the drivers escap'd: ——— Maj. Rogers himself narrowly escap'd being either kill'd or taken, but was so lucky as to be in first sley, which the enemy let quietly pass by them, in hopes thereby to have secured the rest.

NEW-YORK Feb. 25. The following letter is taken from the London Evening Post of December 29, 1759.

Extract of a letter from Albany, oct. 29, 1759.
"Cayanquilliqoa and Rattlesnake Sam, two Mohawk Indians came here Yesterday. They were about 14 Days ago at Oswegachie, in Canada, on a visit to some relations who have many years settled with the french. They say they endeavoured to persuade their relation, and the other Mohawks at Oswegatchie, to leave the French in good time, and return to their own country, telling them, "that the English, formerly women, were all turned to men, and were as thick all over the country as the trees in the woods. That they had taken the Ohio, Niagara, Cataraqui, Ticonderoga, Louisbourg, and now lately Quebec; and that they would soon eat up the remainder of the French in Canada and all the Indians that adhered to them." But the French Indians answered: "Brethren, you are deceived; the English cannot eat up the French; their mouths are to little, their jaws too weak, and their teeth not sharp enough. Our father Onotio (that is the Governor of Canada) has told us, and we believe him, that the English, like a thief, have stolen Louisbourg and Quebec from the great King, while his back was turned, and he was looking another way: but now he has turned his face, and sees what the English have done, he is going into the country with a thousand great canoes, and all his warriors; and he will take the Little King, and pinch him till he makes him cry out, and give back what he has stolen: as he did about ten summers ago, and this your eyes will soon see." The same notions and prejudices, we find, are industriously spread amongst the Six Nations: God grant nothing may happen at the peace to confirm them; for the Indians have no Idea of exchanging conquests, of delivering up what is once taken, but for motives of fear or weakness; and they know little or nothing of what passes in other parts of the world."

CHARLESTOWN S. Carolina Feb. 27. Part of a Letter from Augusta, Feb. 9, 1760.
"If my capacity would permit to do it, it would be too shocking to paint the melancholy scenes that were presented to us in our little march

to the Frontiers. ——— Poor families in droves removing, not knowing where to go; several of them wounded and scalped, who were left by the savages for dead, even little infants two and three years old, strong new houses, and well cultivated plantations, the effects of much labour and industry, deserted, with plenty of provisions exposed to the fury and flames of those barbarians: ——— Surely we should be roused by the great call of nature to take ample vengeance to those destroyers of our fellow creatures? there is not a house or plantation above Mr. Germany's 15 miles off, but what is deserted.

MARCH 1760

CHARLESTOWN S. Carolina March 1. Letters from Prince Georges of the 24th past, contain the following advices; that Ocunnatota, the great warrior of Chote, had beset that fort with 30 gun men, and had wounded Lieut. Coytmore, the commanding officer of that fort, in the left breast, which 'twas thought would prove mortal: two others were also wounded, tho' not dangerously: That Ensign Milin upon this judged it improper and unsafe for the garrison that the hostages should continue any longer only confined to a room, ordered the soldiers to put them in irons; and the soldiers accordingly set about executing these orders, when the first who attempted to take hold of an Indian, was killed on the spot, being struck on the head with a tomahawk, stabbed in the belly with a knife, and his jaw broke; another was wounded in the forehead, this outrage so alarmed and incensed the garrison, that it was tho't expedient to put all the hostages to death immediately, which was accordingly done: That in the night, the Indians which were without the fort, drew near and fired two signal guns, and several times cried out in the Cherokee language, "Fight strong, and you shall be assisted," soon after which the Indians began firing on all sides of the fort; and hence it was suspected, that it had been concerted between the hostages within, and their friends without, to attack and massacre the garrison that night; for upon searching the apartment in which the hostages lay, there was found, a bottle of poison, which they designed to have emptied into the well, several tomahawks buried in the earth, which their friends had privately conveyed thither; so that putting the hostages to death has proved a very critical event, the garrison being freed from the future apprehensions within.

BOSTON March 3. By the South Carolina Gazette of the 9th ult. bro't here on thursday last by Capt. Gardiner from that Port we learn, that the Cherokee Indians had again broke out in open Hostilities, as soon as the Governor and his Army had left Keowee and returned, notwithstanding the Treaty of Peace and Friendship lately concluded and agreed upon between Governor Lyttleton, and that Tribe. —— That they had already kill'd and massacred about 50 Men, Women and Children; and on the 25th of January, a Body of them were gone to besiege Fort Prince George, and then to fall on the back Settlements of that Province: That a great many French Indians were come into the Cherokees; and that the latter had cut one Kelly's Body into pieces, which they hung upon Poles. That one Indian called the Mortar was arrived among the Cherokees, with 100 Creeks, but on what Errand was not known. —— That these Accounts were bro't and deliver'd under Oath by several Persons who were taken and escaped from the Indians: That the General Assembly has been sitting upon this Account; and it was tho't the Governor would make a Campaign against the Cherokees of quite a different Kind than the last: that Expresses were forwarded Northerly to all the Governments, to come as far as New-York. —— It is said two Regiments are to be sent from thence to South Carolina.

On Thursday the 21st Instant Mr. Montrefor, second Engineer at Quebec, and Lieutenant in the 48th Regiment, escourted by Lieut. Butler and a Party of Rangers, arrived at Brunswick from Quebec, across the Land in 26 Days: and on Monday last, Mr. Montrefor arrived at this Place with Dispatches for the Governor; and Wednesday set forward for General Amherst. —— We hear that the Troops are healthy and the Garrison in good Order: —— That all Lower Canada, to the Number of 6000 fighting Men, have delivered up their Arms, and taken the Oath of Fidelity; and that the Militia in said Parts hold their Commissions now under General Murray. —— That the People of the Country supply the Garrison with fresh Provisions as far as the distress'd State of their Settlements will admit of. —— That the Labourers and Artificers work at the usual Price, for the Garrison; and that the People are very happy and contented under the British Government. —— That the Troops having no spiritous Liquors, except a Jill of Brandy whenever they work; but drinking only Spruce Beer, are free from Scurvy. —— That General Murray has given out of the French Stores, taken there, to every Man, Socks, Mauckisans, Leggins, Shirts flannel Jackets, Coats, and Caps laced with Furr: —— which is the Dress of the Soldiers from the General to the Private. —— That as to the Enemy about the Town, so far from any hope of making any Impression on our Folks, wou'd think themselves happy, could they be next Spring in any Posture of Defence to oppose us. —— We hear, the General has turn'd all the Jesuits out of Town, and had made a Store of their College. —— Of eleven Merchant Vessels that attempted to pass the Town in November last. on a dark Night, three were cast away.

We hear, that one of the said Vessels blew up and another a Lieutenant of the Troops and a Number of seamen, said to be 48, had got on board to take possession.

BOSTON March 17. Extract of a Letter received from Charlestown in South Carolina, Feb. 4, 1760

"We lately wrote you, that the Cherokee Indians had submitted to our demands of satisfaction for the former insults, by surrendering some and leaving hostages for the delivery of others of their people, who had been concern'd in murdering some of our back settlers, and had also entered into a firm treaty of peace with this government: but no sooner was our army withdrawn from their country that they showed their insincerity first by cruelly murdering every white man they could lay hands on (for a few happily escaped) in their towns; surrounded Fort Prince George; cut off all intercourse with our upper Fort Loudoun, and followed the bloody stroke, by massacring numbers of families in the remote Parts of the province, and now have penetrated within 60 or 80 miles of this town, leaving the marks of savage cruelty and devastation wherever they go. We are making head against them, and hope in a few weeks to repel them, and prevent further incursions; and when we receive succours from General Amherst, and the neighbouring provinces, we may chastise and humble them; but, in the mean time our distress is great, and greatly aggravated by the small-pox, which spread among us. Some thousands are now under inoculation, and many taken down in the natural way; or the latter a pretty large proportion has died. We shall know the effects of the former in about 10 days hence. These calamities united, throws us all into great confusion, and we shall feel the effects for a long time."

By other letters from South Carolina, we also learn, that by accounts which are daily received from their back settlements, of the incursions and cruel murders committed by the Chrokee Indians on the inhabitants of those places, added to the prevalency of the small-pox, had almost stagnated all business there: ——— That it was suppos'd to present Indian war has been long since fomented by French missionaries among the Cherokees and that all their late shews of friendship were deep laid dissimulations in which the Indians seem as well versed as politer Nations.

BOSTON March 17. Extract of a Letter from Halifax, February 27, 1760.

"Our Government has settled a Treaty of Peace and Commerce with the Chief of the Indians of St. John's River and a Chief of the Passanaquadie Tribe. ——— Large quantities of Goods for the Trade are brought up and shipped on board Capt. Cobb, who will sail in a Day or two with the above Indians for the River St. John's. Yesterday 5 Indians of the Tribe of Micmac came to Town to settle a Treaty of Peace with our Government."

Yesterday Capt. Smallage in a Sloop arrived here in 7 Days from Louisbourg, by whom we learn, That the Garrison at that Place are well, and have plenty of good provisions: The Winter has been very severe at Louisbourg, but moderated much when Capt. Smallage came away.

We also learn by the above Vessel, That the Provincial Troops of this Province who have been garrison'd at Louisbourg the Summer and Winter past, have nearly all inlisted again for the ensuing Campaign, being well satisfied with the large Bounty and Encouragement given by the Government.

Also arrived here Yesterday a Sloop in 6 Days from Halifax, by whom we have an Account that most of the Provincials at that Place and up the Bay of Fundy, have again chearfully inlisted for another Campaign.

We hear from the Penobscot Tribe of Indians are come in to Fort Pownall, and are very desirous of making Peace with the Government upon any Terms.

BOSTON March 17. Last Monday se'nnight Lieut. John Momtresor arrived at New-York from Quebec, with verbal dispatches from Brigadier General Murray, to his Excellency General Amherst, as has been formerly mentioned, and gives the following further account of the situation of our affairs there; that our Troops were in good health and high spirits; had plenty of all kinds of salt provisions, and were tolerably supplied with fresh by the French, 6000 of whom have taken the oath of fidelity to the English, that we had two advanced posts, one at St. Foy, and the other at Loretto, seven miles from Quebec, where our People remained in the greatest security, not one person being killed since the surrender of the place; that a Drum-major in the Colony troops of Canada, who had permission to supply the garrison with greens, &c. was found out in endeavouring to enlist some of our soldiers in French service, and persuading other to desert, being tried by a court-martial, and found guilty of treason was immediately hanged up; that the river St. Lawrence was not froze over at Quebec, the 26th of January; and that the following articles would fetch a great price to those who arrive there first this Spring, viz. Candles, Salt, Tea, Chocolate, Coffee, Sugar, &C. &C.

Lieut. Butler, who escorted Lieut Montresor, set out from Quebec, for this Place in December last, but was obliged to return, after being 21 days in the woods, being pursued by a party of Indians from whom they were secured by the French Inhabitants, in their return, and were extremely well used by them.

NEW-YORK March 17. A Detachment of Colonel Montgomery's Highland Regiment, consisting of 600 Men, destined for South Carolina, arrived here from Epsopus, last Saturday, and immediately embarked on board the following Transports in the North-River, viz. The ship Amherst, the Nicholls: Ship Two-Friends, Spellen, and Brig Swan, Waddell.

The Detachment from the Royal Scotch, consisting of 600 Men also, are to embark at Amboy, on board the Ship Thonton, Gildrist; Snow Albany, Breton; and the Ship Carolina Boyd.

We hear the General Assembly of this Province Have come to a Resolution to raise the same number of Men this Year, as they did the last, and that the Bounty for Volunteers will be the same also.

CHARLESTOWN S. Carolina March 18. His Excellency Governor Lyttleton embarks soon for England in the Frigate Trent, commanded by John Lindsay, Esq; at his departure, the administration will fall on hon. William Bull, Esq; whose commission appointing him Lieut. Governor of this province, came over in the Live Oak.

BOSTON March 22. To His Excellency Thomas Pownall, Esq; Captain General and Governor in Chief in and over his Majesty's Province of the Massachusetts-Bay, and Vice-Admiral of the same,

The humble Address of His Majesty's Council for the said Province.

May it please your Excellency,

His Majesty having thought fit to appoint your Excellency to the Command of the Province of South Carolina, We the Members of the Council for His Majesty's Province of Massachusetts-Bay think ourselves bound on this Occasion, however unwelcomed, to present this our address to your Excellency.

Gratitude, without Acknowledging the many Advantages which have accrued to his Majesty's Service in general, and to this His Majesty's

Province in particular, by means of your Excellency's Administration: an Administration, short indeed, but active, vigorous and filled with affairs great and important. The public Good has evidently been your Excellency's chief and constant View. To promote it you have engaged Harmony between the several Branches of the Legislature has been a natural Consequence of such Views and such Measures. The Approbation of Your Royal Master, has been the great and just Reward.

And although Taxes and other burdens heavy and unprecedented have been brought upon the People, yet they have born them chearfully, sensible that their Burthen's were Necessary, and that their Monies were applied by your Excellency with Faithfulness and the best Occonomy.

A Regard to the Interest of the Province, Obliges Us to whish that such an Administration might have longer continued. His Majesty has a Right to employ his Servants where he thinks proper; and it is our Duty to submit to his Royal Approbation.

May your Excellency's Services in your new Appointment, be as important and extensive as they have been in this: and may they be as gratefully Accepted.

Your Excellency's Relation to us as our Governor, must cease. Your Affection for us we hope will not. It is very probable Opportunities may present of Recommending and Advancing the Interest of the Province, and we doubt not that we shall yet Experience further Instances of your Regard and Favour.

PHILADELPHIA March 27. A Letter from Pittsburgh, dated 20th ult. mention one Giles Collins belonging to the Artillery, being killed and scalped a few Days before, about four Miles from the Fort; and that some Wyondott Indians had come there, and brought with them a Prisoner.

BOSTON March 31. In our Paper some time ago, we mentioned the arrival of a number of Indian chiefs at Louisbourg, from Pictou, to treat for peace, but had then no account of the Terms on which they submitted; we have now received a copy of a letter sent to them, with the articles of capitulation, which we are requested to publish at this time.

The following is the copy of a letter sent by Lieutenant Henry Scomberg, commanding against Pictou, to the Rev. Mr. Maillard grand Vicar to all the Savages.

Rev. Sir,

His Excellency Brigadier General Edward Whitmore, Governor of Louisbourg. ——— and my General, having thought proper to confer the honor upon me to convey his sentiments to you, I now profit of this opportunity to deliver you his thoughts.

The white flag I send in my boat, is an emblem of the innocence and friendship. I come with; tho' too a body of people the least deserving my Royal Master's favour. I also must tell you, that your capital Quebec is surrendered to the King my Master's troops, your army is entirely routed: So that should you, or your people, persist in your rashness, you must inevitably perish by famine, since you can have no succours.

If therefore you would, as I heartily wish you may do, accept of the Olive Branch I send you, and put me in possession of the vessels your people have taken, and surrender your selves to me, I am Authorized by the King my master's commands to assure you, that you shall enjoy all your liberties and properties, with a free excise of your religion, as you will perceive by the inclosed manifesto I have the honor to send you.

Should you doubt the sincerity of my heart, I am ready to treat with you, and exchange hostages: My intentions being humane, equal to my orders, and the generosity of the British nation, to which I have the honor to belong, shall then be fully display'd.

But if, Sir, contrary to my hopes, you should refuse this my christian-like offer; on the white flag's return, you may expect to see the red flying, a token of my King's great indignation; which if you compel me to do, my troops once landed, I will not answer for the cruelties that may ensue, for I deal plainly; I am fully determined to put all to the sword without mercy.

These Sir, are no rash promises, but my real sentiments: Therefore let me pray you not be the instrument that may oblige me to shed human blood. ——— and carry the horror of War Towards a people who have still in their power to enjoy peace and plenty.

ARTICLES OF Capitulation.

Granted by Lieutenant Henry Schomberg, of His Majesty's fourteenth regiment of foot, commanding an Expedition against Pictou, Malogomiche, or any other harbours where the Savages and French are in arms against his Britannick Majesty, to the Reverend Mr. Maillard, Grand Vicar to all the Savages and French in their behalf.

Article I. The Savages and French lay down their arms to me.

II. To send six Indians Chiefs with me to Louisbourg, to pay homage to his Excellency General Whitmore Governor of that fortress and town.

III. To surrender up all their effects to me.

IV. The Savages to stretch along the sea-coast to endeavour to save part of such ships and vessels as are cast on shore, to save the people's lives, and to protect and maintain them with what the Woods afford.

V. The Savages to run all about the Woods to acquaint other Savages, who do not know of the peace, to prevent any accident that may happen.

VI. That Capt. Paul Le Blanc, of a Privateer, who has taken many of our vessels, and whom is now at Riscibucto, deliver them to me.

These Articles ratified,

I promise the Savages, &c. good quarters, and treat them as friends and allies, and to enjoy a free exercise of their religion.

20th of November 1759.

BOSTON March 31. Last Thursday Morning arrived here Capt. Dorrington from Halifax in 8 Days. We learn, that a Number of Frenchmen had lately come into Fort Cumberland at Chignecto, and surrendered themselves. They gave an Account, that they belonged to a large French Ship of 20 Guns, bound up the River St. Lawrence; but they being catched in the Ice at Gaspee, and frozen up, they left her there and travelled over Land to Chignecto. We hear that Commodore Lord Colville has ordered two of His Majesty's Frigates to sail immediately to take Possession of her.

The following information was given to Joseph Frye, Esq; Col. Commanding His Britannic Majesty's Garrison at Fort Cumberland, by the Coxswain of the Barge of a French Frigate now at Gaspee, from whence he deserted, viz. ——— That she is a Frigate built Ship, of between 4 & 500 Tons Berthen, formerly English, and called King George, but now Two-Brothers, commanded by Mons. Bushee, pierc'd for 26, but mounts only 22 9 pounders, man'd (when she sailed from Bourdeaux) with 64 Men, 25 only of whom are French, the rest composed of disaffected Spaniards, Italians, &c. who are ready to revolt upon the first Occasion, by Reason of their Treatment from the Captain; that many of her Crew have deserted since her being at Gaspee. ——— Her Cargo consists of Provisions, Arms, Ammunition, Wine, Brandy, Blankets, &c. and that she is quite unrig'd and hawled up into a Creek for the Winter, not knowing (when she sail'd from Bourdeaux) of the Surrender of Quebec: that the Captain is in great Expectation of the retaking of the City, in which Case he intends to land his cargo there according to his first Orders; but if not, he intends to push out as early in the Spring as possible, either for the West-Indies or Europe.

The General Assembly of the Colony of Connecticut have ordered Five Thousand Men for the Service of the ensuing Campaign, And, The Province of New-Jersey have agreed to raise the same Number of Men for the ensuing Campaign that they did the last, and to give the same bounty. viz. 12 pounds Proclamation Money, to all who shall voluntarily inlist.

NEW-YORK March 31. A letter from Oswego, dated the 25th ult. mentions their receiving a trading visit from the Oswegatchie Indians; that they expected another party on the same account every day; and that those that had been with them behaved exceeding well.

APRIL 1760

CHARLESTOWN S. Carolina April 2. On Thursday an express from the Creek nation brought the most agreeable answers from the different parts of that nation, to a talk dated the 5th of February, which was sent up to them on occasion of the fresh hostilities committed by the Cherokees, by Mr. Atkin his Majesty's agent and superintendent of Indian Affairs. The disposition of the Creek nation in favour of the English may be seen by the answer they returned to the talk sent them by the Cherokees, in order to induce them to commit hostilities against the English, viz. "That Cherokees were mad, and had spoiled the best friend they had; that the Creeks would not help them; but as they had begun the War they might end it themselves; for that they the Creeks were not so mad as they were to kill their traders whom they loved. Advised them not to make a practice of coming with lies to the Creek nation; and beware of spoiling the path to Augusta, if they did, they should repent it; for that they would guard any English traders up and down the path, and if any of their blood should be spilt therefore, they would mix their own with it."

We hear the rangers are now compleated, and continue to scout for the protection of the back settlements. The forts at Ninety-six, Saluda, &c. are all safe, several scouting parties have come up with divers parties of Indians, some of whom they killed and scalped. The levies for a new regiment go on. They are reports of a second attack of Fort Dobbs in N. Carolina. There have been no accounts from Fort Prince George, keowee or Fort Loudoun, since those published of the 5th and 12th ult. nor have we been able to learn what, or if any assistance, the province of

Virginia, and North-Carolina will afford in reducing the Cherokees.

BOSTON April 7. Extract taken from Governor Bernard's Speech to the New-Jersey Assembly he delivered the 25th ult.

"When I received his Majesty's command to attend his service in the province of Massachusetts-Bay, I was ordered to stay here till Mr. Boone, appointed to this government, should arrive. I have been advised by his letter, dated from Charlestown the 14 day of February last, that he will set out for this province with all convenient dispatch."

NEW-YORK April 7. On Friday last arrived here at Sandy-Hook, the schooner Polly, George North master, in five Days from Charles-Town, South-Carolina, bound to Amboy, having on board his Excellency Thomas Boone, Esq; captain general and commander in chief of the province of New-Jersey, who quited the schooner at the hook, and came up to this city in one of our pilot boats; and we hear, designed to set out for his government in a day or two.

NEW-YORK April 7. Our advices from Carolina are, That the Cherokees still continue their depredation on the frontiers of that province, that 'twas thought the whole action would be in arms. That Capt. Coytmore was dead of his wounds; That several bodies of Creeks were gone out against them, leaving their marks upon all they killed.

PHILADELPHIA April 10. In a Letter from South Carolina dated the 20th ult. there is the following Paragraph.

"Tis to be presumed that you will naturally expect some News relative to the present Situation of this Colony, which you will, in a few Words, conceive, when I assure you, that no Description can surpass the Calamity. ——— What few escape the Indians, no sooner arrive in Town, then they are seized with the Small-Pox, which generally carries them off; and from the Numbers already dead, you may judge the Fatality of the Decease. Of the White Inhabitants 95; Accadians 115; Negroes 500, were dead two Days ago, by the Sexton's Account. About 1500 White

Inhabitants, 1800, Negroes and 300 Acadians, have had the Distemper, and chiefly by Inoculation."

BOSTON April 14. Yesterday Capt. Reed arrived here from Penobscott, in whom came four Indian Chiefs of that Tribe in order to Treat with this Government for a Lasting and honourable Peace. We hear there are now 28 of that Tribe, Men, Women and Children at Fort Pownall.

CHARLESTOWN S. Carolina April 16. On Thursday last came to town some of the people who were at the engagement with the Cherokees on Catawba river, and further inform us that the number of Indians was forty, and the white people thirty. None of the latter were killed. Several of the dead bodies of the Indians have been found in the woods by different scouting parties. Nineteen of the Indian scalps were ready to be sent down when the people came away. Colonel Waddell was at Fort Dodds, about 27 Miles N. E. from the place; the Indians that escaped, and some others, attacked the said fort, but were repulsed; and it is believed, that all the forty Indians, not more than one is left alive, or will get back the nation. One of the Indians that was shot had no less than six green white scalps which the white people here have now in their possessions.

About the middle of last Month a party of the inhabitants near Catawba river that were out on scout came, came up with 30 Indians, who after exchanging a few shots, took to a deserted house, which our people soon set on fire, and obliged the Indians to scamper, tho' not without the loss of nine of them, who were shot as they attempted to get out of the house.

A number of inhabitants from almost all parts of the province are gone out in quest of the Savages, and are determined to spare none that fall into their hands. The Creeks have determined several of the Cherokees, bloodied the pain so much, and made the breach between the two nations so great, as to render it a most important piece of service to all the southern provinces.

PHILADELPHIA April 17. Fort at Pittsburgh,

March 2, 1760.
"This day major-general Stanwix set out for Philadelphia, escorted 35 of the chiefs of the Ohio Indians and 50 Royal Americans. The presence of the General has been of the utmost consequence at this post during the winter as well for cultivating the friendship and alliance of the Indians, as for continuing the fortifications, and supplying the troops here and the communications. The works are now quite perfected, according to the plan from the Ohio to the Monongahela, and eighteen pieces of artillery mounted on the bastion that cover the Isthmus; and casemates, barracks, and store-houses are also completed for the garrison of 1000 men and officers; so that it may be now asserted with very great truth that the British dominion is established on the Ohio. The Indians are carrying on a vast trade with the merchants of Pittsburgh; and instead of desolating the frontiers of these colonies, are entirely employed in increasing the trade and wealth thereof. The happy effects of our military operation this way are also felt by about four thousand poor inhabitants, who are now in quiet possession of the lands they were driven from, on the frontiers of Pennsylvania, Maryland and Virginia.

From Winchester we are informed, that several parties of the Cherokees have made incursions into Augusta County in Virginia; that a detachment of the Virginia regiment, under Capt. Gist, has had several skirmishes with them, in which he always repulsed the enemy, and always kept the field, tho' with great loss of men; and that in these skirmishes several of the Cherokees have been killed and scalped.

We have advice from Albany, that two men had made their escape from Fort de troit, and got safe to Niagara; who informs, that the French there were in great want of provisions, and had sent all the soldiers and most of the inhabitants to Missisippi for a supply.

CHARLESTOWN S. Carolina April 20. Yesterday we received letters, from Georgia, dated the 10th inst. and we are informed, that Governor Ellis had sent off another party of Creeks against the Cherokees, and that it consisted of 9 resolved Fellows, who are very ambitious of distinguishing themselves.

BOSTON April 21. Wednesday last the General Assembly of the Province met according to adjournment.

Extract from the Journal of the Hon. House of Representatives:

Mr. Secretary Oliver brought the following Message from his Honour the Lieut, Governor to the House. viz.

Gentlemen of the Council and House of Representatives: By the Post I received a Letter from His Excellency the Governor, dated New-London the 10th Instant. There were included two other Letters which the Governor received at New-London, one from His Excellency Gen. Amherst, and the other from the Honourable Governor Fitch; both which, at the Governor's Desire, I am to communicate to you.

You will find in the General's Letter several Matters which well deserved your consideration, especially what relates to the Levies which you have determined shall be raised for the Service of the ensuing Year.

The Returns of the Men enlisted within the Province shall be laid before you, You will perceive that notwithstanding the very proper Measures taken by His Excellency to forward the Inlistment, we are yet very far from compleating the Number of Five Thousand, which are proposed should be raised.

From Nova-Scotia there have been no regular Return made; but by advices which have been received from the several Posts there, we have no reason to suppose that one half that Number which was generally expected will have Enlisted.

You are sensible Gentlemen, that you can continue to sit for a few Days. I would therefore recommend it to you to engage in no other business until you have determined upon the Way and Manner of making up the Deficiencies.

I Hope this Recommendation will be all that shall be needful from me, that His excellency will return before you can have made any great Progress, and that you will have the Benefit of his Advice and Assistance. But Many Things should occasion his Absence to be longer than is expected. I shall be ready to join with you in every Act of Government that shall be convenient and necessary.

Council Chamber 16th April 1760.

T. Hutchinson.

BOSTON April 21. Our advices from South-Carolina, relating to Indian affairs are continued in the following extracts, viz.

That in the 1st of March Lieut. Coytmore of fort Prince George died of his wounds; the Indians continue firing upon the garrison, but only one soldier was killed in the fort. ――― On the 3d 250 Cherokees attacked the fort at Ninety-six for 36 hours without intermission at 60 Yards distance, one of the Cherokee, was killed and scalped, whose body was given to the dogs, and his scalp hoisted along-side the colours to provoke them to come nearer: next day the fort was reinforced with Major Lloyd and 11 men; six Cherokees were killed and many wounded; only two wounded in the fort; on the 4th the enemy withdrew ――― The 6th six men were attacked going from Turner's to Pennington fort, by about 40 Indians, 2 were killed, 2 missing, and two got back to Turner's. ――― Capt. Grinman immediately set out with 33 rangers; in crossing the river were surrounded by about 70 Indians, which obliged them to retreat back, which he did without loss, by the time he got back the fort was surrounded by 100 Indians, who only viewed it and went off without firing a gun, they burnt every thing on their going off. ――― On the 9th a man was killed in Saxe-Gotha township by the Indians; on the 10th Jacob Trests and one Jenkins were killed and scalped: the same day 25 other persons were murdered on the forks of the Edisto River, about 10 miles from the head of Congaree creek. ――― On the 11th Mr. Gillivray's plantation was attacked by the Indians, Capt. Tobler, who was killed had about 50 guns fired at him, the Indians chiefly aimed at him; his loss is great at this time; it is suspected some discontented Creek under Cherokees took his life.

On the 18th a half breed who is a leader and head warrior of three squares of the Oakfuskees, with another warrior and their attendance came to to fort Augusta, to see the behaviour of the Cherokees; but as they had no power to engage with the English, they set out next day under assurances of endeavours to assist their friends the English; for which they received presents.
——— The Chicasaws, when the Creeks endeavvoured to persuade into a neutrality, has promised to assist our cause, upon receiving some presents, and pretend to be very hearty. ———
That the Creeks, who were uneasy when German's fort was erected, seemed more reconciled; the several gentlemen among them were zealously active and afficacious in endeavouring to interest that nation in our quarrel ——— That the trees and bushes were ordered to be cut down for 50 Yards on each side the great road from Mr. Rae's to the Douglas's to make the travelling faster.

BOSTON April 21. We learn from Albany, that Capt. Tute of the Rangers, with 4 or 5 others were lately taken and carried off by the Indians near Crown-Point.

CHARLESTOWN S. Carolina April 23. We hear the design of the Cherokees in seeming desirous of peace, is to try to get things passed over till the fall, when after their harvest Season, they may fall upon us with redoubled fury, but their scheme have been happily discovered.

A party of Chickasaws that lately went to the war from Augusta, returned thither the 11th instant, with two Cherokee Scalps which they had taken near Estatown.

An account is just been received, that a Catawba woman and child have been lately killed and scalped in their own country; and that two very large gangs of Cherokees are set out for the frontier of North-Carolina and Virginia, while they pretend to treat of peace with us.

Most of the letters from fort Prince George, observe that the Cherokee either artfully disguise some very deep laid scheme, the execution of which cannot be very distant or that something has lately happened, which has put them into a terrible fright: they add, that abundance of Cherokees are dead of the small-pox, and the ammunition of the rest are near exhausted, and some observe, that it the war be immediately carried into their country, most of the Nation must perish for want of subsistences, or submit.

BOSTON April 28. Extract of a Letter from Crown-Point, dated April 4, 1760.

"On the 31st of March there was a small party of 9 men across the lake fishing, who before they could get their boats, were all taken by a party of French and Indians, without firing a gun on either side: in this small party there was three officers, Capt. Tute of the rangers, Lieut. Fortiscue, and Ens. Steward of the 21st regiment; the private men consisted of 3 rangers and 3 regulars, those savages have killed none of the party. The lake is almost clear of Ice, and in a few days we expect the sloops and brigs down from Ticonderoga, which will cruize about and watch the enemy's motions."

NEW-YORK April 28. Tuesday last four deserters from the French at Nut Island, on Lake Champlain came to town from Albany; they say that 15,000 men are collected together at Montreal in order to attack Quebec in the spring, in case a fleet arrives from Old France to succour them; otherwise 'tis said they intend to submit to the English.

CHARLESTOWN S. Carilina. On Friday we received the following, dated Agusta April 2, About three weeks ago the first party of Creeks sent out by Governor Ellis and Mrs Bosomworth, returned here with 3 Cherokee scalps; two more have likewise been brought in by the Chickasaws sent from this palce, neither Creeks or Chickasaws lost any of their people. Ten days ago nine Euchees and two Creeks set off from this place, and attacked about three miles above German's fort, by a superior number of Cherokees, three of whom they killed but could get only one scalp; one Euchee was wounded, and is since dead, the others are gone to Savannah with their scalps, and intend to get a sufficient force and return for satisfaction from the Cherokees.

MAY 1760

BOSTON May 5, We have advice from Springfield, That 'twas last week reported thereby a Person from Albany that Mons. Vaudreuil, was, with his Army advancing, from Montreal, St. John's, &c. towards Quebec, in order to attack it, and had got his Cannon a considerable Way; but imagine there is nothing more to be depended on, than what is inserted in the New-York head.

From the Westward we learn, that a small party of Indians had been near the fort at Hoosuck: That yesterday 7-night at the time of a heavy rain and thunder, a flag was stuck on a pole, and fired in a plain at a small distance from the fort; a party was sent out to see the occasion, and discovered a few Indians in ambush, who made off, suppos'd on seeing of large number come out than they expected: It is thought they were St. John's Indians, and wanted to decoy out of the fort one or two men to gain intelligence.

BOSTON May 5.   Province of Nova-Scotia.

An Act to prevent private Trade of Commerce with the Indians.

Whereas Articles of Peace have been concluded by and between His Excellency the Governor, in behalf of His Majesty, and the Indian Delegates from the Tribes of St. John's River and Passamaquadie, in the Bay of Fundi, and Part of the Tribes of the Michmacks; Whereby said, Tribes have obliged themselves not to trade with any Person or Persons whatsoever, but such as shall be appointed Truck-Masters, or Licensed for that Purpose, by the Governor, Lieutenant-Governor, of Commander in Chief of the Province for the time being:

And for the better and more effectual carrying on a trade and Cormmerce with the said Indians, according to the said Articles; and to prevent private Persons from carrying on any separate Trade, Commerce, or Dealings whatsoever, with the said Indians;

Be it enacted His Excellency the Governor the Council and Assembly and by the authority of the same it is hereby enacted, That from and after the Twenty-first Day of May 1760, no Person or Persons whatsoever, other than such as shall be appointed Truck-Masters by His Excellency the Governor, Lieutenant-Governor, or other commaner in Chief for the Time Being, or Persons Licenced by them or either of them for that Purpose, shall or may presume by themselves or any others for them, directly or indirectly, to Buy, Sell, Truck, Barter, Exchange, Give or receive in Gifts, any kind of Provisions, Goods or Merchandize, whatsoever, to or from any aforesaid Indians, or to or from any Person or Persons in their Names, or from their Accounts, on the Penalty of forfeiting the Sum of Fifty Pounds, Sterling, for each and every Offence, and also the Commodities so clandestinely bought or bartered for.

And be it further enacted by the authority aforesaid, That from and after said Twenty-first of May 1760, the Master of any Ship or Vessel, or any Mate, Master, or Passenger, on board any Ship or Vessel, in any Bay, Harbour, Fort, River, or Creek, within the Province, or upon the Coasts thereof, who shall be found, or Convicted of, Trading with the said Indians, contrary to the Tenor of Effect of this Law, that then the Master of such Ship or Vessel shall forfeit the Sum of One Hundred Pounds Sterling, and suffer Twelve Months Imprisonment; And the Vessel (Carrying such Goods for Trade with the said Indians,) with all her Appurtenances shall be forfeited, together with all such Goods as shall have been so illicitly purchased of, or bartered for with the said Indians. And it shall and may be lawful for any of His Majesty's Justices of the Place in the said Province, or any officer commanding any Fort or Garrison in said Province, or any of the said Truck-masters, in Case no Justice be resident at or near such Fort or

Garrison, upon information either by the said Indians themselves, or any other Person or Persons whatsoever, made of such illicit Trade, to apprehend the said Master and keep him in Custody, and to detain the said Vessel and Goods so illicitly purchased of, or bartered for with the Indians, until the said Matter be fully enquired into and finally determined. And all His Majesty's Justices of the Peace, Officers of Forts and Garrisons, and Truck-Masters, and all His Majesty's Subjects within said Province, are hereby required and directed to aid and assist in the Execution of this Act.

And it is also hereby Enacted, That all Fines, Forfeitures, and Penalties, incurred by this Act, shall be recovered, by Bill, Plaint, or Information, in any of His Majesty's Courts of Record in this Province, (except in Case where any Ship or Vessel may be deemed liable, in which Case, the same shall be Tried and Determined in his Majesty's Court of Vice-Admiralty) and shall be paid, on Half to the Treasurer of this Province, for the use of the Government, and the other Half to the Informer, who shall sue for and recover the same.

And it is also further Enacted, That this Act shall continue and be in force for and during the Term and Space of Two Years from and after the said Twenty-first Day of May 1760, and no longer.

CHARLESTOWN South Carolina May 10. From Georgia we learn that Governor Ellis has dismissed the first Party of Creeks which he engaged to begin Hostilities against the Cherokees, presently satisfied: That he gave the Chiefs Silver Gorgets, and Bracelets, with their Names, Exploits and favorite Figures engraved thereon; and to the Rest Silver Bracelets, which highly pleased them, and 'twas believed would have a very good influence on others: That some of them were gone Southward to secure their Women and Horses; and the Rest returned to War by Way of Augusta: The Fool Harry, since his Son and Nephew had rebelled against him, who declared they could not bear the Sound of War without participating in it, and if he was displeased, they would adopt the English for their Fathers, was hourly expected at Savannah to have a Conference with Mr. Ellis; and that every Thing was now in so good Train amongst the Creeks, that it was hoped, the greatest Part of the Nation, would soon be brought to act vigorously against the Cherokees, entirely owing to the Vigilance, and wise and prudent Measures pursued by Mr. Ellis, and Mr. & Mrs. Bosomworth, and Mr. Gray continued to be very serviceable to his Excellency in his tranlations with the Indians.

The Troops commanded by the Hon. Colonel Montgomery, arrived at Congarees on Thursday the 1st Instant, Waggons were immediately dispatched to Monck's Corner, to bring up what Stores, &c. they had left there, and by the 20th at fartest he expects to move for Ninety-Six, which Place he may reach about the 26th. The Officers and Troops were all in good Health.

We hear that near 400 Rangers are reassembling at Ninety-Six, where they will wait Col. Montgomery's.

An Account came the Day before Yesterday, that two very large Gangs of Cherokees has been discovered on Sunday the 4th Instant, in the Forks of Edisto, about 80 Miles W. from hence, near Capt. Glover's and Mr. Ford's Cowpens: that they had killed some People, and had several Prisoners: One Gang consisted of 60, the other could not be counted. Capt. Samuel Elliott was then near the Enemy with 18 Militia and a few Negroes being then out on their Turn of Duty to Scout that Part of the Country, and prevent their incursions; but not having Force sufficient to go in Quest of them, he sent for a Reinforcement of Men, which we hear he has since received.

Yesterday another Account was brought of some Cherokees having on Friday the 2d Inst. surprized, tied, and carried off all the Negroes belonging to Mr. Henry Young; they came upon them in a Field where they were planting Corn: Amongst the Negroes were six working Hands, one of whom has since escaped. They likewise destroyed Mr. Young's Furniture, and did other Damages, but he being out to dig a Chest which he had buried in the Beginning of the present

Trouble, by that Means happily escaped falling into their Hands himself.

The Nation of Indians that surround us are so numerous and the French so near the Creeks and Chactaws, that it required the greatest Attention to the whole System of Indian Politicks, to extricate ourselves from this critical Situation in which we are at present entangled.

NEW-YORK May 12. Extract of a Letter from Half-Moon dated April 18, 1760.

"This day arrived here, escorted by a party of the Royal Highland regiment, four French deserters from the fortified island they have at the other end of Lake Champlain. By them we are informed that it is guarded by only 450 men, under the command of Mons. Bouganville; and that there is an army of at least 15,000 men, under the command of Mons. Vaudreuille, going against Quebec. These deserters left the island the 10th of this month; and further say, that they were hard put to it for provisions in Canada: That the troops under M. Vaudreuille were to set out from St. John's, Montreal, &c. for Quebec, the latter end of this inst, or early in May; and that they had, if they find it improbable to recover Quebec, give over all hopes of keeping Canada, as they are fully sensible, from the experience they have had since the city has been taken from them, that it will be impossible for them to procure the necessaries of life, or those of war, especially if the mouth of the Missisippi should be guarded during the summer by an English squadron."

Friday last Transports fell down to Amboy, in order to take on board 400 of the Royal Scotch; They are bound for Quebec, and are to be convoyed by the Lizard, Capt. Doake.

By a Sloop that arrived here Yesterday from Albany, we learn, that his Excellency General Amherst arrived safe there last Thursday Morning and that he was taking all posible Measures for an early Beginning of the Year's Campaign.

PHILADELPHIA May 15. By letters from Niagara, of the 15th of April, and from Oswego, of the 24th, we have advice that all was quiet at those Places; that there was great Trade carried on at Niagara; and that the Traders having dispursed of all their Goods, have come down for more, one of which returned with 90 Packs of Beaver.

CHARLESTOWN South Carolina May 17. Advices from the Creek Nation of the 20th ult. present Things are still unsettled from, notwithstanding their late promising Aspect. There are great struggles in it, between our Friends who endeavour to effect a Rupture with the Cherokees, and the Majority of the Nation, who oppose it, and persist in their scheme of maintaining a Neutrality; but it begins to be apprehended, that neither this Government nor Governor Ellis can prevail against the united Efforts of the French and Cherokees advocates, ——— We have however have some Advices from Georgia, that raise our Hopes a little, viz. That Sympoyassee, (Fool Harry) himself was arrived at Savannah with 20 Warriors of the Coweta Town, and has positively promised Governor Ellis, to go out with them against the Cherokees immediately, for which purpose he and his Gang were fitting out the 10th Instant: We have upon the gaining of this Indian to be of great Consequence, and he has Interest enough to justify his Actions, and sufficient Authority to influence others to imitate them, and it is also a favourable Circumstance; that this Chief of the Coweta Town reckoned the most disaffected of any in the Creek Nation.

BOSTON May 19. Friday last in the afternoon, the Race-Horse-Bomb, Capt. McCartney, arrived with Dispatches from Quebec to his Excellency General Amherst, which was forwarded immediately; and the next Morning Capt. McCartney set out for Albany.

BOSTON May 19. When the Governor was at Penobscot the last Spring, in order to take possession of the Country and build a fort therein, he sent the following message to the Penobscot Indians by some of the tribe who had come in.

——— Tell your People that I am come to build a fort at Penobscot and will make the land English ——— I am able to do it ——— and I will do it; if they say I shall not, let them come and defend their land now in time of war ——— take this red flag to remember what I say:

When I have built my fort and set down at Penobscot, if ever they be an English man killed by your Indians ——— you must all from that hour fly from the country, for I will send a number of men on all sides the river, sweep it from one end to the other and hunt ye all out.

Gave them a red Flag.

As to people of Penobscot I seek not their favours nor fear them, for they can do me neither good nor harm ——— I am sorry for their distress and would do them good, let them become English, they and their wives and families, and come and live under the protection of the fort, and I will protect them, they shall have wigwarms and planting ground near the fort, and may hunt as usual, but the English shall hunt also; they shall not interfere, with one another's hunt, when they hunt separately; and they may hunt together when they choose it. If they will live under the English laws I will make such of their Sungama's as they shall choose justices, to do justice ——— to right what may be wrong, and to keep peace among yourselves ——— and when any thing happens wrong between the English and Indians an English justice and an Indian justice shall meet and do right between them, you shall have a free market for your furs and skins, and the price shall be set for agreement.

Take this white flag and remember this.

Gave them a white flag.

And this spring a number of said Indians came in following terms of accommodation being agreed upon were signed in the Council Chamber on Tuesday the 29th day of April, by his Excellency on part, and by four of the Indians who came as deputies from the tribe on the other.

I Thomas Pownall, Esq; his Majesty's Governor of the Province of Massachusetts-Bay, do hereby in his Majesty's Name, and on behalf of the Province aforesaid, receive into his Majesty's protection within and under this his Government, all such Indians of the Penobscot Tribe or their allies as do or shall enter into the engagements of these presents specified, and as do or shall sign the same, and I do hereby promise to them all the rights, benefits, privileges and advantages which British subjects do or ought to enjoy: ——— furthermore, for the encouragement to employ themselves in hunting they may be assured of a constant supply of goods necessary or convenient for them, either from fort Pownall or from such other places as may be appointed for that Purpose.

T. Pownall.

We the under-written Indians in consideration of the protection we are hereby admitted to, and of enjoying the rights and privileges hereby granted, do for ourselves and families agree as follows:

1st. We acknowledge ourselves to all intents and purposes, and without any restrictions or limitations, to be subjects of the Crown of Great-Britain: And do hereby promise and engage to be and to remain true and faithful to his Majesty and to the Government of this Province.

2d. That as we have been in open rebellion and hostility, and have thereby forfeited our lands, and as possession has been taken of all our lands in this our time of open rebellion, and is now rightfully held, that we acknowledge this right and relinquish all claims to said lands, and only pray that we may have a privilege to hunt, fowl, and fish, within such limits as shall be assign'd us, but not to the exclusion of any other of his Majesty's subjects; and also to erect Wigwams and other buildings to dwell in, and to plant or otherwise improve such land as may be assigned for our support, and we do hereby engage to fix our dwelling in such a place near unto or in sight of Fort Pownall, and to remain there;

3d. We promise and engage that we and each of us will utterly quit and relinquish all alliance and correspondence with the French, and in case of any invasion or attack made by the French, or any other enemy on the Eastern frontiers of this province, we will join with the English in every act of duty and loyalty towards the Government.

4th. If any one who now enter or shall enter into these engagements shall commit any hostility or injury upon or against any of his

Majesty's English subjects, the offender shall be delivered up to the authority of this Government, and shall be subjected to such and no other punishment as by the laws of this province, an English subject in such case would be liable to suffer.   Kehowret, Zachetien, Joseph Marie, Zachebrsen.

As none are actually admitted to the terms of protection and answerable for the conditions of the submission but those who do actually sign, ⎯⎯⎯ The Indians desired that the instrument might be sent down and kept at Fort Pownall, that all the rest might sign, and that it might remain there as a memorial to which they might always have access. ⎯⎯⎯

The Indians say that at present their tribe consist of 5 Sachems and 73 Warriors.

The foregoing is an Abstract of his Excellency the Governor's Transaction with the Penobscot Indians, as a Record.

Attest, A. Oliver Sec'y.

NEW-YORK May 19. By letters from Niagara the 15th of April, and Oswego on the 24th, we have advice, that all was quiet at those places; that there was a great trade carried on at Niagara, and that the traders having dispos'd of all their Goods, have come down for more, one of which returned with 90 packs of Beaver.

Saturday and Sunday last, several Sloops sailed from hence for Albany; with the troops raised in this province for the ensuing campaign.

Yesterday sail'd hence (which arrived here since our last) the Forces belonging to Rhode-Island destin'd for Albany.

Saturday Afternoon the Quota of the Forces appointed to be raised by an Act of this Colony, for the City of New-York, embark'd for Albany.

CHARLESTOWN South Carolina May 24. By an Express which arrived here on Sunday last from Fort Prince George, we have a communication of the firing of Keowee, by two Chickasaw Indians on the 30th of April. ⎯⎯⎯ We have also the following Advices by said Express, viz. That on the 5th Instant, as Richard Ratcliffe, late of Long Cane Settlement, with a Boy of his, Mathew Abenthin, a Servant of Doctor Murray's, and a

Negro Boy belonging to said Murray, were gathering together some Cattle that had been collected for the use of the Army, they were fired upon by 17 Cherokees, from an Ambuscade (near Wilson's Creek, between Ninety-Six and Saludee River) who killed Ratcliffe and Abenthin on the Spot, and took Rathcliffe's Boy Captive; but the Negro escaped as he had done thrice before. That on the 8th Instant another Boy belonging to Mr. Greduedy at Fort Ninety-Six was missed, and had not been heard of the 14th, so that it was believed he also had fallen into the same or some other Gang's Hands. That the Day after the firing of the Town's House and some other Houses at Keowee by the Chickasaws, a great Number of Cherokees, and some of the Tistowe, came down from the Sugat-Town to see what mischief had been done, and appeared much concerned. That from that Time to the 8th instant, many more Indians were daily observed to come down by the Over-Hill Path, all on Horseback, and many are advanced to the River side. That Time one Tistowe once came over the River, with several attendants; desired a Talk with Mr. Milin, still pretending to prefer Peace and Friendship to war and plunder; and promised to deliver up a white Boy after Time, as a token of his Sincerity, which however was not done. That Ratcliffe's Boy being carried to Sugar-Town and showing no Sign of Fear when he was taken, but telling the Indians "That as some out in Consequence of their having set up a white Flag near Fort Ninety-Six, with white Wampum he was sure to be soon released for it would take place in a little Time, the Governor whom they had offended by the late Breach of Treaty being gone over the great Water, and as now one appointed, who always lov'd the Indians and would soon Treat with them," they began to entertain fresh hopes, that they could be able once more to impose upon us, and, another temporary Accommodation, 'till they planted, reaped, and got fresh supplies of Ammunition: whereupon 210 of them came on the 9th mounted, ranging along the Keowee Side of the River, putting on chearful Countenances and expressed Desire to have some talk with Mr. Milin who consenting that they should, Eight of their Men immediately divested of their Arms crossed the River, and came pretty near the Fort. Mr. Milin went out and asked them if they would talk, they answered Yes; and while that Ceremony was performing he amused them with hopes that much should be made up:

At length he observed to them, That we had been long quarreling together like Children, about trifles, that these Things would be soon forgot; told them, that he has plenty of good Beef, Flour, and Bread, assured them they should be welcome Guests, if they would accept of such Entertainment as these would afford, and he had Rum they should have it also: They accordingly consented to dine with him, where; upon he ordered a large Marquis to be brought out and pitched just without the Fort Gate, with the entrance into it placed facing the Gate: The Indians went in with him, & Mr. Dogharty, Mr. M. Donald, Mr. Bell, and two or three more; mean while, a notorious Villain, the Raven of Estatowe, came riding along, without any other Weapon than a Bundle of Arrows in a Bear Skin Quiver and a Bow, upon which they pretended to wait Dinner till he had joined the Company; when he came pretty near, Dogarthy invited him in, told him what headmen were there, and that all were to dine together, for it would soon be Peace; after some Hesitation the Raven was prevailed upon to enter likewise, but Dogarty observing that the Bow and Arrows were too cumbersome, took them off with one Hand, and immediately seized the Raven with the other, as did Mr. Milin at the same Time Tistowe and others the Rest; the Raven made some resistance, but at last was passive, saying he had a bad Dream the Night before; 25 Men then rushed out of the Fort, and brought in all the Prisoners that was made by this Stratagem, and they were put in Irons immediately; except the Wolfe of Settique (or Keowee) who was first shown all the Magazines that they were well filled, and then sent off, to tell the Nation what had passed and he had seen, and with a message from Mr. Milin to the Standing Turkey, acquainting him, "That having been well informed, that notwithstanding they pretend to desire Peace, the English Prisoners in the Cherokee Nation were very ill used, he had seized 9 Headmen above mentioned and would keep them confined 'till those Prisoners were bro't in to him, for doing which he alloyed them 12 Days, which expired last Thursday; that since the white Flag has been hoisted on Keowee Town House, he had desisted firing upon that Town, or upon any of the Indians; but that they had not behaved in like Manner, for the Discharge of Guns, the War and the Death-Whoop had been continually sounding in his Ears; that therefore, he would take Satisfaction on his present Prisoners if he heard of one gun more being fired against Fort Loudoun, or any more Gangs going down against our Settlements; or of any Prisoners being ill-treated, or a single Gun more thereafter fired against the Fort he commanded; or the Prisoners were not delivered up in the Time demanded."

When the Wolfe went over, he was immediately surrounded by some Hundreds, eager to hear the Talk; after hearing which, they seemed to depart without any Disturbance or Discomposure whatever. That soon after this Affair (on the same Day) one Welch ventured out of the Fort with a Boy, to more than a Mile's Distance, to catch some Horses belonging to the Garrison which the Indians on the other Side observing. Ten of them laid down their Arms, came over, helped to catch their Horses, and brought them to the Place where they were usually kept, behaved with great Complaisance, and returned over the River in a very orderly Manner. ──── That all was as well as could be expected at Fort Loudoun, where the Little Carpenter and his Family had been 30 Days, and proved himself an honest Fellow. ──── That notwithstandig the Rebuff the Chilhowe People lately met with in Virginia, a fresh Gang of 30 Men were gone from that Town the same Course to seek Revenge. ──── That most part of the Rangers were encamped with Col. Richardson, at Turkey-Creek, a little below Ninety-Six, so as to cover the Settlements below, while the rest are partly escorting the Cattle and partly with Col. Montgomery.

The Waggons from Mock's-Corner, having reached the Army sooner than was expected, Colonel Montgomery set out from the Congarees the 17th Instant, and expected to reach Ninety-Six as last Night ar farthest, when we hear, he will not halt above one Day or two if the Waggons can be got up in time.

BOSTON May 26. By return of several expresses from Albany, we are informed, that General Amherst, upon the news of the French marching with a large army collected from all parts of Canada, to attack Quebec ordered all the troops, as fast as they arrived at Albany, immediately to proceed forward. That on the 17th ult. nine companies of the Provincial of this Province (being the first of the Provincials from any of the provinces that had arrived there this season) march'd from thence for Fort Edward and Crown-Point; other companies of the troops raised by this Province, are on their march from Worcester and Springfield for Albany. ——— That last Thursday an account was received there, that a party of the enemy was discover'd near Saratoga: and that a man was taken prisoner near Fort Edward; also that two of our Battoes going down Still-Water Falls, by accident both sunk, and 16 lives lost in them, besides provisions, &c. That two regiments of the regulars march'd from Albany last Wednesday, but that the General still remains there.

We learn by Capt. North from Georges Fort at the Eastward, that on the 4th Instant he received an express from Pleasant Point, Acquainting him that the Indians had killed two of our hunters on Penobscot river;. that some of the Penobscot Indians informed Col. Prebble, that they saw 120 Canadian Indians pass them, while on an island in that river; and that their intent to fall upon St. George's, Broad Bay, and Sheepscut; and that those men, supposed to be Indians, were seen by our hunters within about two miles pf George's Fort, upon Capt. North fir'd an alarm, expecting an attack; but the enemy not appearing, there went out a party of 21 men, who returned without so much as to find a single tract: So that the report of our losing a number of cattle is without foundation. no disturbance having happened in those parts before the 8th instant, at which time he came from thence. 'Twas generally thought at the Eastward, that the above reports were owing wholly to disputes arisen between the Indians and our hunters; and it was also reported that some of the latter plundered some of the former.

FORT LOUDOUN, May 29. About 11 days ago I wrote you fully by Negro Abraham: We all long eagerly to see a message from the Army, for our provisions run very short, and the Indians are much exasperated by the seizure of Tiftoe, and other headmen, and the certainty of their hostages, being killed, so that they now talk of going down and giving the army a meeting, which we were in hopes they had laid aside all thoughts of. The Little Carpenter this morning came to the fort and told us, that he had done every thing in his power to bring his people to reason, but that as he had perceived all his efforts to be in vain, he was determined to let them take their own way; he hoped that the troops would make no delay, but push forward, and not be deterred by the mountains, which they would not find so difficult as has been represented, that nothing but correction can bring the Indians to a sense of their interest and duty.

JUNE 1760

CHARLESTOWN South Carolina June 1. "The Cherokee Party is stronger, and has been more successful with the Creeks than ours; so that they have actually engaged them to begin and, commit Hostilities against us, by the Slaughter of all our Traders they could lay their Tomahawks on; of that we have certain Intelligence within these few Days past ——— The Chocktaws are a very numerous and powerful Nation, laying just behind the Creeks and commonly reckoned about 7000 fighting Men, and have hitherto been prevented from falling on the Creeks, a very warlike Nation, and till now were devoted to our Interest; but they have left us and are generally said to be about 2500 fighting Men and the Cherokees are suppose to be 3700 to 4000: so that you will easily see from this what the number of our external Enemies may be, while we have 70,000 Negroes in our Bowels. ——— You may think how these Things will end. ——— We do not exactly know our Situation, but a few Days more will open our Eyes."

BOSTON June 4. By the HOnorable Thomas Hutchinson, Esq; Lieutenant Governor and Commander in Chief in and over His Majesty's Province of the Massachusetts Bay in New-England.

A Proclamation

His Excellency Governor Pownall having embarked for Great Britain, and the Administration being devolved upon Me;

I have thought fit to issue this Proclamation for establishing and conforming all such Commissions as would otherwise cease and determine. And I do hereby authorize and require all Officers bearing such Commissions, to continue in the Exercise of their respective Powers and Trust, until they shall be otherwise ordered.

Given at the Council Chamber in Boston, the Fourth Day of June 1760. In the Thirty-third Year of the Reign of our Sovereign Lord George the Second, by the Grace of God, of Great-Britain, France and Ireland, King, Defender of the Faith, &c.   T. Hutchinson.
By His Honor's Command   A. Oliver, Sec'ry.
             God Save the King

BOSTON June 6. Province of Massachusetts-Bay, June 6, 1760. By the Honorable Thomas Hutchinson Esq; Lieutenant Governor, and Commander in chief.

The General Assembly having voted that every effective Man who before the 20th Instant, shall inlist into His Majesty's Service, to compleat the Five Thousand Men proposed to be raised, shall receive Three Pounds Lawful Money Bounty, over and above the Encouragement already granted: And also that each enlisting officer shall receive three Shillings for each Man inlisted, over and above the three Shillings already granted.

It is thought to make this Encouragement public.

And to encourage Persons to proceed with Vigour in the business of inlisting, the Lieutenant-Governor in granting his Commissions for each Company, will give the Province to such Persons as shall have inlisted the greatest Number of Men.

Each Company to consist of Fifty Men, including Officers.

By His Honor the Lieutenant-Governor's Command,   Wm. Brattle, Adj.-General.

BOSTON June 9. Last Tuesday about Noon, His Excellency Governor Pownall, attended by his Honor the Lieut. Governor, the Honorable Gentlemen of His Majesty's Council and the House of Representatives, and a great Number of Civil and Military Officers, and other Gentlemen, set out from the Court-House in this Town, and being escorted by the Company of Cadets, under Arms, walk'd in Procession thro' King Street, down the Long-Wharf, where the Castle Barge lay ready for the reception of His Excellency: And after receiving the most respectful Salutation upon his

Departure from us, His Excellency was received into the Barge; the barge of the Province Ship King George also attended, a Number of Gentlemen accompanied His Excellency: Upon the Barge Putting off the Wharf, in order to proceed to Nantasket, His Excellency was saluted by the Discharge of the Guns of the Batteries of this Town; as also by those of the Castle upon passing the Fortress: ———— Upon arriving in Nantasket Road, His Excellency went first on board the Province Ship King George, Capt. Hallowell, the Guns of the said Ship being discharg'd upon his Excellency coming aboard; and after a very elegant Entertainment at Dinner, His Excellency put off in the Barge, (the Guns of the Ship being again discharged) and embarked on board the Ship Benjamin and Samuel, Capt. Patten, lying also in Nantasket Road, and about 8 o'Clock came under sail and proceeded on his Voyage to England.

After his Excellency's Departure, his Honor the Lieut. Governor made the following speech to both Houses, viz.

Gentlemen of the Council and House of Representatives,

His Excellency Governor Pownall having embarked for Great-Britain, and the Administration being devolved upon me, by virtue of His Majesty's Commission for Lieutenant Governor, I shall endeavour to improve what Opportunity may be allowed me in promoting His Majesty's Service and the Interest of the Province: And I will immediately apply myself with all Diligence to that important Affair, the compleating the Levies as far as the Provisions you have already made will permit; and as the Thing should occur to me necessary to be further done by you, I will recommend it to you.

You will find, Gentlemen of the House of Represenetetives, That the Establishment for the Forces on the Frontiers will expire the 20th Instant. For the Eastern Frontiers it will undoubtedly be necessary you should continue the Establishment; and if you should apprehend any of our Settlements Westward to be exposed to the Enemy while the Army is without, you will make provisions accordingly. The State of the Treasury you will likewise take into your consideration, and make such Supply as the Circumstances of the Government may require.

I am Sensible of the very heavy Tax engaged to be laid on the People this present Year; and that the Warrants for levying it must soon go forth, unless by some Act of Government they are prevented. If you think it necessary to go into any Measures for the Relief of your Constituents, they must be such as shall give no reason to the Creditors of the Government to complain, and shall be consistent with the publick Engagements.

To these Matters, Gentlemen of both Houses, as well as ordinary Business of Legislature, which may lye before you, I desire you to give all convenient Dispatch. Nothing shall be wanting on my Part, that can be reasonably expected from me.
T. Hutchinson.

WHEREAS THE Ship King George, under my Command, is now ordered, and will sail in a few Days on a Cruize against his Majesty's Enemies:

This is to inform all able bodied Seamen, who are inclined to serve his Majesty on board the said Ship, now lying in Nantasket Road, that if the repair on board, or to my Dwelling House in Boston, they shall be kindly receiv'd, and shall enter into immediate Pay of Fifteen Pounds old Tenor per Month, and for their further encouragement, they are hereby informed that the whole of all Prizes, taken by aforesaid Ship, will be shared among the Officers and Seamen, that are on board at the Time of the Capture, in the same proportion as Officers and Seamen share on board his Majesty's Navy.

Benj. Hallowell Jun.

BOSTON June 9. On Friday the 30th of May arrived at Albany on express from Crown-Point, who informed, That two Indians formerly of the New-York regiment, and taken at Fort William-Henry, and one Stockbridge Indian, who was taken with Capt. Jacob (as formerly mentioned) made their escape from Montreal the 18th of May, and informed on the 10th the inhabitants there were all in tears --- that the French Army before

Quebec had met with three repulses on the Plains of Abraham, and lost between 4 & 5000 men; and that afterwards the made two breaches into the wall of Quebec, and attempted to storm it; but by means of a mask'd battery they were repulsed with great loss, and obliged to raise the siege, and were returning home. ——— That on the 1st of June one of said Indians arrived at Albany, and confirmed the above; and that the same day an express arrived there from Crown-Point, and said, That a party of ours being out on a scout, had taken a Frenchman or Indian, with a canoe, who inform'd that the three above Indians, who had left Montreal in order to take a prisoner; which said Indians at first denied; but upon their being commended for deserting from the enemy, they acknowledged the above to be fact.

BOSTON June 9. The following preliminary Articles for a general Peace, have been handed about at the Hague.

I. That France shall withdraw her armies from Germany.

II. That Britain shall likewise recall her national troops from that Country, and discharge those of the Allies at present in her pay.

III. That the French shall entirely evacuate Canada, and absolutely cede that territory to the British Crown; that all their encroachments in North-America shall be, bona fide, evacuated and delivered up; and that new limits and boundaries berwixt the settlements of both nations, in that quarter of the world, shall be marked out by commissaries, on both sides, appointed for that purpose.

IV. That the fortifications of the Royal, or Cape Breton, shall be demolished, and the island entirely abandoned by both nations; and that the settling there of any of the natives of Britain or France, or those of any other country, bearing a commission, from either of those crowns, shall be understood as a declaration of war.

V. That the possessions of the island of Guadalupe, Marigalante, &c. be confirmed to Brittain; and the West India isles, commonly called the neutral Islands, be abandoned by France, as stipulated by the treaty of Aix-la Chapelle.

VI. That the island of Minoca be yielded to France.

VII. That Senagal and Gorce, on the African coast, be ceded to Great-Britain.

VIII. That the English East-India Company shall be indemnified for the demolishing of Fort David's and the bombarment of Madrass.

IX. That all the ships taken before or since the declaration of the war shall remain the property of the captors.

X. That the prisoners of war on both sides shall be exchanged, one for one and as after said proposed exchange, there will remain in Britain upward of 20,000 prisoners, France shall, in consideration of their being set at liberty make payment of the sum of ———— as their ransom.

XI. That France shall give hostages for evacuating Canada, and the Neutral Islands, and for payment of the sums, &c.

BOSTON June 9. We hear from Albany, that Maj. Rogers has lately made an excursion from Crown-Point, in one of the sloops, which went up within 3 miles of Isle de Noix, where he and two rangers went on shore: That on the enemy's seeing the sloop, they dispatches 2 birch canoes, in which it was computed they were 70 men, but the sloop firing on them, they immediately turn'd tail, and landed near where Rogers and his men lay, and said he narrowly escaped. All the discovery he made, was, that they appeared to be numbers on the island. All the regular regiments are gone from Albany to their different destinations; and the provincials, arrived their daily.

Remarks at Quebec, from October 27, 1759 to May 8, 1760.

Oct. 27. Came down, two French schooners from Montreal, with flag of truce.

31. Came down a Spanish ship.

Nov. 22. The French fleet fell down the river and came to an anchor above the town. The Magaret and Betty schooners were sent to reconnoitre them and make signals.

24. Some of the French vessels having run

ashore, Capt. Miller and Lieut. Cox, with 23 of the Porcupine's and 21 of the Racehorse's people, were up the river in the scooner and boats, intending to burn the French vessels; they boarded one which blew up: Capt. Miller and Lieut. Cox being dangerously wounded, the rest were instantly destroyed by the explosion, except 7 of the Porcupine, and 5 from the Racehorse, who are now prisoners in Montreal.

25. The French ships passed the town.
28. Capt. Miller died of his wounds.
Dec. 1. Lieut. Cox died of his wounds.
5. The river began to freze over.
[1760] Feb. 13. Discovered a body of the enemy at Point Levy: A party of the garrison were immediately detached over the river on the ice, who defeated them, and took post at the church.

24. The enemy endeavoured to storm the church at Point Levy, but a party from the Town coming seasonably to their relief, repulsed the enemy and took 11 prisoners.

26. A party of our men march'd over the ice, and burnt all the houses from Gorhams to Point Levy. Compleated 7 blockhouses round the Town this month.

March 20. A party from the Town attack'd the French out-post at St. Augustine's, and having destroyed them took 79 prisoners.

22. Finished 2 blockhouses, and 2 loghouses at Point Levy.

April 8. The river clear of ice from Quebec downward.

24. The French army having landed at St. Croix. Two frigates and seven other vessels fell down the river and anchored off St. Sallery, where they landed their artillery and ammunition. The same day we deserted our out-post at St. Croix, and Lotetto, and burned the Church at St. Foy, with the blockhouses at Point Levy.

28. The General and the garrison marched out of the town, and gave the enemy battle on the height of Abraham, and after a sharp fire which continued two hours, we were forced to retreat, with the loss of 1061 killed, wounded and taken prisoners, and 20 pieces of cannon lost.

29. In the morning found the enemy entrenched

across the height, from Point Diamond to the Wind-Mill, near the Royal Hospital.

30. Our grand blockhouse of the height, in which we had two pieces of cannon, blew up by some accident; both the officers were wounded, and several men but none killed. All our men employed night and day, in strengthening the works and harassing the enemy.

May 1. Capt. McCartney, and the Porcupine company came on board the Racehorse, which fell down the river with an express to Gen. Amherst.

8. Off Louisbourg, but forced to bear away for Halifax.

CHARLESTOWN S. Carolina June 10. Extract of a letter to his Honour the Lieutenant Governor, giving an account of the success of his Majesty's Arms under the command of Col. Montgomery.

Camp near Fort Prince George, June 14, 1760.

"We arrived the 1st at Twelve-Mile river, and the same morning passed it without opposition, in the afternoon our carriages got to camp, having been bro't up those steep rocky banks by the force of men; the horses could not do it, being worn out with a march of 84 miles without a halting day.

As we met with no opposition at Twelve-Mile river, and our scouts finding no Indian tracks near us, we were convinced they knew nothing of our march, so were resolved to take the advantage of their negligence, by a force march that night, tho' the troops had marched 20 miles that morning; and leaving our tents standing, with about 300 men as a guard to out camp, waggons, &c. we marched thro' the woods, in order to surprize Estatoe, Estatoe which was 35 miles from our camp. After marching 16 miles, a dog was heard to bark, and our guides informed us, there were a few houses about a quarter of a mile from the road, called Little Keowee; to prevent any inconvenience from those houses, the light infantry of the Royals was detached to surround the houses, and put the Indians to death with their bayonets; which they accordingly did, putting to death all they found either within or without the houses, except the women and children.

We then proceeded to Estatoe, and found a few houses on the road just deserted, their beds warm, and every thing left in the houses. We arrived in the morning at Estatoe, which was abandoned about half an hour before; ten or a dozen of them who had not time to escape, were killed; the town consisted of about 200 houses, well provided with ammunition, corn, and in short all the necessaries of life, which we soon laid in ashes, many of the inhabitants who concealed themselves in the houses, perish'd in the flames. We then proceeded on our march, took all their towns in our way, and every house and town in the lower nation, shared the same fate with Estatoe; their villages were agreeably situated and their houses neatly built. Estatoe and Sugar-Town consisted of 200 houses each, and every other village at least 100 houses. After killing all we could find, and burning every house in the nation we marched back to camp, and arrived the second of June, at four in the afternoon at Fort Prince George, after a march of 60 miles without sleeping. We killed from 60 to 80 Cherokees, and took 40 prisoners. Those that escaped must be in a miserable condition, as they can have saved nothing, some of them had but just time to run out of their beds: they had in their towns plenty of ammunition, and every where astonishing magazines of corn, which were all consumed in the flames: the soldiers found money in many of the houses; 3 or 4 watches were got. We intended to have saved Sugar-Town, where they even had a stockade fort; but finding the body of a dead man, who they had put to torture that very morning, it was no longer possible to think of mercy, We had but 3 or 4 men killed, and Lieut. Marshal and Hamilton of the Royals wounded.

We shall make use of Tistowe and the old Warrior of Estatoe, by setting them at liberty, to inform their nation, that tho' they are in our power, we are ready to give them peace; and have also sent to Little Carpenter, that he may come down with some other headmen to treat, which must be done in a few days, or they may expect to see all their towns in the upper nation in

ashes."
                                              I am, &c.
                                            James Grant.

   PHILADELPHIA June 12. The General Assembly of Virginia have granted Thirty-two Thousand Pounds for the Relief of the Garrison of Fort Loudon, in the Cherokee Country.

   CHARLESTOWN S. Carolina June 14. There is no further advices from Augusta on affairs to the Creek nation. Whence we concluded that nothing has happened yet, more than the murder of about 16 or 17 Traders in some of the upper towns; however every prudent and necessary measure is taken to prevent and repel their incursions, in case that nation is for war. Expresses have been sent with dispatches to the Northward and Westward, other dispatches gone by sea to General Amherst, &c., and some will go in a day or two to Adm. Holmes at Jamaica: The provincials and independents doing duty here are under marching orders. And this morning an alarm was fired at Granville bastion, and one half of the militia of the whole province draughted, to be ready to march on the first notice, with 14 days provisions, to several places of rendezvous that are appointed. One half of the artillery company is likewise draughted, with a small train of artillery, stores, &c.

   CHARLESTOWN S. Carolina June 14, 1760. By dispatches from Fort Loudoun we are informed, That the garrison was very miserable and their provisions reduced to two ounces of rotten meat, and a pint of corn per day, at which allowance they had not more than would last them six weeks: The Little Carpenter has sent down a good talk, and says his countrymen will ask for peace, but he believes they will not be sincere. Captain Demere had ransomed a woman and three children from the Indians, but the poor woman had been so cruelly used that she died soon after. The Indians burn all their men prisoners; they had lately burnt six at Canasatchee, (the Sugartown) among them John Downing whose arms and legs they first cut off, and otherwise tortured him.

   BOSTON June 16. We learn from Nottingham, That on Tuesday last about Ten o'Clock before noon,

The Alarm Gun was fir'd at No. Four, but on what Account we have not yet heard; and that near one Hundred of the New-Hampshire Provincials were on the Road coming back, but for what Reason we pretend not to say.

NEW-YORK June 16. By the Albany post arrived last night we have advice that the brave Major Rogers has had another brush with the French: He, with 200 Rangers being out on a Scout landed about three miles from Nut-Island, the 4th instant, but were soon attacked by 300 of the enemy, when a smart engagement immediately commenced, and ended greatly to the disadvantage of the French, they being soon obliged to fly, having between 40 and 50 men killed and wounded. The Major brought off three Indian scalps, but had 10 men killed and 9 wounded: Among the former were Capt. Johnson of the Rangers, and Ensign Wood of General Monckton.

By letters and new-papers brought hither from South Carolina, down to June 3d, we are informed, that the Cherokee Indians still continue desperate in their designs, carrying all before them, by murder, rapine, &c. —— That even the Creek Indians, at least the upper tribe, who were thoughr to be friends to the English, have commenced hostilities against us, by killing and cutting to pieces all the English traders among them, save two who happily escaped by the goodness of their Squaws: —— That the Lower Creeks seem to be still, in our favour, but lay under great suspicion: —— Thar Fort Moore and all the private forts about Augusta, were either destroyed of abandoned by the garrisons; and men women and children flying from all quarters in most deplorable circumstances. In short, that the desolation and distress of those parts of Georgia and Carolina that are most exposed, is hardly to be conceived, much less to be discribed. —— That Col. Montgomery was gone from Fort Ninety-Six, and determined to ruin and distroy all he meets with till he arrives at Fort Loudoun, which is in a most piteous condition having only a pint of corn per day each man.
    —— That on Thursday the 5th of June a Draught was to be made from the province of South-Carolina

when it was thought every 2d or 3d person must be draughted, and hold themselves ready to go off, with 14 days provisions in order to save Georgia. [That it appears that the french and their agents have not been inactive on the side of the Missisippi.]

We further learn, than an insurrection was apprehended in the province of South-Carolina.

Our Account by last night's post from Albany, are, ——— That on Wednesday last the 11th instant, an express arrived there from Sir William Johnson, with the agreeable news that the siege of Quebec was raised with the loss of 5000 of the enemy: That the intelligence was brought from La Galette by a party from thither, where the head warrior of the enemy acquainted our Indians, that an express from Montreal had informed the commanding officer at La Galette, that two of our ships had intercepted a French fleet, consisting of six store-ships, near the Town of Quebec; but notwithstanding this, the enemy continued to push the siege with vigour, until the arrival of 8 English men of war, which occasioned the enemy to quit their works and cannon precipitately, and marched back to Montreal.

CHARLESTOWN S. Carolina June 18. We learn from Enoree, in this province (situated between 30 and 40 miles N. E. of Ninety-six) that on the beginning of the month a party of Cherokees, in a number 60 at least, made an inroad into that settlement, and attacked a family, the master whereof, one Donolly, they killed, but the mistress with one of her children escaped; the enemy plundered the plantation of everything, which they carried off with six children; a party of militia next day came up with them, and retook most of the booty with four of the children; the eldest a girl of 14, the Indians carried off the youngest an infant, and the night before put to death the eldest boy, about 12 years of age. Also that 7 of the above party of Indians, attacked the plantation of one Miles, which they destroyed, and killed the whole family, except Miles himself and three negroes.

According to letters from Savannah in Georgia, dated the 9th and 10th inst. those Creek headmen who escorted the traders thither out of the lower towns, assured Governor Ellis that the traders were not cut off by consent of the headmen, and that they had not the least previous knowledge of it; and declared, that they believed matters might be accommodated, if we did not ask to high a satisfaction: Upon which his Excellency sent a talk by them, to this effect: "That the treaties subsisting between the white and red people pointed out in what manner accidental quarrels were to be made up; particularly that which he had made with them, whereon was stipulated, that the irregularities committed by the mad people of either side, should not be deemed a sufficient motive for the two nations to make war upon each other, until after the party aggrieved should be refused satisfaction: That it was in regard to that treaty, that he did not immediately take satisfaction of the many Creeks that were in Georgia when the accounts came to him of the loss of the traders. And that in conformity to another article of the same treaty, he required satisfaction of their nation, thro' them, in a friendly manner; which satisfaction, as a proof of his great regard for, and unwillingness to break with them, he left to themselves." for obvious reasons.

The late alarm had done incredible damage to that province; most of the inhabitants of the back settlements having moved off, and left forts with swivel guns, arms and ammunition, besides large quantities of provisions. We are daily more and more convinced, that the talks sent to the Creek nation will have good effects; and we hope that Col. Montgomery's success against the Cherokees, will rather excite terror than jealousy; but the latter seems likely as the former, the French having persuaded both Creek, and Cherokees, "that the English only set the Indians together by the ears to diminish their numbers so that their armies might afterward more easily extirpate the rest, in order to enjoy their land quietly." ――― Nothing less than the reduction of Louisiana, seems to be our general opinion, will ever establish the several Indians and nations firmly in our interest.

BOSTON June 23. Friday last arrived here Captain Gowell in 9 Days from Louisbourg, and informs, That about 150 French Neutrals from Picto, who went off some Time since had arrived there, in order for protection from the British Crown; but as no great Dependence could be put in their Fidelity, they are going to be sent to France in a Cartel Ship: These Neutrals inform, That about 50 Indians were also coming in to surrender themselves to the English. —— And that the Miners lately arrived from England, together with Part of the Garrison, were daily employ'd in making the necessary Preparations for demolishing the Works of that Place, in such a manner as not to leave one stone upon an other.

In our last we mentioned on alarm being given at No. Four since which we learn, That one Mr. Willard, his Wife and Five Children, were taken and carried off from that Place the 7th last, by the Indians: Scouts were immediately sent out after them, and was in Pursuit when the Express came away.

A few Days ago sail'd from New-London, the Snow Earl of Halifax, Capt. Taggart, having under Convoy 8 Sail of Transport with 500 Inhabitants, Men, Women and Children, going to settle in Nova-Scotia.

BOSTON June 23. Great and Good News from Quebec.

We have had various uncertain Reports, from a Fortnight past, of the favorable state of the Garrison at Quebec, but on the 21st instant at about XI in the Forenoon, we were relieved from all suspense, by the arrival of the Schooner Lawrence. Job Harris, Master, in 26 Days from that City. In this Vessel came Lieut. Calder, with Dispatches from His Excellency General Amherst. We are now inform'd and from the best Authority. That the Siege of Quebec was raised the 18th of May; that the Enemy had lost 3000 Men all their Magazines, Baggage, Tents, Scalin Ladders, 36 pieces of Cannon, 4 Petards, and 1000 Stand of Small-Arms; in short, every thing that was necessary for their Defence. The Labours and brave exploits of the Garrison are without Parallels. His Honour the Lieutenant

Governor order'd the Guns at Castle-William, and the Battaries in Town to be discharged on this Occasion; and indeed this happy event seems to have diffused joy as great and as universal as from the surrender of that Place last Year.

Our Friends have suffered greatly by Scurvy during the Winter, and stand in Need of refreshments of every Kind. A ready Market may be had there. Not interest alone, but Compassion, and especially Gratitude, will we hope, excite a speedy and sufficient Supply.

Our other Account from Quebec are,

That on the 9th they were agreeably surprized to see Capt. Dean in his Majesty's Frigate the Loestaff of 22 Guns arrive there which gave great Spirit to the Officers and Soldiers: ——— That about 6 Days after Commodore Swanton in the Vangard, and Capt. Scomberg in the Diana, arrived there in the Dusk of the Evening; and the next Morning the three Ships weigh'd Anchor and stoad up the River to attack the Enemy's Ships, which were 4 Frigates (Com. Votang) from 44 to 22 Guns, besides several Store Ships; That they made a running Fight of it till our Ships got up with them, when our Ships run them all on Shore; That the French Commodore fought bravely, and did not strike till all his Ammunition was exhausted; this is the man that commanded the Arathusia at Louisbourg, but we have him at last safe on board Capt. Scomberg. In the Affair we lost the Loestaff, which by Accident run ahore; ——— That on the 17th three Deserters came into the City, half drunk, and reported that the French Camp were in the greatest Confusion, and their General was so discourag'd that he intended to raise the Siege very soon; That on this Intelligence, Gen. Murray order'd a Sally at midnight, between the 17th and 18th, and as soon as the French Guard discover'd our Men, they ran to the Camp, and acquainted them therewith, on which the French Army decamp'd immediately and leaving every thing behind them: The Enemy's Encampment was within 600 Yards of the City Walls: The Enemy had 15,000 Men, and afterwards were reinforced by 5,000 more, the last of which were all young Fellows and not a Married Man amongst them. The Siege lasted three Weeks and two Days, and our Men behaved so well, that the very mention of their Brave Behavior would appear romantic; That we took 2 Mortars and about 40 Battoes laden with Poultry, and pursued the Enemy 9 Miles: The Enemy 'tis said can raise 20,000 Men, but have not 50 Barrels of Powder in all Canada: That on the 22d all the French Ships above the City except one, were taken and destroyed, And that by the Assistance of the Fleet from England they were unable to raise the Siege, obliging the French to leave 6 Mortars, 32 Pieces of Brass and Iron Cannon, Shot, Shells, Intrenching Tools, Ammunition, Scaling Ladders, and Stores of all Kind innumerable.

We lost on the Field of Battle on the 28th of April, 10 Officers Kill'd 85 wounded, two of which died; and 10 taken Prisoner.

NEW-HAVEN June 27. Our Troops had not arrived at Albany on the 10th Instant for which the Colony was blamed. The Army had not march'd from Albany the 17th but was expected to move next Day. It was tho't the Connecticut Troops with the main Body of the Army would go to Oswego; the Massachusetts, New-Hampshire, and Rhode-Island Forces, with two Regiments of Regulars to Crown-Point.

BOSTON June 30. Extract of a Letter from an Officer of Distinction to his Friend here, dated Quebec, May 18, 1760.

I Embrace the first Opportunity to inform you of our present Situation at Quebec: ——— We march'd into this Garrison the 19th of September last, with 7,700 Men. ——— By the inexpressive Fatigues in bringing Wood to the City, fortifying the Place, &c. the severe Winter and the great Want of Fresh Provisions, our Troops are now greatly reduc'd. ——— During the Winter we were often threatened with a Visit from M. de Levy with 14,000 Men. ——— And accordingly the 27th of April he landed with all his Regulars, and as many Canadians as made up 12,000 Men about 3 Miles to the West of Quebec; at the Time we did not know his Number; and on the 28th General Murray march'd out of the Town with 3,000 Men (being all we had capable of bearing

Arms) to give them Battle upon the Plains of Abraham, which was accordingly done about 11 o'Clock the same Day: The Enemy had grately the Advantage, ―― both as to Situation and Numbers; In short we lost the Battle, our Cannon and 1060 Men killed and wounded; as the Field was warmly disputed, the Enemy lost on their side 1500 Men. ―― As soon as we got beck to Town, we began to strengthen the Fortifications and remove the Guns from the Grand Battery, on the Water Side, and made the Whole Front on the Land Side towards the Enemy one entire formidable Battery, which kept them at awe: however they immediately invested the Town, and entrench'd themselves about 800 Yards from the Walls; and on the 10th of May they opened three Batteries, consisting in all 13 Guns and 2 Mortars, and play'd pretty smartly for 2 or 3 Days, but made no further Approaches waiting for the Arrival of the Ships, as they had not Ammunition or Provisions to carry on the Siege; ―― On the 9th (May) the Loestaff arrived here, and the 16th the Diana and Vanguard, which made the Ennemy despair of Succour: the next Morning our Ships went and destroy'd three of the Enemy's Ships by running them on Shore, and Yesterday the Canadians dispers'd, and left their Arms on the Plains ―― The Regulars are gone off to Montreal.

Names of Officers Killed, Wounded, and taken Prisoners without the Walls of Quebec, 28th of April 1760.

XVth Regiment.
Lieut Maxwell sen. killed.
Capt. Lieut, Colburn, Lieuts. Makey, Maxwell, Catburn, Viater, Ervin, Lockhart: Ensign Montgomery, Barbut, Mills, Barker, Monneypenny all wounded, and Ensign Hamilton wounded and Prisoner.

XXVIIIth Regiment
Colonel Walsh, Major Dalling, Capts. Spann, Maccorsson, Kepple, Lieut. Fassfail, Brown, Phipps, Ensign Gilmer, Shepherd, & Seal, all wounded.

XXXVth Regiment.
Capt. Ince, wounded and Prisoner, Lieut. Brown, and Ensign Lysaght wounded.

XLIIId Regement.
Capt. Skey, wounded, Capt. Maitland wounded and Prisoner. Lieut. Clermens, wounded, Lieut. Lysalt and Ensign Maw, both wounded and Prisoners.

XLVIIth Regiment.
Major Huffrey killed. Capt. Archibald and Lieut. Sheriff, both wounded and Prisoners, Lieuts. Forester, Basset, Stretford, and Ever, wounded, the last died of his wounds. Lieut. Gibson killed, Ensigns Eushion and Henfield wounded.

XLVIIIth Regiment.
Captain Convay killed.

IID Battalion of Royal Americans.
Ensign Steel and McDonalds wounded.

IIId Battalion.
Colonel Young Prisoner, Capts. Fash & Chartres, wounded, Lieut. Forbes killed, Lieut. Fash wounded and Prisoner. Lieuts. Campbell, Grant, Stephenson, Lewis, Fortes. Ensigns Pickney, Hill, Stuart, and Mackay wounded the last died of his wounds.

LXIIId Regiment.
Colonel Fraser, Capts. Cameron, John Campbell, Alexander Fayer, McLead, wounded, Capt. Lieut. Donald wounded. Ensigns Cofine, Gordon, killed, Archibald Campbell wounded, Hector McDonald killed, Donald McBean, Alexander Fraser, Senr. Alexander simon Fraser, Senr., Simon Fraser, Junr. Malcolm Fraser, Alexander Fraser, of the Grenadiers, and Donald McNeal, wounded. Lieut. Alsxander Campbell wounded and prisoner, Ensigns Henry Munroe, Robert Menzier, Charles Stuart, Duncan Camoron, William Robertson. Alex. Gregorson, Arthur Rose, wounded. Ensign Malcon Fraser killed.

Royal Artillery.
Major Goodwin, 2d Lieuts. Heathers & Scott, Lieuts. of the fireworkers, David & Cock wounded.

Chief Engineer Major Mac Keller wounded.

Ranger. Capt. Hazzen wounded.

The Return of the killed, wounded and Prisoners, of the privates belonging to each Regiment is not come to Hand.

BOSTON June 30. A Letter from Albany dated the 12th Instant, says That three or four Battoes landed with Sutler's Goods, have been taken near

Oswego, by the Enemy.

Our Advices from Albany that since the Skirmish of Major Rogers mentioned in our last, he has been to a Place called St. Peter (Between Nut Island and Montreal) and burnt about 16 or 20 Houses, being all in the Village, and brought off 35 Men Prisoners, leaving the Women and Children behind: That he was pursu'd by between 4 and 500 of the Enemy, who were in half an Hours March of him, when luckily for the Major and his Party, they came across a Number of the Enemy's Battoes which were provided to bring the Officers, who were taken at the Battle of Quebec on the 28th of April last, to Crown-Point, who were all discharged upon their Parole of Honor, except Col. Young, who is still with them, and is treated in a very polite Manner, by Mons. Vandreuil, and all the Officers of the Army: in the above affair Rogers did not lose a single Man.

We also learn, that General Amherst with his Army were march'd from Albany, in order to persue the operations of the ensuing Campaign.

Our Advice from Montreal on the 14th inst. when the French Army was return'd from the siege of Quebec: That they have Bread, fish and Pigeons in plenty, but no other Provisions; That near all their Ammunition was expended, and the French is in just a Situation as we could wish: ——— That they daily sent our Scouts in Order to take a Prisoner to gain Intelligence of the Operations of our Army, but they return'd unsuccessful, till about 10 Days since, when they took two Men near Crown-Point, one of which they kill'd and scalp'd, and the other they carried to Montreal; that the Fields were planted before they went to attack Quebec, and since their Return the Inhabitants had Leave to go and take care of the same, but were ordered to appear at an Hours Warning with 8 Days Provisions, in case of an Attack.

Extract of a Letter from Fort Frederick at St. John's River, dated June 6, 1760.

"The Indians of several Tribes are come in, and signed a Treaty of Peace, which they say shall last forever. ——— They all behaved exceeding well. ——— A few Days since 20 Canoes arrived here with Men, Women and Children, they were honoured by the discharge of several Cannon, which pleased them very well.

JULY 1760

BOSTON July 1. We hear that an Express arrived over Land from Quebec at Albany the same Day Lieut Calder arrived here from thence by Water, with the same Intelligence of the French Army retiring from before Quebec.

CHARLESTOWN S. Carolina July 5. An Express is arrived from Savannah, with advice, that Mr. Joseph Wright, with the Tellasee's king's son, and two other Creek headmen, are arrived there with talks from both the upper and lower Creeks, to governor Ellis; that ten headmen more were on their way down, to receive and carry up his answers; that some Coweta people from the Cherokees, had bro't the small-pox into their town; that the Mortar had likewise that distemper introduced into the Oakehoys, and that it was reported, the Miser was going against the Cherokees with a gang of 50 men.

The Talks delivered to governor Ellis are as follows; that from the upper Creeks nation is dated at Mucculassa, and runs in these words.

Present the headmen of the upper Creek nation, The Gun-Merchant acquainted the governor, that an accident has happened between some of the red people and the traders; but he hopes, that the governor will not think, what fell out was a concerted thing of the nation in general, and assured him to the contrary; for, neither the headmen nor warriors had forgot the talks sent from time to time by the governor; and, that this affair gives them the greatest uneasiness and concern, as is known to the white people present. He further adds, as a proof of what is said before, that had this been a concerted thing, some of the white people now alive, would ever have got to their country; and desires, that the governor may believe thet the Creeks have no malice in their hearts, and their own wish is that a good understanding and friendship may be renewed, and firmly preserved as formerly. The reported Mischief was done by a few young fellows, without consulting the headmen of the nation; who think it not prudent that any satisfaction should be demanded at present, lest these desperate fellows should be pushed to greater lengths. The Gun-Merchant continued; that he himself is a thorough judge of this affair, and protests, that they were no more in it than what he has related; and intreats the governor, to let the traders return speedily with goods, to quiet the minds of the young people, who would be alarmed at the traders being stopped on this occasion. He desired, that the governor may give particular attention to what he sends him; and consider with himself that the innocent should not suffer for the sake of a few guilty people; and hopes, he will think of nothing but the former friendship that subsisted between the two nations.

He hopes the governor will not take amiss the white people's being detained so long in the nation, and their goods and leather had been distributed amongst the people; but that the headmen would use their best endeavours to gather every thing together, and the traders may go down as soon as they are ready.

He again request in behalf of his nation, that the governor may not harbour a thought that any of the headmen were privy to what had happened; and desire, that an answer may be sent to the nation as soon as possible.

Signed by Gun-Merchant, in the name and the presence of the heads of the Upper Nation.

The talk of the Lower Creeks is dated the 7th of June at a meeting of all the headmen at the Hitcheta's.

Notwithstanding that our old wise men are dead, yet what remains of us, though not so wise as them, are assembled together and agreed to be at peace with the English; for, notwithstanding the mischief done by a few mad people, yet all that, we desire nothing but peace and quietness. We say, there is nothing shall put us against the English, as long as the sun shines or the master of breath is above us. We hope our friends the English don't think that any of our headmen had any hand in this, nor do we think it the least that the English will throw away our nation for the murder committed by a few young people: As the difference between you and the Cherokees, we declare against taking part on either side; for we want to have peace with all nations. As for the Cherokees we have forwarned them from spoiling our path, and we take care to send guards with the horses for fear of mistakes. We of the Lower Towns are the same people with those of the Upper; and we have all agreed, to continue our peace and quietness with all the English.

As all the talks that came from the English are good, ours are the same. We desire that our people may be well used below, and that our traders may come and go as usual with goods to us. We conclude here, and desire nothing but peace and quietude with all People, for that is best. Old Stump says, he don't forget the talk at Savannah, and the Governor's talk; he promised we should never want for goods: He says, they are now in want of goods, and desire that they may have goods up as soon as possible.

CHARLESTOWN S. Carolina July 5. An Account of the proceedings of the Army under Col. Montgomery, from their return to the Camp at Fort Prince George, after destroying the Cherokee Towns to the 25th ult.

Fort Prince George, June 5, 1760.

On the 7th of June one of the Highlanders was still missing, and supposed to be taken or killed seeking plunder. ——— That on the 10th most of the Catawba's and some of the people in the pay of the Province, went to Little Keeowee in quest of plunder, and bro't off all the corn they found, and burnt the remaining houses. The same day a soldier of the provincials coming from the camp at Mile-Creek, about a quarter of a mile from it, was fired at by 4 or 5 of the enemy, who shot him thro' the arm and immediately rushed upon him with their tomahawks, and took off his scalp with some of the flesh; He defended himself as well as he could, but being much chop'd about the hands they at last overpower'd him; the Indians had but just time to escape, and left a bloody-tomahawk by him: He was alive and is likely to do well. —— That on the 11th one of the Royals was killed and scalp'd near the grass-guards, early in the morning the picket-guard saw several of the enemy, but neither molested each other; as it was not intended to fire on the Indians during the 10 days allowed Tiftowee. —— That on the 12th an account was bro't that lieut. Webb's horse was found killed at Twelve Mile river: —— That on the 13th lieut. Webb returned to the camp almost naked and starved, having been attacked on the 8th, at 11 at night, as he was crossing Twelve Mile river, on his way to Ninety-six, but by favour of the night made his escape; which he betook himself to the woods, he says he fell in with Indian camps one after another, for four days and nights, successively, and at last had strayed almost down to 18 mile branch; he supposed the Indians to be the late Inhabitants of the Lower Towns, moving down towards the settlements to revenge their losses sustain'd by the army. —— That on the 14th the grass-guard discovered some Indians over the river, 5 of the Regulars were chased by 13 of them to the guard. —— This day Tiftowee should have returned with an answer from the middle Settlements and over-hills, but did not appear. —— That on the 15th the army began to bag up flour and make other dispositions for the proceeding further into the enemy's country, and the day was even fix'd for Marching; but towards evening came in, half-breed Tom, with a white flag which put a stop to further proceedings. He reported that the headmen of their town being much dispersed, it had not been possible for Tiftowee to execute his commission; that he had however communicated his instructions to such as he met with; was gone over the hills; and would be back to the army after six sleeps more. Col. Montgomery accordingly gave him that further time to make his appearance, and the runner set off again the same evening; he likewise reported, that the

Middle Settlement people had reproached those of the Lower Towns with cowardice, and as being the authors of their own misfortunes, and told them that should the army march thither, they would meet it with a white flag. ——— That on the 16th the Raven of Estahtowih, and three more of the Cherokees, that had been for sometime confined were released, and told, "that they were not looked upon as prisoners of war, but at liberty to do as they pleas'd; that if the nation were for peace, we were willing to accomidate matters with them; but if for war we were ready for them; and that if at any time they had a mind to speak with Col. Montgomery, the bringing of a white flag should protect them." This day the Catawba's returned homewards with their plunder, and now arrived at Pine-Tree Hill with 30 horse loads. That on the 17th, 10 or 12 Indians beset three of Captain Brown's rangers who were seeking their horses near the camp, two of whom were killed and scalp'd the third got away. ——— This day the time prologued to Tiftowee expired, without any news coming from him or the nation. And at night a half-breed Indian arrived express from Fort Loudoun, who reported, "That the upper towns did not choose to make peace; had invested the fort; put several of their prisoners to death; and threatened the Little Carpenter's life, who was looked upon as an Englishman, and no longer admitted into the councils; that the people of the lower towns and middle settlements were starving and naked, and almost destitute of ammunition; that the overhills towns were ill provided with corn; that the Indians in the middle settlements seemed desirous of peace, but afraid to treat, and that he with great difficulty and artifice made his way good. ——— That upon this Intelligence, the army moved their camp, and leaving all the tents, waggons, and unnecessary baggage at Fort Prince George, on the 22d cross'd Keeowee river, with six days provisions per man, to take with them a gang of cattle, and 40 pack-horses laden with flour. ——— That on the 23d the army was getting ready to begin the march the next morning, for the middle settlements and were all healthy and in good spirit, and eager for an opportunity to humble our Savage enemies.

From Fort Loudoun. That the garrison had not enjoyed two hours rest since the departure of the former express, the 29th May. ——— That on the first of June, in the night, Ocunnastorah, with the warriors of Chotih, Settiquo, and Chilhowih, set out on a secret expedition; to disguise their intentions, they pretended to have discovered some enemy Indian tracks, which they were going on quest of. June 2d, The Little Carpenter came and informed Capt. Demere, that no enemy's tracks were seen; cautioned him to be strictly on his guard; expressed great concern that he was no longer able to give intelligence as formerly, of what passed in his countrymen's councils; and wished the army would make haste up that he might see the hot headed people of his nation, well beaten and humbled. June 3d, a lieutenant of the provincials and another man went out, but had not got 50 yards before they were fired at, killed and scalped by some Indians who had concealed themselves behind a log, 40 or 50 men sallied out of the garrison, but too late to be of any service; immediately after the Indians fired upon the fort on all sides from the hills around, and were so well concealed, that returning their fire was in vain. June 5th, the Little Carpenter gave information to Capt. Demere, that it was the Great Warrior that had invested the fort; and that he had sent for the warriors from the towns of Talliquoh and Chatugui, to come to his assistance, and intended when they came to set fire to the fort in the night and storm it, and put to death every soul he should find there. June 6th, the Little Carpenter sent word, that a runner was just arrived from the Creeks, with a painted wooden hatchet, (as a token of war) and a talk, in which he acquainted the Cherokees, "That many Creeks were coming to their assistance, and would arrive at Hiwassih in a few days, and that he was ordered to ask them (the Cherokees) for powder and bullets for those allies." From June 6th, to the 8th, the enemy continued skulking about the fort, so that it was impossible to get further intelligence, or refreshments from any of the towns; and the warriors had orders to kill all women that should attempt to go to the fort, that when the express came away (the 9th at night) provisions again ran very low, so that on the 10th the garrison was to have an allowance reduced to one quart of corn for three men per day.

Mr. Dempsey from fort Prince George, informs us, that the army marched forward from Keohwee the 24th ult. and halted at 12 miles distance, for the horses and cattle to come up.

On Tuesday the Sloop Hawke, Capt. Tucker was sent express to Governor Fauquier of Virginia, upon the movements of Col. Montgomery's army, the state of affairs in the Cherokee nation and to hasten the march of the troops from that colony for the relief of Loudoun.

We are length relieved from our apprehensions of a general Creek war, at least for some time, by the arrival of Jerone Courtonne from the Breed Camp, who on his way down, came thro' all the upper Creeks towns, the beginning of last month; when all was apparently quiet there and he saw the traders in several of them gathering up their effects and about their usual business. ——— He gives the following information of the late outrages committed there; that there were no more than 11 people killed in those towns, viz. John Ross, William Mitchell, and Tom (Ross's Negro) at the Sugespogas, where the mischief first began; that the gang increased here and went next to the Oaksuskees, where they killed William Rae, and William Robinson, making the people believe, that the headmen of the Lower Towns had killed every white man in them, and the Sugespoga headmen had done the same in theirs, this insinuation brought more Indians into their gang, with whom they went on to Caiologies, where they murdered Lachlan McIntosh, John Johnson, John Roberts, George McCullough and William Franks; repeating there what they had told before, and that the Oaksuskee headmen themselves had killed their own traders; hence they proceeded to Fushatchies, where they where they killed Richard Hughes, and their murders ended. That several traders fled to the Wolf's town, who caused them to be hid in a swamp, and arm'd and painted all his warriors, declaring, that his attachment to the English was unalterable, and that he would defend them to the last. The Wolf soon got intelligence how the affair happened, and recalled the hidden traders, and kept them under his protection, till the headmen of the nation were summoned and had a meeting at Mucculassa; at which them and the warriors all disavowed having any knowledge of, or consenting to, the murdering of the traders; and resolved that the living traders should be protected, and the effects of the same be restored to their friends; he even sent runners to recall the traders that had fled to Pensacola, where naked and distressed as they were, relief was refused then by the Englishmen! who were there in two vessels from New-York and from Rhode Island trading with some French gentlemen from Mobille, while even the savages (the Yamasee Indians took off their shirts and covered them.) Mr. Courtonne is in the opinion, that notwithstanding the friendly professions of most of the Creek headmen a national rupture has been long since premeditated and resolved on, at the instigation of the French, by means of their known agent the famous Mortar of Oakehoy, who is using all his influence to engage his countrymen, to join and assist the Cherokees, and to carry his Point affirmed, that Capt. Montgomery's army had been entirely defeated, and that even the old Cherokee women with their corn pestles, knock'd many of the soldiers on the head as they stoop'd to cool their mouth with water out of the runs; and left such talk should have any bad effect, the Gun-Merchant advised the traders to go, for safety, out of the nation, till the Mortar should be proved a liar; many traders accordingly took his advice, and were conducted to Augusta, with part of their leather. That the traders who had returned from Pensacola, heard that three English men of war were cruizing off the mouth of the Missisippi and had taken an English vessel bound in there. And that Capt. Brown with several white men, and about 50 Chickasaws sent out on the 29th ult. on an expedition against the Cherokees. ——— It is likewise said, that the Talasee king's son, has declared, that if his nation were for war against the English, he would with 117 gun-men join against his countrymen.

BOSTON July 7. By return of an express from Albany, we learn, that Gen. Amherst had set out from Fort Stanwix, and had proposed to be at Oswego last Thursday, where all the troops destined that way was already arrived.

We learn from Montreal that the Indians were very insulting to the French since their late bad success and threaten to join general Johnson with the Mohawks, when they should receive intelligence of their approach: ——— That the French being short of warlike stores, very much lamented the loss of one of their store-ships, in which they had the greatest quantity ——— That as they expected General Murray up from Quebec, 'twas tho't they would soon give up on the approach of General Amherst with his army, and general Murray with his. ——— That and officer from France arrived at Gaspee in a Dunkirk cutter in 28 days, and landed there, from whence he got to Montreal; what news he bro't had not transpired, but by the countenances of the French people it seemed to be something very discouraging. ——— That the French acknowledge to have lost at the siege of Quebec 114 officers and 1500 privates, tho' the people of the country say they miss 3000, ——— That a bushel of salt sold for .25 pound sterl. and a quart of brandy for 42 livres. ——— That Capt. Ince of Otways, Capt. Archibald of Lascelles, and 3 other officers, who were taken prisoners on the 28th of April, died of wounds at Montreal. ——— That Mons. Bourlimac lies dangerously ill of a wound in his thigh. ——— That Mons. Longe, a famous partisan, fell thro' the ice sometime ago and was drowned; his loss is greatly lamented by all Canada, and his equal is not to be found in that country. ——— That the Cachnawaga Indians are divided among themselves, half of them declaring they will join us, the other half saying they will retire into the woods and remain neuter.

Extract of a Letter from Quebec, dated May 22 1760.

"We are likely to have another battle with the French; as we are ordered to hold ourselves in readiness to march at a moment's warning, where to, we have nor yet heard, but we are mostly of opinion that it is Trois Rivere."

BOSTON July 7. We hear that Colonel Young was taken prisoner, after the battle on the plains of Abraham, on the 28th of April last, in going so far in pursuit of the enemy, and by getting inro a boggy piece of ground. He cold not prevent himself from falling into their hands: His servant seeing the Indians coming towards him, ran to extricate his master out of the danger; but was forbad, as it was impossible to assist him; and very likely the Indians would have killed the servant, tho' at the same time they might save his own life, being an officer of distinction. ——— As soon as the Indians had seized the Colonel, they began to strip him, which they did all to his breeches, and were carrying him off to butcher him, when a French grenadier came up, who with great difficulty (after making use of his arms and bayonet) prevented the putting their bloody design in execution, till a party of French soldiers came and rescued him out of their hands. ——— As soon as the Colonel was relieved, he offered his purse, whenin were ten guineas, which he had in his breeches pocket, to the grenadier for his behaviour, who generously refus'd the reward, thinking himself happy in relieving a gentleman, tho' an enemy, when in the hands of such cruel savages; ——— The Colonel was then escorted to Mons. Levy, the French General, and after informing him of the circumstances of his being taken; and of the behaviour of the grenadier, requested that the 10 Gunies might be delivered to him; which after great importunity, he accepted, tho' with reluctance, having done no more than his duty. ——— Happy would it have been for many had the late M. Montcalm and the officers under him, at the capitulation of Fort William Henry in the year 1758, being such a noble Spirit as the grenadier, when the gentleman (Col. Young) and many other officers and soldiers felt the same effect of not being rescued from the bands of a blood thirsty crew!

——— Perhaps many will say, happy would it have been for some hundreds in America, if some of the late French Governors of Canada had had but half the sense of human and generosity of this soldier.

BOSTON July 7. These are to give Notice, That Joseph York and John Griffin, both of Glocester in the County of Essex, on the 16th Day of June Currant, inlisted with me, they subscribed into His Majesty's Provincial Service for the total reduction of Canada, and receiv'd five Dollars each, and they have both since deserted. These are therefore to warn all Persons not to entertain, or conceal them, or either of them, and if any person shall so do, they may depend upon being prosecuted with the utmost Rigor of Law, And if any Persons will apprehend them or either of them, so that they be convey'd to his Majesty's Castle William they shall have all the necessary charges paid, and shall have the further Sum of Forty Shillings Lawful Money paid them (for each of the said Deserters) by Boston, June 30, 1760. Humphry Bradstreet, Capt.

NEW-YORK July 7. Many letters received last Wednesday from Albany, mention that his Excellency General Amherst was much indisposed, but we are credibly informed, his indisposition was not so bad as to retard his march.

On board the Devonshire came his Majesty's commission appointing his Excellency Thomas Boone, Esq; Governor of the Province of New-Jersey, and his Excellency Francis Bernard, Esq; Governor of the Massachusetts-Bay. Agreeable to which his Excellency Thomas Boone, Esq; who arrived some time before in this city from South Carolina, set out early on Thursday morning last and arrived the same day, safe in his Government.

CHARLESTOWN South Carolina July 12. On Thursday afternoon arrived the Negro Abraham, express from the army commanded by Colonel Montgomery, with an account of their return to fort Prince George, on the 1st instant and from its setting out from thence on the 4th, & marching down into the settlements. ——— The following letter dated the 2d Inst, at the fort contains a full an account of the transaction of that army, as any we have seen.

Extract of a Letter from Fort Prince George, dated July 2, 1760.

The 24th of June we marched from hence, and continued marching the 25th and 26th without any interruption from the Indians; but on Friday the 27th, about 6 miles from Etchowee the first town in the middle Settlements, the advinced party under Capt. Morrison, discovered three Indians, one of which he made prisoner: who pretended that the Middle Settlements were for peace, and knew nothing of the army's coming up. ——— The Colonel did not give much credit to what the prisoner said, but marched forward with the greatest precaution, and when they had got about a mile further, the advanced party under Capt. Morrison aforesaid, were fired upon by the Indians from the thicket; he nevertheless went forward till his party retreated, and he himself was unfortunately killed. ——— The Colonel on hearing the fire, ordered the light infantry and grenadiers to advance, which they did, and met with some of Capt. Morrison's party, who told them, that there were seen about 500 Indians in ambush; they however still advanced, but could see nothing, tho' they were often fired upon; coming to a rising ground they at length discovered a body of the enemy, whom they immediately fired upon, and obliged them to retire into a swamp. The Colonel then ordered the whole to advance, himself at the head of the Royals, and Lieut. Col. Grant at the head of the Highlanders. The Indians continued firing whenever they had an opportunity, and the army always pushed forward and firing, but at too great a distance to do execution. When they got as near the Indians as possible, seven platoons were discharg'd amongst them, which must have done execution for they retired and left off firing. In this affair the Colonel was struck with two spent balls, on the shoulder and ancle.

The army was then ordered into the path, and

go for the Indian Town, a flanking Party being our on the left, and a deep river on the right: this path was so narrow that the army was obliged to move thro' it in an Indian file. The Indians observing this motion went off, and came round upon the rear of the army, fired frequently and wounded several men, but several platoons being fired among them, they ran off, some dragging others away by the feet, arms and legs. ——— The front was fired upon two different times before the army reached the town, but little damage done: the inhabitants were all gone when we entered there, they had their doors lock'd: we found nothing there but some Indian corn. ——— The army encamped on a plain surrounded with hills, and made huts of boards from the Indian houses. The Colonel had his little tent pitched in the center, and we formed a square. ——— Several shots were fired on our camp from the hills around, some of the balls falling within 3 yards of the Colonel's tent, but were spent. About 5 in the afternoon an express came to the camp, with advice, that the picquet, and guard with the provisions were lately attacked by the Indians, but that they defended themselves bravely and killed several of the enemy, The Colonel immediately ordered Capt. Sinclair with 200 men to their assistance, and they return'd to camp about 12 at night, the enemy having been beat by the picquet and guard before Capt. Sinclair's party got to them. The fore part of the 28th was taken up in dressing the wounded, and putting every thing in a proper posture of defence; and all was quiet till about four in the afternoon when a shot fired from a hill at a small distance from us, which was followed by vollies from a body of Indians, for the space of half an hour without ceasing. Capt. Southerland was immediately ordered to the river's side with the Colonel's company; but when he arrived there thinking he was at too great a distance to do execution, he crossed the river, and fired several of the platoons upon the enemy, which obliged them to run off. We received little damage from the enemy; they wounded only two or three of our people slightly. Several of our horses being killed and others wounded, it was hard to determine what should be done, for if we proceed further, either provisions or sick must be left; the first we could not go without, and the sick could not be left in a place of no defence, to be prey to the Savages: It was therefore resolved that the whole should return; and carriages were immediately made for those that could not go on horseback. The whole marched about 12 at night, the Col. thinking it was the safest way from being disturbed by the Indians.

We accordingly marched about 25 miles that night and next day, without hearing any thing of them, till on the 30th, when several shots being fired of which could not be drawn, having been wet by the rain in the night, at assembly beating, a party of the enemy, who had come thro' the woods by a near path (emerging the camp was attacked by some other of their party) advanced and fired upon the center of our picquet who were posted at some distance in the woods; but they were soon made sensible of their mistakes, and obliged to get off in great haste. After our flanking parties were placed, and every thing got in readiness, we began our march, and before the rear had come off the ground of encampment, lieut. Montgomery, who was on the flanking party of the front, came upon a body of about 60 Indians, who were lying in wait for us and drying their baggage, blankets, &c. in the sun, which had been wet the night before. Upon giving them a fire they all ran off, those that were wounded they threw on horses and carried away with them: before all Lieut. Montgomery's party could come up, it being on a hill, and the men walking in an Indian like file, the Indians had left every thing (except their firelocks) which our party seized, and what they could not bring away, was cut to pieces and destroyed. Another party of the enemy attacked our rear, but were beat off, and several of them killed. We encamped that night about 9 miles from hence, and arrived here the 1st current, whence we shall proceed in a day or two down the country. Capt. Williams of the Royal infantry and 8 of the Royals rank and file were killed, and Capt. Peter Gordon, Ensign Eddington, one serjeant, 32 rank and file wounded of the Highlanders, two serjeants and 6 rank and file were killed; Lieut. McMarton, and M'Kennon surgeon's mate, J. Monro, one serjeant one piper, and 25 rank and file wounded, some slightly. No Indian have been seen or heard of since they were beat off on the 30th in the morning.

The following Particulars are mentioned in other Letters, viz.

That the action between the army and the Cherokees on the 27th ult. began at 8 or 9 in the morning and continued between 4 and 5 hours, with little intermission. That some of Captain Morrison's company supposed the number of the Indians in the thickets that day, to be about 500 that they were soon some men killed of the provincials and rangers, and two of Morrison's company slightly wounded. That Morrison behaved like a gallant good officer till he fell; and his company returned with the regulars to Fort Prince George, who offer to continue in the service under the command of Lieutenant Patrick Calhoon. That Capt. Grinnan and O'neal of the rangers, and some other of our officers behaved with great spirit. That there was at least 500 bushels of Indian corn found in the town of Etchowee. That some of the army's flour was thrown into the river, in order to get horses for the wounded. That Capt. Williams (who is much regreted in every letter) loss his life in going to supply Capt. Morrison. That the number of Indians killed may be about 50; and that having many rifles among them, they did execute at a greater distance than our people could. That many more men must be lost in the difficult passes on the return to Keeohwee, had not the Indians been deceived, by lights left in the houses at Etchwee when the army came away from that town, whence the enemy supposed them to be still there, till they had stole near a day's march. And that, when the army set out for Ninety-six, good stores of provisions was left with the garrison at Fort Prince George.

There is no news whatsoever from Fort Loudoun;

but we hope only Byrd has before now marched from Virginia to relieve that distressed unfortunate garrison.

The General Assembly of this province have voted 5000 pounds at the disposal of his Honour the Lieutenant Governor, towards the relief of such helpless people as have suffered by the present Indian war, and taken refuge in the several forts on our frontier.

BOSTON July 14. From Quebec we have these further particulars, viz.

That from the Battle of the 28th of April, to the raising of the siege, the Garrison had not above 50 Men killed and wounded: That the General hearing the enemy designed to escalade, called his Officers together, and told them, that if they would stand by him he would not give up the Place while he had ten Men left; in which the brave Men immediately agreed, and with the great chearfulness: That the Garrison would soon be strongly reinforced, the Battalions at Louisbourg being shipping off for that purpose, as they were destroying the works of that place. The fleet of new Provision Ships had got up; That the Rochester Man of War, with 15 or 20 more Provision vessels from England, they met going up the River: And that it was said some of the Men of War, of the same Convoy, had taken two French Frigates on the Passage.

Last Week one Chamberlan belonging to Fort Drummer arrived there in about 10 Days from Montreal, after a tedious Captivity: He says, that the Indians despairing of all Succours from France, were packing up their All in order to go to the Missisippi, and were going to carry all their Prisoners with them: That he had several Times attempted to make his escape, but was discover'd till the last, when in their conditions, not keeping such a strict Watch over him as usual he effected it.

BOSTON July 14. Our advice from Oswego are as follow, viz. That about the middle of last month a number of foreign Indians came to the carrying place above Niagara to trade: That two soldiers of the 44th regiment met with some of them, when they were seized by two of their warriors; but one of the soldiers being a stout fellow got away, and alarmed the fort; upon which the picquet marched in pursuit of them: That one Lucas, a private centinel, who had been some time among the Savages, and six others, went a-head of the guard, and overtook the Indians, just as they were going into their canoes, at Lake Erie, when said Lucas made a speech, in which he told them, that tho' he was in a common dress, he was a great warrior; and that if they did not immediately return the prisoner, and deliver up the aggressors, he would go back to the fort, and the commandant would put to death those of their tribe that were still trading there. That at first they would not harken to him; but on a repetition, and solemnly declaring his treat should be put in execution, and taking leave of them, they delivered both the prisoner and the offenders, who were brought back to the fort: That the two offenders were of the Tawa's who said, that Mons. Bellerre, at Detroit, told them, he would make them the richest men in Canada, if they would bring him two English prisoners, from Niagara: And that one of the chiefs made a speech to the commanding officer, expressing much concern that the young Warriors had behaved so ill, and desired he would keep them as hostages, till such time as they should give convenient proof of their friendship to the English, which they determined themselves would be very soon in their power to do.

The report we have lately of some cattle being taken on their way to Crown Point, was without foundation: One of the persons who went with them returned here last week, and informed, that the Indians had way-laid them, but while they were preparing to fall on the guard, a party came from Crown Point to escort them, whereby the enemy were disappointed in their design.

———— Col. Haviland commands at Crown Point ———— Major Rogers with his rangers was there, and was filling up his companies with such as had a mind to inlist out of the Provincials: Our Troops were hearty and in high spirit: some of them are employed in getting the battoes and other things in readiness to go down the lake, while others were employed in making a good waggon-road from Crown-Point to No. 4. At the same time the New-Hampshire troops are making the road fron No. 4 towards Crown-Point.

NEW-YORK July 14. Wednesday last arrived here from Albany, near 80 of the soldiers taken prisoners by the French at Quebec, the 21st of April. The Lieutenants Cox, Lison, May, and Hamilton, are in this party. Mons. Bonneau, who conducted this flag of truce from Montreal to Crown-Point, to be exchanged for French prisoners, was Ordered down, and now here.

NEWPORT Rhode Island July 15. On Saturday arrived here by land, Mr. Joseph Pike, of this town who was at Oswego in the year 1756, when that place unfortunately fell into the hands of the enemy. He, with thirteen more English Prisoners, were, by order of the French General, St. Luke, delivered to 25 savages (natural allies of the French) twelve made their escape. Pike and another were conducted into the woods by the Indians who employ'd them in hunting for six months, in the fall and winter. after which, those two unhappy persons were conducted to a town called Conassatego, inhabited by part of the Indian Nation. The next season their execise was hunting. The third they were commanded to perform the same duty, but were obliged to return in four months, beaver proving so scarce, and not to afford the Indians, sufficient game; during the return there only sustenance was bark of trees and roots. In the summer of the fourth year, their business was to clear the land, and raise corn. In the fall Pike and his fellow sufferer were sold for 3 years to two French merchants, for 150 Pistereens of each, one of which died in two months; when they were conducted to a prison in Montreal, where they continued in a miserable condition, upon a nauseous and slender allowance, till a flag of truce was prepared to receive them and 128 other English prisoners, who were safely landed at Crown-Point.

PHILADELPHIA July 17. Extract of a letter, from Pittsburgh July 4, 1760.

"General Monckton arrived here on the 29th of June, and immediately gave orders for the march of a large detachment of the army to Presque-Isle, every thing being provided for that purpose. The troops appointed for this service, are to set off on Monday morning next. Our Magazines of stores, provisions, forage, &c. are most amply supplied, and every thing wears a smiling countenance this way. The Indians, to all appearance, are hearty in our cause; and a number of them go, under Mr. Gogham; with the troops designed for the Lake."

Since our last came to town 29 Indians from Machmid, an Indian town, about 60 miles above Wyoming; they brought with them three prisoners, a boy and two girls; and appears to be a religious sober well behaved sort of people.

CHARLESTOWN S. Carolina July 19. Extract of a Letter from Augusta, June 24.

"In my last of the 16th inst. I flattered myself and you with hopes and prospects that now seems vanished into the air. Indeed things here are so mutable and quick in their revolution that we have scarce time to consider one circumstance or piece of intelligence, till the arrival of another entirely destroys all conjectures. ―――― After the first fatal stroke all was quiet for about 20 days in the Upper Creeks, and the Indians were gathering together all the horses, leather, and other goods that had been dispersed and divided: Some white people got out with part of their effects, and either were preparing to follow them; but the Gun-Merchant, who had all along been their good friend, and persuaded them to stay till they had got collected, when the people should have been ready to come off in two days at most, came and told them to go off directly, for he could no longer prevent them, the Mortar being just come in, and had spoiled all his good talk; and on their answering, that they had not yet got horses enough to carry off their leather, he told them that if they loved their leather better than themselves, they might stay, and pushed them from him: Away they came, and arrived here yesterday in 8 days. They say the Mortar, when he came in, cried out, "What, do I see still these fowls (meaning the white people) crawling about, &c." He likewise told them many lies about Fort Loudoun and concluded with telling them, that the Cherokee women knock'd the white people down with junks: They are nothing says he, you may kill them with your very looks. In short, it is in vain to think a peace with the Creeks, till they are in some measure humbled; they despise us to the utmost, and are exasperated against us to madness; all the talks sent to them about making up differences, and forgetting what is past, serves only to make them more insolent. I am even afraid Col. Montgomery's success against the Cherokees, however great will not have sufficient weight to tame the Creeks unless they feel a little of it themselves.

The private forts that are kept up here, and in which duty is done, are five: Were there is only 20 or 25 men in each of those, this place, which is more the frontier of South-Carolina than of Georgia, might defy all the attempts of the Indians. I have not mention'd Mr. Golphin's fort, as it is so far from the rest."

A Letter from Fort Prince George dated july 5 1760.

"An account of the operation of the army under the hon. Col. Montgomery, I make no doubt, had been communicated to you long before this, I therefore shall not trouble myself or you with the recital of what passed, from their leaving Keeohwee to go to the Middle Settlements, till their return to this fort. I most heartily lament the situation of our poor friends at Fort Loudoun, but it is absolutely impacticable to relieve them this way the difficulties of the passes, even to the middle settlements, can hardly be imagined; before I saw them, I had no Idea of them; but the traders tell us, that these are not to be compared with what we must have gone through to the Over-Hills towns. The return of the army was certainly a well judged thing altho' I see some bad consequences that must follow: Had there been a fort in the middle middle settlements, where to have lodged the sick and wounded, and to have secured a retreat in case of defeat, and that properly supplied with men and provisions, then we might have carried our operation further; but as we were situated it was impossible.

The 3d inst. the army left us, and marching downwards in order to re-imbark for New-York.

Yesterday one Jefferson, a soldier in the Buffs, strolling about the hills where the army had been encamped, was shot and scalped by four of the enemy, whom we saw running away just after we heard the report of the gun. In the evening the centinels discovered 7 or 8 more skulking about the same place; so that we begin to undergo a second confinement, which I wish may not be as long, and more disagreeable than the first. Not a man of the rangers, or the new raised regiment, could be prevailed on to remain here, alleging that their time was up, &c. This morning about 9 o'clock, arrived here Capt. John Brown from Augusta, with 13 white men that were dressed and painted like Indians, and 43 Chickesaws, who come with intent to join Col. Montgomery, not having heard of his return. They propose to stay till the Colonel is informed of their arrival, which he will be this evening, by the bearer. Not a word from Fort Loudoun since the 9th of last month."

CHARLESTOWN S. Carolina July 19. Part of a letter from the camp near Ninety-Six, July 8.

"Mr. Wilson is dispatched on a purpose to get the transports ready, in order to take the troops on board as soon as they arrive at strawberry. ——— When we returned from Etchowee to the field of battle, I had the mortification to see poor Capt. Morrison's head cut off, and scalped and his body cut in several pieces; even his eyebrows were cut off; other carcasses lay stripped, and many infamous marks of cruelty and contempt upon them. Since that affair we have seen the miscreants dressed in regiments of the slain. Considering the many difficulties we must have encountered, and the great inconveniencies we laboured under, I think we had not force enough to attempt the relief of Fort Loudoun."

"It is a great error that the Indians were furnished with rifled barreled guns, for what we suffered was chiefly owing to that cause, they wounded our men at such a distance as our carbines could scarcely do execution. —— The Day after we left Keowee 42 Chikesaws, and 15 white men came into the fort, to be revenged on the Cherokees for the murder of two of their people: —— They are provisions at Prince George for eight months."

It is said that the Young Warrior of Estatoe, our inveterate enemy, was killed in the action near Etchoey, for he was seen encouraging his men, whereon two platoons were ordered to direct their fire that way, and he was not heard or seen afterwards. It is said a tomahawk, blanket and gun, known to be his were found on the field of battle, and are now in possession of some of our people.

On the 4th inst. one of our provincials, was shot within 100 yards from Fort Prince George, scalped, and his belly ripped open by the Indians.

Col. Montgomery sent down orders for the transports to be ready to carry the troops back to New-York, by the 10th of July.

Mr. Williamson who left Ninety-six last Sunday we are informed that the troops marched from thence for Congarees on Friday morning: Captain Bell the commandant of that fort, had 40 men in garrison. Mr. Williamson also informs, that the garrison of Fort Loudoun had been supplied with 300 bushels of corn, and a quantity of bacon, which the Little Carpenter had procured by a negotiation with Occonastata.

BOSTON July 21. We learn from Louisbourg that two regiments of that garrison had sailed from thence for Quebec, under convoy, and that the Mines were almost finished, for the blowing up the fortifications and the other works there, agreeable to his Majesty's positive orders, received some time since.

The following Letter from Quebec, contains many particulars of the Battle of the 28th of April which have not been published here.

Extract of a Letter from Quebec May 20, 1760.

"Ever since the departure of the British fleet last year, every discerning person of this garrison expected an assault from the enemy before succours could arrive from any part of the British dominions. The enemy were numerous by land, and the river commanded by seven French frigates, which reduced us to the necessity of establishing our posts to watch the enemy, and secure the garrison from surprize; also, to mount numerous guards in every weak part of the town, ready to act if the General should be disappointed in his intelligence. Their military preparations and many different advices brought, were, that Gen. de Levy would attack us from time to time: but every disappointment gave less credit to ever attempting it. This together with many shameful instances of their bad behavior in small attacks about our out-posts during the winter, gave an insulting kind of an opinion to the officers and soldiers in this army, who soon forgot that Wolfe fell the 13th of Sept. 1759, and still thought the remains of his little army every way equal to the whole force of Canada. In this security we remained to the 20th of April following, when a serjeant of the French artillery who past the garrison not unheard, but unnoticed, driven by the tide to Orleans and back again, and was taken up, on a small sheet of ice, who tho' expiring with the cold of the night told us. That Gen. de Levy, with an army of 14,000 men, covered by 3 frigates and some victuallers, were at hand to attack us, and that he was in the headmost boat with some pieces of artillery, but was cast away 10 leagues above Quebec. This man the soldiers call the messenger of God. I don't know the dispensation of Providence but if the night of the 20th had not brought on a continued storm, and the man they call God's messenger arrived as he did, our outposts, some of which were far detach'd, and occupied by 800 of our prime troops, must inevitably been cut out.

The posts were directly called in, and 3 regiments with some pieces of artillery sent out to retard the march of the enemy who we knew were landed, and had established bridges across at Cape Rouze, but had not yet pass'd. Our light troops gall'd them on their march, but the regiments went only 4 miles to St. Foize, when they took possession of the house commanding the road, and drew upon the ground securing the pass, between them and the plains of Abraham, but night came on and it rained hard all day, the enemy declined to force the pass, and the troops after some skirmishes, retired into town. The next morning the enemy appeared on the plain about 2 miles from Quebec, when the whole garrison amounting to 3,700 men, officers included went to meet them, drawing up in two lines, with the light Arm'd troops and rangers on the wings.

——— The enemy retired a little and we kept advancing until we came within musket shot of the woods, where we came to an engagement, which lasted three hours and a half: The fire on the flanks and wings of the line was exceedingly hot: The French claim a victory, they kept the field, but they lost 2,000 men, and near 200 officers, we lost 1,100 men and 102 officers with 20 pieces of brass field artillery. 'Twas impossible to restrain the officers and soldiers of this little army from giving battle, they were use to victory, had been once before under the command of Wolfe with only 2 pieces of artillery; and I must say, had not some mistake or other happened in the disposition of the cannon and situation of the ground, we could that day have given an example to the whole world.

"At our retreat the French continued their march in columns to the high ground where Gen. Wolfe fell, and a little advanced, they drew their first line about 600 yards from the walls, at which time we had not three pieces of cannon bearing on the enemy, the last resource to save the town was, flanking out embrazures thro' the curtain and mounting all the guns on the ramparts, which was done with incredible swiftness, that in four days 130 pieces of cannon bore upon them. They opened 3 batteries of 13 guns and 2 mortars and persisted in a siege of 19 days, but meeting with great loss, and finding the walls converted into an intire battery, they raised the siege the 19th inst. The Leostaffe man of war was sent up the river to destroy the French frigates, which she did, burnt two and ran one ashore, but she unluckily struck on some rocks and immediately sunk. At the time of the siege a fire broke out by accident and consumed a great number of houses."

By the return of the courier last Thursday evening from Albany, we learn that his Excellency General Amherst with his army had got to Oswego, and were making the necessary preparations to proceed forward. —— That they had lately launched a snow of 18 guns at Niagara, it being more convenient to build there than Oswego. —— That from crown-Point they had advice, that Major Rogers with his men being out opposite the fort cutting faggots for fascine for the use of the army, their own guard was fired upon by the enemy, who killed one and wounded five, among whom was Captain Brewer, slightly; that the Major immediately detached a party in pursuit of them, but were not returned when the last advices came from thence.

NEW-YORK July 21. Extract of a Letter from Albany July 10, 1760.

"I take this opportunity to acquaint you of our worthy friend Denormandei's being drowned on his passage from Oswego to Niagara, almost at the latter. A sea struck his whaleboat and split her, he depending on his swimming strip'd his coat and jacket off and plunged in, the rest of the crew staid upon the wreck and were saved. The waistband of his breeches gave way, and fell to his feet, and was the immediate cause of his death. His body was cast ashore at Niagara and buried the next morning.

The General and most of his troops are at Oswago, and Major Godwin with 5 or 600 men are set off from Niagara for Presque-Isle upon secret expedition, which time must bring to knowledge."

PHILADELPHIA July 24. We hear from Pittsburgh that on the 7th Instant four Companies of the Royal Americans marched for Presque-Isle under the Command of Colonel Bouquet; as did also Captain M'Neil's Company of the Virginia Regiment: That on Wednesday following Capt. Hugh Mercer was to march for the same Place with three Companies of the Pennsylvania Regiments, viz. Capt. Clapham's, Biddle's and Anderson's: And that two Days after, they were to be followed by two Companies more of the Pennsylvanians, Commanded by the Captains Atlee and Miles. The Destination of these Troops were not known, but from the nearness of Presque-Isle to Detroit, it was hoped the Enemy would not be long in the possession of that Place.

BOSTON July 28. Monday last arrived here Col. Arburthnot, who has commanded at Fort Frederick in St. John's river, the year past; also several other officers and a number of soldiers belonging to this province, who have garrisoned his Majesty's forts up the bay of Fundy, and now discharged, arrived here, being relieved by a number lately enlisted in this province, for that service. We hear the Indians behave well, and still continue to come in to the several forts at Nova-Scotia, and carry on trade very peaceably.

The same day a person came to town from Albany, which place he left the Friday night before and says, that there was no advice from Oswego since the arrival of the General there. —— He informs, that one of Major Rogers's men lately wounded, died of his wounds; and that one our provincials was lately drowned.

We hear from Portsmouth in New-Hampshire, that an express arrived there last Wednesday from their regiment at No. 4. and informed, That an express came to Col. Goffe the 17th inst. from Maj. Rogers, with advice, that a large body of French and Indians had landed upon the East side of Lake Champlain, and it was feared were designed to attack their regiment, who were encamped on Goffe's road, 18 miles above No. 4.
—— That their men were all well and in high spirit, having lost but one man out of the regiment; and that they had finished the road 23 miles.

Yesterday morning arrived here Capt. Andrews in 18 days from Louisbourg, and informs, that the miners have been somewhat retarded in their work, by the caving in of some of the mines, and that it would be some time before the works are blown up.

Last Friday by virtue of his Honour the Lieut.

Governor's Proclamation, 22 Of the Provincial, soldiers were taken up and committed to goal in for trial: These men have been part of the garrison of Fort Cumberland, in the bay of Fundy, who engaged in that service upon assurance of being discharged at a certain period: This time of service, as they pretended, being expir'd, and no relief appearing, they on the 15th inst. forcibly entered a sloop, one Bragdon master, bro't the vessel under sail, and arrived here last Thursday morning. —— They also bro't their arms with them, on pretence of delivering them at Castle William, from whence, they own they received them: After giving bail for their appearance they were on Saturday last discharged from their confinement, and are now on their way home to their families and friends, from whom they have been long absent.

BOSTON July 28. One of our vessels taken going to Quebec, was Capt. Clouston, from this place, which vessel was retaken, after a Valuable cargo was taken out her: The vessel from Halifax belonged to Rundle and Crawley of this Place. —— Three small vessels, 'tis said were armed and fitted out from Quebec, to cruize in the river, and prevent the enemy from thus seizing the traders. —— And that Governor Murray had given liberty to the French peasants to bring into the city fresh provisions, for which they are very well paid.

Friday last arrived here from Louisbourg and a cruize, the Province ship of war King George, Captain Hallowell. —— from Louisbourg we learn, that the arm'd vessel lately fitted from thence, had been at Pictou and burnt 5 or 6 of the vessels which the enemy had taken from us last year, and bro't off some plunder. —— That the Indians from St. John's, who bro't the account of the 5 French men of war being in the Bay of Chaleurs, also informed that they had landed 400 men, in order 'twas said, to attack our garrison at Fort Cumberland.

PHILADELPHIA July 31. From Pittsburgh we have advice of the 14th inst. by which Major Gladwin, with 400 men, was arrived at Presque-Isle, from the northward; and that our forces from Fort

Pitt, it was thought, would be there likewise by the 16th of this month.

Extract of a letter from Niagara, July 15.

"This day will sail our two snows the Mohawk and Apollo, the latter mounting 20 and the other 18 guns, They expect to have a blow with the French vessels, who were seen between this and Oswego a few days ago. Great numbers of Savages come here trading, some of them quite from the from the Wabash river; they say the French at Detroit have nothing to give them."

AUGUST 1760

BOSTON Aug. 4. Last Wednesday morning arrived here Capt. Detin 3 days from Halifax by whom we have advice that on the 21st of July arrived there the Repulsive man of war of 32 guns from Bay of Chaleurs, and brought in the Crew of several vessels which had been taken by the French, particularly the Augustus, Barabas Velman, from New-London, but last from Louisbourg. Bangs from New-York coming from casco Bay. Cambell, Swinney and Maxwell, from Halifax, bound up the river, which vessels on the 16th of May last, off Gaspee Bay, fell in with a French frigate and two large storeships, from Boudeaux France, who took them all and carried them into Bay Chaleurs. —— Some of the men that were taken arrived here in Capt. Dean and inform, that the French had fitted out the Augustus as a privateer, but was taken by one of the 5 men of war, which sailed from Louisbourg some time since in quest of those ships; by some papers found on board, they got intelligence where the French ships were, and accordingly pursued them, but when the English men of was appeared in the bay, the French ran their ships into shoul water, where they were defended by 3 or 4 batteries, which they had before erected and planted a number of guns bro't on shore from their ships; and only the Repulsive & Scarborough being able to come near enough to engage, they continued the attack 3 days, when the enemy abandoned their works, and set two of their ships on fire and burnt them; and most of their prizes they either burnt or sunk; they then put the English prisoners, consisting of 59 men, women and children, whom they strip'd and bound in irons, on board the other ship which they ran ashore, at some further distance and left them: —— That soon after they were left they found means to unbind themselves, and one of the men swam 3 or 4 miles to out ships, and informing of their situation and circumstances, 9 boats were mann'd out and sent to their relief, who brought them all away, and set the ship on fire: 'Tis said she had a great quantity of provisions and other stores on board. —— The Repulsive having receiv'd considerable Damage to her Hull, sails, and Rigging, put into Halifax to refit.

BOSTON Aug. 4. Our last Advices from Fort Ontario on Lake Ontario, arrived here Monday last in but 9 Days from Oswego, they are as follows. That General Amherst with about 5000 Troops were were preparing to go from thence and that the Remainder of the Troops were expected at the Lake in a few Days. —— They, with stores having been much retarded, by the want of sufficient Water in the River, there having been no Rain. —— That Commodore Loring was out on a Cruize in the Lake, with two fine Snows, one of 28 Guns, and the other of 20 Guns; That after he sailed a French Snow and a Brig of 18 Guns each appeared in sight of the Fort, just as 8 Boats had put off deep loaded with Stores for Niagara, and whom narrowly escaped falling into their Hands; but they got safe to the Place they were designed for. ——

By a Letter from Aswego, dated July 19th, we have Advice, That 4 Battalions of Regulars and 3 Provincials were encamp'd near the Garrison; and that 3 Battalions of Regulars, with the Connecticut and New-Jersey Regiments, would join them in a few Days: Also, That Sir William Johnson with a large body of Indians, at least a Thousand; some say Fifteen Hundred, were but a few Miles from the Fort, and on their way thither, to join our Army: That the Regulars and Provincials, appear to be a fine body of Troops, and all in high Spirits.

BOSTON Aug. 4. Saturday last about one o'clock, came to Town by land from Providence, his Excellency Francis Bernard, Esq; with his Majesty's Royal Commission to be Captain-General, Governor and Commander in Chief in and over his Majesty's Province of the Massachusetts-Bay; as also a Commission from the Right Honourable the Lord of the Admiralty, to be Vice Admiral of the same, &c. —— His Excellency embarked from his late Government of New-Jersey on board the Massachusetts arm'd Sloop last Tuesday, and arrived at Rhode Island on Wednesday Evening, and the next morning proceeded from thence to Providence in a passage Boat provided for that purpose, accompanied by the Hon. Mr. Secretary Oliver, who waited at Rhode Island to attend him; From Providence his Excellency set out on Friday afternoon, and lodged at Wrentham that night, and from thence set out early the next morning, escorted by a Party of the Troops of the Horse Guard, detached thither for that purpose: and was met at Dedham by the remainder of the Troops, and several of his Majesty's Council; and on the road from hence, by a great number of Gentlemen from Town in their Coaches and Chariots, and proceeded to the Province House, (where the company of Cadets were drawn up) and received the Congratulations of a number of Gentlemen who had repaired thither on this occasion; from thence his Excellency walk'd in procession to the Court-House, being escorted thither by the company of Cadets: The Regiment of Militia in this Town being under arms, and drew up in the Maim-Street, he received their Compliments of the Cheers, by paying the Standing Salute as he passed by, and the Windows of the Houses, were crowded with Spectators on the occasion. His Majesty's Commission, to his Excellency, as also that from the Lords, of Admeralty, were opened and publicly read in the Council Chamber, and the usual Oaths administered by his Honour the Lieutenant Governor: After which he was congratulated by the Council and a great number of Gentlemen there present; which was followed by three loud Huzzas, and a discharge of three vollied from the Militia, &c. as also a discharge from the Guns at Castle William, and Batteries in this Town and Charlestown, and from the Ships in the Harbour; after which his Excellency, with the Gentlemen of the Council. a number of Officers and other Gentlemen were entertained with a Handsome Dinner provided at Faneuil-Hall for that purpose.

By His Excellency Francis Bernard, Esq; Captain-General and Governor in Chief, in and over his Majesty's Province of Massachusetts-Bay in New-England, and Vice Admiral of the same.

A PROCLAMATION

Whereas His Majesty by his Royal Commission has been pleased to appoint me to be Captain-General and Governor and Chief in and over His Majesty's Province of the Massachusetts-Bay in New-England which Royal Commission had this Day been duly published:

I have thought fit to issue this Proclamation hereby Impowering and requiring all Officers, whose Commissions would otherwise cease and determine, to continue in the Exercise of their Trust reposed to them by their respective Commissions, until further Orders: And all Persons concerned are required to conform themselves accordingly.

Given at the Council Chamber in Boston, the Second Day of August, 1760. in the Thirty fourth year of the Reign of our Sovereign Lord George the Second, by the Grace of God, of Great Britain, France and Ireland, King, Defender of the Faith, &c.   Fra. Bernard,

By His Excellency's Command
   A. Oliver, Secr.
            God Save the King.

NEW-YORK Aug. 4. On Wednesday morning last, died at his Seat, the Honourable James De Lancey, our Lieutenant Governor, in the 57th year of his age. This unexpected event, for he was in perfect health the evening before, threw the whole city into the deepest sorrow and amazement. A pain in his breast awakened him at three, and continued without intermission till about nine in the morning, when before he apprehended the necessity of a Physician, seized with a Fit, he suddenly expired. The next Day his remains were honourably interred from his Seat in the Bowery.

PHILADELPHIA Aug. 4. Extract from a Letter from Charlestown, in South Carolina, dated July 18, 1760.

"We are in hopes that at the request of the

Governor, and House of Assembly, joined by the great voice of the People, Colonel Montgomery; with the King's Troops will be prevailed to stay 'till our affairs with the Indians are a little settled. —— In a Letter fron Augusta received on Wednesday there were small Hopes of Matters being made up with the Creeks. Some People are glad of this intelligence; but perhaps the withdrawing of the Forces may make the Indians alter their peaceable Disposition, if they were really inclined."

NEWPORT Rhode Island Aug. 5. On Saturday last arrived Capt. Whitman from Turks Island. Just before he came into the port, he spoke with the Captain of a ship, bound for Philadelphia, who had been 13 days from Quebec; from whom he received the following intelligence. That nine sail of man of war and a number of transports arrived there from England: That General Murray with about 40 frigates and transports, had left Quebec, in order to meet General Amherst at Montreal, who had marched for that place: And, that he met the troops which were in Garrison at Louisbourg, in the river, bound to Quebec.

CHARLESTOWN S. Carolina Aug. 9. On Tuesday last the Lieutenant Governor received an answer from the Honourable Colonel Montgomery, to the letter desiring he would leave a part of the detachment of the King's troops under his command, for covering the frontiers: wherein he acquaints his honour that he shall leave four battalion companies of the royal regiment for that purpose, who will be under the command of the Major Fredrick Hamilton. The express met the troops at Lyon's Creek, and the four companies just mentioned were ordered to return to the Congarees, which they did on the 2d instant. The rest of the detachment is marching down in order to embark for New-York, the transports being ready to return them.

PHILADELPHIA Aug. 11. Extract of a Letter from Pittsburg July 25, 1760.

"This moment the pack-horses, that went with the Colonel Bouquet and Mercer to Presque Isle are returned. —— The troops arrived at the lake on the 10th and on the 17th of May, Walters, with 400 of the Royal Americans embarked in whale boats, and proceeded to Niagara, —— The Indians very hearty at least seemingly in our cause."

PHILADELPHIA Aug. 14. On Monday last Captain Rench arrived here, in 20 days passage, from Quebec. By him we learn as follows, viz. That a week before he sailed, General Murray, with between 2 and 3,000 troops, and about 40 sail of Transports, left Quebec for Montreal, having likewise with him a 40 gun ship, a frigate, and a sloop of war, with several floating batteries, some of which mounted 24 pounders: That about 10 leagues up the river, he landed his men, and took, after a good deal of opposition from the enemy, a 16 gun battery, which is said to be the only opposition of that kind he had to meet with in going up: That it was reported a French Army (about 10,000 men) designed to give Gen. Amherst battle, to hinder his joining Gen. Murray. —— That an express of rangers had arrived from Gen. Amherst, who were 20 days from Crown-Point: but in crossing the river St. Francis on a raft, they were carried down the falls, by which they lost their packet, and all their arms; so that General Murray could receive but little information from them: That one of our ships above Quebec had received some damage from some of the French floating batteries and lost some men: —— That a French Indian came in from Trois Riviere, and said, the French told him, that Maj. Rogers had burnt two villages on the Island of Jesus, within five leagues of Montreal: And that our troops went off from Quebec in high spirits, the officers, it is said, striving and partitioning for leave to go on the expedition.

BOSTON Aug. 18. The Express which went from hence with the letters that came in the Earl of Leicester Packet Boat from England, for General Amherst returned here last Wednesday from Albany, by him there is advices from the army at Oswego, of August 4th. that Gen. Monckton from Pittsburgh had joined Gen. Amherst at Oswego, where they were all in readiness to proceed on the intended expedition; and it was tho't they would go forward about the 10th. —— From Crown-Point we learn Col. Haviland with 2500 regulars, and Brigadier Ruggles with 3000 provincials were also ready, and would proceed forward about the same time.

Extract of a Letter from Oswego, dated July 16, 1760.

"There are now here 10 French Indians from Oswegatche, who are come in the name of their nation, to make peace with the Six Nations and us. Some of them that are here now, were at the battle of Quebec the 28th of April: They say they never saw fighting till that day; that indeed the French are great warriors, but the English much greater, as they fought so well and had so few men; They asked whether, our regiment (meaning the Highlanders) were there, as they said saw such a battle, and that they killed many Frenchmen with their long knives (meaning their broad swords) These Indians would readily join us, where they not afraid the French would destroy their Squaws and children; but promise to join General Amherst with 60 warriors in going going down river. They make no secret of their leaving the French, as they plainly see the English will take their country."

Express of a Letter from Crown-Point, July 19.

"Next Week we expect to take our departure from this place, in order to attack the French, who have advanced half way between St. John's and Crown-Point to the number of 2600: They are determined to make the greatest opposition possibly against our party which go from the Lake, as they have two row gallies, each to carry six 24-pounders, ten swivels, and 1000 men, which will greatly retard our joining Gen. Amherst, who goes by way of Oswego: The French will endeavour to defeat us, as they know that they will thereby cut off the provisions which we are to carry to the General at Montreal: However, we shall go with 5000 men from this place, with a brig, which will carry 18 nine pounders, two redoes 16 guns each, 5 floating batteries, well built and doubt not but will be sufficient to repel the enemy's forces: They are very weak at St. John's; and about all their Indians have left them, which will render our conquest easy. —— We are all in high Spirit, and want nothing but to see the flag of Christian Liberty waving on the bastion of Montreal. We are certain the enemy have had no reinforcement either of men, provisions or ammunition this spring, neither do they expect any: They are certainly in the greatest dilemma, and have no way to flee to safety, as General Murray comes up the river with troops from Quebec, General Amherst by the way of Oswegatche, Sir Wm. Johnson, with his Indians, from Niagara, General Monckton by way of Iroquois, and Col. Haviland from Crown-Point by the Bay of St. John's, and all to meet at Montreal. —— I hope by the 7th of August to drink an health to King George in the Bunch of Grapes Tavern at the east side of Montreal town, and at the same time to see the French pledge me. —— We have here Claret (but not the property of the French, as they have none) in bumpers and the sovereign toast is, Success to the British arms, and a final conquest of Canada."

PHILADELPHIA Aug. 21. Advices from Pittsburgh of the 17th Instant, mention every thing going on well there then; that the Day before a Party had gone up the Ohio in Battoes, to take post at Venango; and that another had set off that Day with Cattle for the same place.

From Presque Isle (July 18) we learn, that 400 Royal Americans, who arrived there the 17th of that month, from Pittsburgh had embarked for Niagara, in a number of whaleboats and battoes, sent by General Amherst for that purpose, which 400 with those that came in those boats, made up 900, and it was thought would give the people at Detroit a good deal of uneasiness: That the Indians that way seemed much surprized at the appearance of our forces, but used them very civilly and lent the several horses, to supply those that tired on the road: That the country between Pittsburgh and Presque Isle (distance 140 miles) was generally hilly, and the soil but indifferent, but that between Venango and Presque Isle our people met the finest meadows they had ever seen, some of them two miles and a half long and 1 mile broad, without a tree or brush and the grass 5 feet 5 inches high; and they were told by the Indians, that there were such Savannahs for 20 miles farther up. ——— The distance from Pittsburgh to Venango some 80 miles. ——— Our men are now building a fort at Presque Isle. ——— The Allegheny is said to be very shallow, and hardly navigable for canoes.

CHARLESTOWN S. Carolina Aug. 23. Last Tuesday night arrived here Charles M'Lamore, with dispatches from the Lieut. Governor from Capt. Paul Demere, Commandant of Fort Loudoun, dated the 8th inst. wherein he acquaints his Honour, "That they had agreed to the capitulation that was enclosed, with the Great Warrior, and other head men of the Creek nation; which, considering the great distress they were in he hoped would not be disapproved of: That nothing but the inclinations those Indians had for peace, could have saved them, for they would have been obliged to abandon the fort that day, happen what would, and few of them could ever have reached Carolina: That the garrison were to set out next morning, flattering themselves that the Indians meant them no harm; and they would make all the dispatch their starved conditions would admit of: That the Indians expect, that immediately on their arrival at Keowee, the prisoners confined there [meaning those that are now here,] will be released; all thoughts of further hostilities laid aside, and an accommodation heartily set about. That peace and well regulated trade might be established, such as, they say, may last forever: That they could discover nothing in the behaviour of the Indians that contradicted this, and they hoped, at least, that nothing might be undertaken that would endanger the garrison upon the march."

On the 6th of Aug. Capt. Demere held a council of war, to concert the properest measures to be pursued in this present distress, when the officers gave their unanimous opinion, in writing, under their hands, "That it was impracticable to maintain the fort any longer; and that such terms as could be procur'd from the Indians, consented with honour, should be immediately accepted of. and the Fort Abandoned." And in consequence whereof Capt. John Stuart was sent by Capt. Demere, to Choti, the Great Warrior's Town, accompanied by Lieut. James Adamson, and some Indians, to treat with the Warrior: and the following terms were obtained viz.

Articles of Capitulation agreed upon, and assented to by Captain Paul Demere, commanding his Majesty's forces at Fort Loudoun, and the Headmen and Warriors of the Over-Hills Cherokee towns, August 7th, 1760.

Art. I. That the garrison of Fort Loudoun march out with their arms and drums; each soldier having as much powder and ball as their officers shall think necessary for their march, and what baggage he may chuse to carry.

Art. II. That the garrison be permitted to march for Virginia, or Fort Prince George, as the commanding officer shall think proper, unmolested; and that a number of Indians be appointed to escort them, and to hunt for Provisions on the march.

Art. III. That such soldiers as are lame or by sickness disabled for marching, be received into the Indian towns, and kindly used, until they recover, then to be returned to Fort Prince George.

Art. IV. That the Indians do provide the garrison with as many horses as they can conveniently, for the march, agreeing with the officers and soldiers for payment.

Art. V. That the Fort, great guns, powder, ball and spare arms, be delivered to the Indians, without fraud, the day appointed for the march of the troops.

Before the above surrender was resolved on, the garrison found their provisions entirely exhausted. ——— They had subsisted on horse flesh, and such scant supplies of hogs and beans as the Indian women bro't in by stealth, without any bread kind, since the 7th of July, by which the men were excessively weakened, and must soon have become incapable of duty. The Indians blocked them night and day. Considerable parties of soldiers had deserted, and some had thrown themselves on the mercy of the Indians. The garrison in general had threatened to abandon their officers. ——— The Indians had told them, that the detachment of Col. Montgomery had been defeated and driven out of the Cherokee country, while they could know nothing to the contrary, having no intelligence from any British settlement since the 4th of June. They had not heard of any attempt for their relief on the side of Virginia. And they had given over every prospect or hope of seasonable deliverance from any quarter. Thus was the garrison of Fort Loudoun circumstanced, before they Capitulated.

After keeping this paper back till 5 o'clock, P. M. in expectation of hearing from the Cherokees, we have the mortification to learn, that the Negro Abraham arrived at Congaree on Thursday morning, with most disagreeable Accounts. viz. That the garrison of Fort Loudoun was not arrived at Fort Prince George the 31st ult. nor any tiding from them, but Mr. Mile had that morning received a letter (Found by the river side) from some white person in the middle settlements, a confederate of the Cherokees, advising him to desert that fort as speedily and secretly as possible, to march all night and next day, and he should not be hurt; for that, since the surrender of Fort Loudoun, the Indians had murdered Capt. Demere, and 23 more of his command; that Capt. Stuart and the rest were employed to bring down and and manage the cannon taken at Fort-Loudoun, to reduce Fort Price George, which the Cherokees were determined to make themselves masters of; that for this purpose the whole Charokee nation, "All Over Hills, Valley, Middle settlements and Lower Towns people," joined by 100 French Indians (whom they call Nottwegas) 200 Upper Creeks of the Oakeboys, and 200 more from Coosahs, were marching down in a body, and would be at Keowee in four nights; and that they were determined, after reducing Fort Prince George to proceed to Ninety-six, and from thence to Congaree.

BOSTON Aug. 25. Extract from a Letter from a Gentleman at West End of Oneida Lake, dated July 22, 1760.

"An Indian who was taken in Capt. Jacob's

adventure last year and has been ever since a prisoner about Oswacatche, found some means at Strength to escape, and arrived here last night; he bringing advice that the troops at Isle Gallop are struck with such panic, that they have their baggage and most valuable effects embarked on board Battoes, which they have for that purpose, in order to push off on the first appearance. The Troops at Montreal, he says, are thoroughly convinced of their inability to make a long stand, as Vaudreuil had determined to make the best terms in his power, on the first approach of our Army; he having heard that one of the chief pilots taken by Lord Colville, has actually engaged in our interest, having undertaken to conduct any vessel vessel of 36 guns up to the very walls of the town.

  I imagine you might have a curiosity to know The strength of the Armament with Gen. Amherst on the present expedition. I have therefore anexed an account thereof which I dare say, differs but little from the truth, as I have been more tham commonly curious to ascertain the strength of each corps, that have passed this Season, viz.

XLIId, Royal Highlanders Regiment	1300.
XLIVth, ---- ------------ --------	900.
XLVth, ---- ------------ --------	600.
LVth, ---- ------------ --------	600.
LXth, or 4th Batt. Royal Americans	500.
LXXVIIth, Montgomery's Highlanders	700.
LXXXth, ------------ -----------	1500.
New-Jersey Regt, with their Rangers	1000.
New-York; that has passed this station,	1000.
Connecticut Regiment ---- ---- --------	3000.
	11100.

  I have not included the Indians, as Sir Wm. Johnson told me himself that he was uncertain of their numbers but believed they would not be less than 1500 or 2000 warriors, which, in conjunction with our other troops, will make an army, who with the divine protection, will shortly have it in their power to prescribe such terms to our perfidious and barberious enemies, as to them shall seem most advantageous for our country, and have the greatest tedency our future peace and tranquility.

Camp at Lake Ontario, July 29, 1760.

"We embark'd on board our boats At Schenectody the 24th of June, and arrived here the 22d July, continuing our march all the time; the navigation was bad in the Mohawk river the water being swift and in many places so low that we were obliged to get our boats over by lifting by man strength; the Wood Creek was still worse, it was filled with logs, and the water so low, that we were obliged to lift over the logs. I was eight days going the length of the Creek, which is not 40 miles; that brings us to Oneida Lake, which is a most beautiful water, in length about 30 miles, from the Onondago river leads to this Lake, the distance about 60 miles. 'Tis a wide rapid river, full of riffs, and difficult of navigation, especially now, as the water is very low. The country is generally from Schenectody is very good, especially on the Mohawk River, The land hereabout is poor and broken, but the view of the Lake is very pleasant, the sight is bounded by the water, which is 15 miles broad, and 270 in length, and in time of a storm the water runs as in the main Ocean. —— We hear the French Army is entrench'd on an island near La Galette. —— Two French vessels appeared off the fort, about a fortnight ago, at which they fired several shots, which was returned by the fort, when they sheered off; about 4 days ago they again appear'd off the fort, but two of our vessels coming from Niagara they were pursued and came in sight of another near Frontenac, but it being calm our vessels could not come up with them, so they escaped and got into the river towards La Galette. —— We have here about 6 or 700 Indians; Gen. Johnson is going to the three Rivers, there to wait the arrival of the Seneca and Cayogas."

By the return of an Express from Albany, who came to town on Friday last, we have intelligence, that the troops under General Amherst had embarked from Oswego in three divisions; the first commanded by Col. William Amherst set off the 7th inst. the General with the second 10th, and Col. Gage with the third proceeded the next day; The number of troops the General has with him, we can't yet learn, some say 10,000, others not quiet so many ——— Also that Col. Haviland and Brigadier General Ruggles of the Provincials with 5,000 men proceeded from Crown-Point on the 11th ——— We have no account where the main body of the French are; nor can we tell the particular routs and stoppages either of our armies will make: There is no doubt considering the great abilities of our commanders with troops that have gone thro' many difficulties, and behaved with courage and conduct becoming British soldiers, but that the well laid plans will be executed in such a manner as that, by the blessing of Heaven, all Canada will soon be under the Dominion of the Britannic Majesty.

By Capt. Gardner who arrived at Casco Bay last week in 25 days from Quebec, and who came to town from thence on Saturday last, we have the following advices, viz. ——— That General Murray with above 2500 men, in a number of sloops, Schooners, &c. with the Diana, Penzance, Porcupine Frigates, left Quebec on the 14th of July, and on the 23d at night, an express came from them with the following Intelligence, viz. That on the 15th the whole anchored between Point Platon and De Chambeau: The 16th the Pocupine with the floating batteries, and the greatest part of the fleet went thro' the rapids Richlieu, without any damage, tho' a Snow and a Brig went ashore, but got off again; That Lieut. Campbell of the Highlanders (the only one hurt) was killed by a cannon shot as they pass'd De Chambeau: The 17th in the evening Major Carry with 200 men and 70 rangers, were ordered down the river, to land on the South shore, opposite Jaque Quartier, from whence he was to detach a Captain and 100 men with all the rangers, to surprize a guard at the Platon, about 5 miles above where they landed; Capt. Leslie was detached for this service, and landed the same night, and march'd them about day light; but Mons. Hartett, who commanded the French party had received the alarm, and gave a struggling fire to our people, and run off, but our men were so close upon them that the kill'd two upon the spot, and took Capt. Hartett and two other prisoners, the former was wounded in the belly and died the same night; the troops since that guard was removed, land daily, and the inhabitants of the parish of St. Croix and Larbinare have come in with their arms, and have taken the oath of fidelity, which is tho't will be the case with all the South Shore, as people advance: ——— They bring greens and refreshments of all kinds to our people, who were all in high spirits. ——— The arrival of the Louisbourg troops is impatiently look'd for, when they are immediately to proceed to join General Murray, and doubt not but they will then be able to do something.

Capt. Gardner also informs, that about a fortnight before the troops embarked, a large body of French horse appeared in sight of Quebec, who after riding about sometime went off: ——— That the troops from Louisbourg were arrived at Isle of Coudre, the 29th of July, and would proceed up the first favorable opportunity: ——— That Capt. Barbut of the 48th regiment, died there the beginning of last month, of the wounds he received in the action with the enemy near that place last spring: ——— That Capt. Inglish in a ship from this place, in whom went a number of officers joined their respective regiments: ——— That 'twas publicly reported at Quebec, that the French had strongly entrenched themselves at the Isle Way, a little below La Galette, where 'tis said they have 130 pieces of cannon, and where Gen. Amherst must pass in his way to Montreal.

Extract of a Letter from Louisbourg Aug. 4.

Mr. John Moss, returned here with 14 Indians, who came to pay their submission to his Excellency General Whitmore, and sign articles of peace: His Excellency received them with great marks of friendship, and ordered them all to be cloathed. There are one chief and 12 more indians expected in every day on the same account.

N. B. said Mr. Moss was the hostage left at Pictou last winter, and the person who bro't the first Indian into Fort Cumberland, and sent the first to his Excellency General Lawrence."

NEW-YORK Aug. 25. On Monday Afternoon arrived here, in 5 Weeks and 3 Days from Bristol, the Sampson, Capt. Greatrakers of 20 Guns and 67 Men. As she came up, his Majesty's Ship Winchester, Capt. Hale, lying in the Bay, gave Signal for her to bring to, and sent a Boat with an Officer and 13 Men to go on board her; but the Ship kept on her Way, without any regard to the Signal, when the Man of War fired at her, and continued to fire successively several shots, one of which struck her just below the fore Chains, and went thro' her; but, none of her People received any Hurt. Mean Time the Man of War's Boat being head of the Sampson, and at some distance to one Side, hail'd her; and advanced to board, but the Sampson's Men, being confused the Captain and Mate, fired a Volley of small Arms into the Boat when the Officer desired them to desists, and did his Men, but to no purpose, for they fired a second Time, killed three outright, and a fourth was wounded he died soon after: ———— The Magistrates of this City, having received Information of the Affair immediately issued Warrants to apprehend the People belonging to the Sampson, and when she was land'd in to the Dock, the Sheriffs and Constables, who was upon the Watch, in Order to execute the Warrant in the most effective and peaceable manner, staid still the Captain and Mate came on shore, and then took them into custody; but the rest of the Men on board armed with Cutlasses and fire Arms would not suffer themselves to be taken, nor any Person to come on board. Their Resistance being noticed to Capt. Hale, he weighed Anchor, and brought the Winchester into the Harbour along Side the Sampson, whose People, on this Appearance of the Man of War, got into such Boats as they could find, and dispersed, different Ways, some to Long Island and some up the River, leaving none on board but only one or two Men, and three Boys, who are supposed to have no concern in the tragical Affair. After Examination of Witnisses the Captain and Mate were admitted to Bail.

SEPTEMBER 1760

BOSTON Sept. 1. By the return of the Courier from Albany, who came in last Friday afternoon, we have the following important News, viz.

Extract of a Latter from the commanding Officer at Crown-Point, dated August 22, 1760.

"We have News from the Encampment by Express, with the following intelligence, viz. That they landed at the Isle ou Noix, the 16th inst. with the loss of Capt. Glegg of the Train, who was killed by a cannon shot, having both his Legs shot off; 5 others of the train had each of their legs shot off by the same ball, one of which has since died of his wounds; That our Army had erected 3 batteries with in 400 yards of the enemy's fortifications, and that they were well entrenched. —— And a deserter which came to our camp the 19th inst. informs that they were but 1500 strong, French and Indians, and but 12 pieces of cannon, and were short of ammunition. —— That Gen. Murray was very near Montreal and had cut to pieces a battalion of the enemy, and had taken one Captain and all his company prisoners. —— This deserter further says, that Gen. Amherst was within two days march of Montreal. We are all well, our army is in high spirits, and we are in hopes that within about 10 days to be able to give you an account of the surrender of all Canada. —— The Express left our army at Nut-Island the 20th instant.

While the Courier was at Albany he heard a letter read, wrote by Col. Haviland to Mr. Lake, paymaster to the forces at Albany, which agrees with the above letter from Crown-Point, excepting that he says, "Gen. Murray would have to cut to pieces a battalion of the enemy had not night prevented."

We hear one of the boats overset on the Lake soon after our army set out from Crown-Point by which accident 9 men were drowned.

In Capt. Gardner who arrived here last Saturday se'nnight from Quebec, came passenger Capt. John Malcom of this town, who with one of his hands was taken on the 6th day of November last by 9 Frenchmen, as they were endeavouring to get wood off the Island of St. Barnaby for the use of the vessel: After he was taken, he was immediately stripped of all his cloaths and barbarously used by the enemy for four days at that place; and then obtained liberty to go to Quebec, was taken twice in 28 days; and that before he got to Quebec, he was often threatened by the French to be given to the Indians to be massacred, they thinking him to be a spy. And that on the 14th of November his sloop, called the Sally (his mate being then on board endeavouring to ger to Boston) off Gaspee, was taken by the ship Two Brothers, Francis Boucher commander, mounting 20 carriage guns, by which accident the said Malcom not only lost his vessel, but likewise to the amount of near five hundred pounds sterling in cash, and other effects then on board.

BOSTON Sept. 1. Friday last at the Superior Court of Judicature, became on the Trial of Thomas Frast (a Matross in the Train of Artillery that winter'd here) for breaking upon the House of Mrs. Magarett Wright, and stealing from thence in Money and Plate to the Value of .250 Pounds L. M. when he was found guilty and sentenc'd to be whip'd 35 Stripes, and to pay treble Damages and Cost. ——— If unable to pay, he is to be sold for 14 Years ——— If anybody will buy him.

BOSTON Sept. 1. Monday the 18th ult. Captain Greatrakers arrived at New-York from Bristol, by whom we have the following, viz.

WHITEHALL June 27.

This Morning arrived Major Mantland and Captain Schomberg, with the following Letters from the Honourable James Murray Governor of Quebec, to the Right Honourable Mr. Secretary Pitt.

Sir,   Quebec May 9, 1760.

Having acquainted General Amherst 3 Weeks ago that Quebec was besieged by an Army of 15,000 Men, I think it necessary of doing myself the Honor of addressing directly to you, the most agreeable News of the Siege being raised, lest by your receiving the former Intelligence before the latter, some of the Inconvenience may arise to his Majesty's Service.

By the Journal of my proceedings since I have had the command here, which I have the Honor to transmit to you, you will perceive the superiority we have maintained over the Enemy during the Winter, and that all of lower Canada, from the Point au Tremble was reduced and had taken the Oath of Fidelity to the King. You will not doubt be pleased to observe, that the Enemy's Attempt upon our Posts, and ours upon theirs all ended to the Honor of his Majesty's Arms, as they were always baffled and we were constantly lucky.

I wish I could say as much within the Walls; the excessive Coldness of the Climate, and constant living upon Salt Provisions, without any Vegetables, introduced the Scurvey among the Troops, which getting the better of every Precaution of the Officers, and every Remedy of the Surgeons, because as universal as it was inveterate, in so much that before the end of April 1000 were Dead, and about 2000 of what remained totally unfit for Service.

In this Situation I received certain Itelligence that the Chevalier de Levi was assembling his Army, which had been cantoned in the Neighbourhood of Montreal; that he had compleated his 3 Battalions, and 40 Companies of the Troops de Colonie, from choice of the Montrealists: had formed these 40 Companies into 4 Battalions; and was determined to besiege us the moment the St. Lawrence was open, of which he was intirely Master, by Means of 4 King's Frigates, and other Crafts, proper for this extraordinary River.

As I had the Honor to acquaint you formerly, that Quebec could be looked upon in no other Light, than that of a strong Cantonment, and that any Works I should add to it, would be in that Stile; my plan of defence was, to take the earliest Opportunity of entrenching myself upon the Heights of Abraham, which interely command the Ramparts of the Place at the Distance of 800 Yards, and might have been defended by our Numbers against a large Army. But the Chevalier de Levi did not give me Time to take the Advantage of this Situation: The 23d, 24th, and 25th of April, I attempted to execute the projected Lines, for which a Provision of Fascines, and every necessary Material, had been made but found it impracticable, as the Earth was still covered with snow in many Places and every where Impregnably bound up by Frost.

The Night of the 20th I was informed the Enemy had landed at Point au Tremble 10,000 Men and 500 Barbarians. The Post we had taken at the Embouchure of the River Caprouge,(the most convenient Place for disembarking their artillery and guns, as for securing their Retreat) obliged them to land where they did, 20 Miles higher up.

The 27th, having broke down all the Bridges over the Caprouge and forced the Landing Places at Sillery and the Foulen. I marched with the Grenadiers, and Piquets, Amherst's Regiment and two Field Cannon, and took Post so advantageously. as to frustrate the Scheme they had laid of cutting off our Posts. They had begun to form the Defile they were obliged to pass, but tho't proper to retreat, and reconnoitring our Position; about four this Afternoon we marched back to Town, having withdrawn all our Posts, with the loss of two Men only, though they did every Thing in their Power to harrass the Rear.

The enemy was greatly superior in Number, it is true; but when I considered, that out little Army was in the Habit of beating the Enemy, and had a very fine Train of Field Artillery; that, shutting ourselves up at once within the Walls, we putting all upon the single Chance of holding our, for a considerable Time, a wretched Fortification; a Chance, which an Action in the Field could hardly alter, at the same time, that it gave an additional one, perhaps a better; I resolved to give them Battle; and if the Event was not prosperous, to hold out to the last Extremity: and then to retreat to the Isle of

Orleans, or Coudre, with what was left of the Garrison, and wait for Reinforcements.

This Night, the necessary orders were given, and Half an Hour after Six next Morning, we marched with all the Forces; could muster, viz. Three Thousand Men and formed the Army on the Heights, in the following Order; Amherst's Austruther's, 2d Battalion of Royal Americans, and Webb's composed the Right Brigade, commanded by Col. Burton; Kennedy's, Lascelles's, Highlanders, and Townshend's the Left Brigade, commanded by Col. Fraser. Otway's and the third Battalion of Royal Americans, were the Corps de Reserve. Major Dalling's Corps of light infantry covered the Right Flank, and Capt. Hazzen's Company of Rangers, with 100 Volunteers under the Command of Capt. Donald M'Donald a brave experienced Officer covered the Left. The Battalion had each two Field Pieces.

While the Line was forming, I reconnoitre the Enemy, and perceived their Van had taken Possession of the rising Grounds, three Quarters of a Mile in our Front, but that their Army was upon the March in one Column, as far as I could see. I thought this the lucky moment and moved with the utmost Order to attack them, before they had formed. We soon beat them all from the Heights they had possesed, though they were well disputed; and Major Dalling, who cannot be too much commended from his Behaviour this Day, and his Service during the whole, formed their corps of Grenadiers, from the House and Windmill they had taken hold of, to cover the Left Flank: here he and several of his Officers, were wounded; his Men however pursued the fugitives to the Corps which were now formed to sustain them; they halted and dispersed along the Front of the Right, which prevented that Wing from taking Advantage of the first impression they had made on the Enemy's Left. The had immediately Orders given them to regain the Flank, but, in attempting this, they were charged, thrown into Disorder retired to the Rear, and from the Numbers of Officers killed and wounded, could again be brought up, during the Action. Otway's was instantly ordered to advance, and sustain the

Right Wing, which the Enemy in vain made two attempts to penetrate. On these Occasions, Capt. Ince, with the Grenadiers of Otway's were distinguished. While this passed there, the Left was not idle: They had dispossessed the Enemy of two Redoubts, and sustained with unparalleled Firmness the bold united effect of the Enemy's Regulars, Indians and Canadians, till last, fairly fought down and reduced to a handful, though sustained by the 3d Battalion of Royal Americans from the Reserved, and Kennedy's from the Centre, where we had nothing to fear they were obliged to yield to superior Numbers, and a fresh Column of Roussillon, which penetrated.

The Disorder of the Left was soon communicated to the Right; but the whole retired in such a way, that the Enemy did not venture trying a brisk Pursuit. We left most of our Cannon, as the Roughness of the Ground, and the Wreaths of Snow, made it impossible to bring them off; what could not be brought off, we nailed up.

Our Killed and wounded amounted to one Third of those in the Field; that of the Enemy by their own Confession, exceeds, 2500 Men, which be readily Conceited as the Action lasted an Hour and 3 Quarters.

Here I think it my Duty to express my Gratitude to the Officers in general, and the satisfaction I had in the Bravery of all the Troops.

On the Night of the 28th, the Enemy opened Trenches against the Town and at the same Time, we set to work within, to fortify it, which we never had in our Power to attempt sooner, from the severity of this Climate during the Winter, and the absolute Necessity of executing Works of more immediate Importance, last Autumn, before the Frost set in. I wanted the assistance of Major Mackellar the chief Engineer, dangerously wounded in the action, his Zeal for, and knowledge in, the Service is well known; but the alacrity of the Garrison made up for every defect.

My Journal of the siege, which accompanies this, set forth in full, what was done; and I flatter myself, extraordinary Performances of the Handful of brave Men I had left, will please his Majesty, as much as they surprized us, who were Eye-Witnesses to them.

Great Praise is due to Commodore Swanton, and the Captains Schomberg and Dean: I have not words to express the Readiness, Vivacity and Valour, they showed in attacking, and destroying the Enemy's Squadron. Capt. Dean has lost his Ship, but it was in a good Cause, and he has done Honour to his Company.

The Morning of the 17th of May, I had intended a strong Sortie, to have penetrated into the Enemy's Camp, which from the Information of the Prisoners, I had taken, and the concurrent Accounts of the Deserters, I conceived to be very practicable.

For this Purpose I had ordered the Regiment of Amherst, Townshend, Lascelle, Anstruthers, and Highlanders, with the Grenadiers, and the light Infantry, under Arms; but then informed by Lieut. M'alpin, of my Battalion, (who I sent out to amuse the Enemy with small Sallies) that their Trenches were abandoned.

I instantly pushed out at the Head of these Corps, not doubting but we must have overtaken and forced their Rear, and had ample Revenge for the 28th of April; but I was disappointed, for they had crossed the River Caprouge, before we could come up with them. However, we took several Prisoners, and much Baggage, which would otherwise have escaped. They left their Camp standing, all the Baggage, Stores, Magazines of Provisions and Ammunition; 34 Pieces of Battering Cannon, four of which are Brass 12 Pounders, ten Field Pieces, six Mortars, four Patards, a large Quantity of scaling Ladders, and entrenching Tools beyond Number and had retired to their former Assylum, Jacques Cartier. From the information of Prisoners, Deserters, and Spies, Provisions are very scarce, Ammunition does not abound, and the greatest Part of the Canadians, have deserted them, at present they do not exceed five Thousand men. The minute I am joined with that Part of the Garrison which was sent from hence last Autumn, I shall endeavour to co-operate with Mr. Amherst, Towards compleating the reduction of this Country; though, if rightly informed, he can hardly act by the Lakes before the Month of July, at which I am more convinced, because of the Intelligence forwarded to him last February, of the Enemy's Designs, by Lieut. Montresor, he would certainly have been upon them before now, had it been at all practicable.

Major Maitland the Bearer of these Dispatches, who had acted as Adjutant General this last Winter, is well acquainted with all our Transactions here; he has a thorough Knowledge of the Country and can give you the best Lights with regard to the measures further to be taken relative to his Majesty's Views in Canada.

I cannot finish this long Letter, without asserting how much I think myself obliged to the Lieutenant-Governor, Col. Burton, his activity and Zeal were conspicuous during the whole severe Winter's Campaign; and I flatter myself you will be pleased to lay this Service before his Majesty.

P. S. Since I have wrote the above a Nation of Indians has surrendered, and entered into alliance with us.

I have the Honour to be with great Regard Sir Your's &c.   Ja. Murray.

BOSTON Sept. 1. Extract of a Letter.

"The reduction of the French colony is generally presumed to be an inevitable event. ——— Some people are not so confident, as to proceed to Lake Erie, to join General Monckton at Presque-Isle, and advance to Detroit. ——— [by this we shall have a free communication from Pittsburgh to Niagara, and 'tis said we are to have a chain of forts between these two last mentioned places] ——— An allowance for this and the General's cautious disposition, and the precarious co-operations of the other troops in Lake Champlain and the River, with the difficulty of keeping up a quick intelligence between the several bodies designed for the attack, seems to render it very probable that the progress of this Arm will be slow. ——— However, it is certain that we are arrived at the most promising juncture that ever offered for the conquest of Canada: It has been often said that the enemy were Straitoned for the necessaries of life; but it is now really the case with them; their Magazines of military stores are very low; our Indians exceed a thousand in number; and tho' Mons. Levy threatens a vigourous and difficult defence, it is highly probable that the people of property may force a surrender upon terms, rather than risque a battle which must expose all to unbridled repine and Slaughter."

BOSTON Sept. 1. Deserted from Col. Whetecomb's Regiment of Provincials, the following inlisted Soldiers, viz. John Williams, of Portsmouth, in Capt. Tafts Company: Edward Sourie and John Biglow of Boston, in Capt. Gray's; Eli Nelson, of Boston, and Solomon Pein of Freetown, in Capt. Crowdin's —— Deserted also from Col. Roggle's Regiment, Robert Trutt of Dorchester, Barabas Evans of Woodstock in Capt. MacFarland's Company: Jonathan Pegan, and Indian of Dudley, in Capt. Small's; Peter Deforge, alias Allen and John Gordon, of Old-York. —— Whoever shall apprehend the said Deserters, or any of them, and convey them to Timothy Paine, Esq; at Worcester, shall have forty Shillings lawful Money Reward for each and all necessary Charges paid, by Thomas Crowdin. Boston Aug. 27, 1760.

One Phineus Goodwin who has practiced enlisting into many different Companies and receiving the Bounty Money at each Time, was taken up by the above Officer, and sent in Irons to the General Officers, where no doubt he will be made an example of. —— He inlisted six different Times receiving the Bounty, and deserted, this Campaign.

Deserted his Majesty's Service from on board the Ship King George, the following Seamen, Viz. Robert Hooper, John Leiverex, James Taylor, Simon Murphy, George Norton, and Mathew Balton, (The four first have robbed the Ship.) —— Whoever takes up aforesaid Deserters and secures them in any of His Majesty's Goal within this Province until the said Ship returns to this Port, which will be very soon, shall have Ten Dollars Reward for each of them and necessary Charges paid by me the Subscriber.

The above People have been seen frequently at

and near the Salutation Tavern, at the North End.   Benj. Hallowell, Jun.

NEW-YORK Sept. 1. Yesterday arrived here the detachment of the Royal, and Col. Montgomery's regiment of Highlanders, from So. Carolina, after a passage of 12 Days, excepting the four Battalion company of the Royal, that were left to cover the frontiers of Carolina, till the Province should have an opportunity of raising their intended compliment of troops. But as no Indians have been seen or heard of near the settlements since the action of the 27th of June last, and that the Cherokees of the lower and middle settlements had sent a message desiring peace, before the embarkation of the troops at Charlestown, its believed the stay of those companies in that province cannot be long. ———
The prisoners taken in the Cherokee country, were left to the care of the lieutenant governor of South Carolina. The Creek Indians are very quiet, and by the latest account, had put some of the murderers to death, as was proof of their desire for peace.

PHILADELPHIA Sept. 4. Our last advices from Pittsburgh are of the 18th ult. when the treaty held with the Indians there was finished, to the entire satisfaction of all concerned. There were present between 6 and 700 Indians, besides women and children. The Delawares delivered up 8 prisoners.

PHILADELPHIA Sept. 4. Our advice from Pittsburgh of the 14 inst. are, that the night before an express came in there from Niagara, via Presque-Isle; that all was presently well at both those posts when the express left them: That the troops under the Majors Walter and Gladwin, arrived at Niagara the 25th ult. the day following the light infantry and the 44th regiment embarked for Oswego, And that Major Stewart and his party got to Venango the 9th inst.

There were at Pittsburgh, at the date of these advices, 600 Indians with the chiefs of almost all the nations, from the upper lake to the lower Shavana town; and no people could seem better disposed than the whole of these Indians were. The General had conferred with the chiefs of all the different tribes, who declared themselves well pleased with all he had said to them. —— The names of the principal nations then there were, Delawares, Shawanese, Twightwees, Wyondotts, Otawas, Pettawatimes, Mingoes, and Chippowees, who were to meet the 15th to answer the General's speech.

CHARLESTOWN S. Carolina Sept. 6. Wednesday morning about 70 Chickesaws came to town from Augusta on a visit to his honor the lieutenant governor, with whom the had some conferances, in the usual friendly strain. They were handsomely rewarded, and are gone home perfectly well satisfied.

About three weeks ago, two persons were killed and scalped, and one wounded, by a party of Indians, about 12 miles above the Catawba town; on the first notice whereof, the neighbourhood of the murdered assembled and went in pursuit, but could not overtake the murderers. We hear that two scalping gangs of Cherokees are gone out against our back settlements.

A report has prevailed for some days, and is not yet contradicted, that a great number of horses were killed last week, supposed by the Cherokees, not far from the camp at Congarees.

We have not a single letter from Augusta or the Creek nation whereby it is so much hinted, that the Creeks have been in the least frightened at any thing that has yet happened to the Cherokees, besides the loss of their trade.

On Wednesday morning his Honor gave his assent to "An act granting to his Majesty an aid of One hundred and twenty five thousand pounds, current money, & applying other money therein, mentioned, to defray the expence of raising, paying and cloating, for six months, a regiment of soldiers, to consist of ten companies, each to be composed of 100 men, besides officers; to be employed in the service of the government, in prosecuting the war againsr the Cherokee Indians and their abettors."

BOSTON Sept. 8. The following Letter, as it contains some particulars worthy of notice, altho' the Substance has already been published, we shall give a Place in this Paper —— It is an Officer who was in Action, and dated at Crown Point, June 26, 1760.

Doubtless the account of our last scout will be common enough in Boston before this comes to your hand; but all reports of such occasions are so various that I dare say you will be glad to hear the truth which are as follows.

The 1st of June Major Rogers went down the lake with 270 rangers and light infantry: On the 3d landed Lieut. Holmes, Lieut. Starks, and Ensign Phillips, with 48 rangers in the Bay of Misco, with orders to proceed to Wigwam-Martincco, where are about 200 houses, inhabited by Canadians and Indians, which they were to destroy if possible: He proceeded himself to the West-side of the lake with the rest of his party, and on the 4th in the Evening landed below Isle au Mote, immediately on landing, he perceived some of the enemies boats of the Isle au Noix, by which he knew he was discovered: He stopped there all night to observe their motions; next day (5th) it rained so hard that the enemy did not think proper to land; but in the morning of the 6th his scouts that he kept out to observe them, sent in word that they were landed 5 miles above him, on their march towards him, the Major immediately put his party in a posture to receive them, when the other party was out to observe their motion, came in, and told him that they was within half a mile of him, marching in very good order, and chiefly Indians, and about 300 in number. They began to attack on the left wing, with usual intrepidity and yelling; which was returned as brisk by our men; the enemy came so nigh to us on the left where our boats lay, that we exchanged shots across the boats, and when the Indians found that they could not load fast enough for our men who had cartridges to load with, that they took up stones and threw stones at us, on which our men haloo'd to them that they would likewise fight with stones, and give them an equal chance, routed them from behind the boats: The enemy then began to retreat from the right to left with the same veracity they attacked us, we pursued them about 3 quaters of a mile, and in spite of the care they always take to carry off their wounded and dead, we got 3 Indian scalpes and some Indians they scalped themselves, because we should not have the benefit of em, as is suppos'd; we got 34 fine Indian guns, and by the blood and other marks we killed about 60: but they say since that we killed no more than 32, and wounded 19, among the last was Monsieur Longville, a famous Partisan: The fight began at 11 o'clock and ended at half after two: our ammunition being almost exhausted the Major ordered that the dead and wounded should be put in the boats, the number of dead was 17, including officers, and 8 wounded of which number was Capt. Johnson: Ensign Wood of the light infantry was killed the first firing: ———— We then proceeded up the lake to join our vessels that lay at Isle ou Mote, where we landed, buried our dead and sent the wounded to Crown-Point. On the 9th Lieut. M'Cormick joined with us with Stockbridge Indians, which made our party as strong as at first: The Major not satisfied at his success, ordered the men to furnish themselves with ammunition and provisions for ten days on board the brig. ———— and on the 11th at night landed again on the west side, and proceeded by land to St. John's and reconnoitered the fort, which was too strong for us to attempt: Notwithstanding, the Major was in hopes of surprizing it by a stratagem, which was this. To send Lieut. M'Cormick, who speaks the French well, with the light infantry under his command, with their coats turned being lined with white: His orders were to tell them he came from Montreal, with an express to the commanding officer; as soon as he got admitted to attack the guard, and secure the gate until the rest as they could be discovered should rush in. Those measures being proposed we marched up to the fort about two o'clock in the morning, in full hopes of succeeding; but when we came within 200 rods of the fort we found there was a camp on the grasses, and by the number of their centries, judged it impracticable to put the scheme in execution, we being too weak, and in the heart of the enemy country; we suppos'd by the regular troops being at the fort the French army had returned from before Quebec: The Major consulted that our tracks would be seen in the morning, and that the best way would be to go to St. Therese, 9 miles below on the river, where we knew was a large village, and a strong stockade fort, and that they used to keep boats there to transport provisions to St. John's and the Isle ou Noix: ——— We marched directly thither, and arrived at ten o'clock undiscovered, we saw the French driving waggons with hay and provisions into the fort; the Major ordered Lieut. M'Cormick with the light infantry to rush down on one side, and Capt. Brewer with some of the rangers on the other side, who met at the gate which fac'd to the river, and made all prisoners without firing a shot: The rest of the party being divided, at the same time attacked the village; which was so well managed that we took all the inhabitants there prisoners also, without the loss of a man: We found to our great satisfaction 14 boats and 5 canoes under the fort, we secured them. then burnt the fort and village, and passed the river with 27 men prisoners, the major having sent off 52 old men, women and children taken in the village. ——— No sooner were we landed the other side, but the French and Indians to the number of 600, came down to the river side, where they had the mortification to see us opposite to them staving their boats, and marched off, without having it in their power to pursue us for want of boats.

——— We arrived at our vessels the 22d, very much fatigued and hungry, but all well.

BOSTON Sept. 8. Tuesday last arrived here Capt. Noble in a Sloop in about 3 Weeks from Quebec, and one week from Louisbourgh. Our Advice from that Quarter, which may be depended on, are as follows. viz.

From Quebec of the 13th of August. That General Murray with his Army had passed Trois Revieres without Opposition, and got two or 3 miles above, while he waited the arrival of the Louisbourgh Troops: In the mean while Parties daily went out on shore the South side of the River

St. Lawrence when Numbers of the Canadians, even whole villages, came in to them with Greens, and laying down their Arms, who were promised Protection, and sent to their Fields to provide for Winter: The parties return'd on board their respective Transports: ——— That they attempted to land on the North Side of the River, but not having sufficient Force, was prevented by the Enemy's appearing as if the chief Body of French Troops were collected there to prevent the Army from proceeding up the River. ———
That the Louisbourgh Troops got to Quebec by the 1st of August, and having only landed the Sick there, sail'd immediately to join General Murray. ——— There is no Account of their junction when Capt. Noble came away tho' it was doubted but they got up in 5 or 6 Days after they passed the City.

We further learn, That Mons. Levi has a drove of Horses out of which he subsists his Troops that 16 Bushels of Wheat has been given for one Bushel of Salt, and that the Enemy are under the greatest Strain for almost every Thing.

BOSTON Sept. 11. The following Advices from His Brittanic Majesty's Armies on this Continent, with an account of their late successes, are here published in order, we received them, viz.

From General Murray's Army.

By a Vessel from Quebec last Monday we have a more particular Accounts of the Proceedings of the Forces that we had before received, viz.

That General Murray has passed the Rapids of Richlieu, without any other Loss than of the Officer killed by a Cannon-Shot from a Battery on the North Shore. ——— That some Days after the Fleet passed Trois Riveres without any Loss. ——— The Enemy had erected Batteries on the North Shore, within a Musket-Shot of which the common Channel lies; but by sounding with Boats a very good Channel was discovered in the Middle of the River, by which the Ship passed. ——— Lord Rollo with the 22d and 4th Regiment from Louisbourgh sailed from Quebec the 4th, to join Gen. Murray.

The above Vessel in her passage put into the

Louisbourgh, from whence we have the following further Intelligence.

"Louisbourgh, Aug. 27. A Vessel is arrived here in 5 Days from Quebec, by which we learn, That the whole Force of Canada, consisting of near 14,000 Men, are assembled at Montreal, in order to make the last general Stand: It is tho't that upon the appearance of Gen. Amherst, Mons. Levy will make an honourable Capitulation for the whole Country." —— Gen. Murray with the Army from Quebec and the Forces from Louisbourgh, [5,000 brave Troops] were within five Leagues of Montreal, convoyed by the Sotherland, Diana, Pentance and Porcupine."

From Colonel Haviland's Army.

Tuesday last several Letters were brought to Town by the Way of No. IV. from Crown-Point. dated the 30th of August and the 1st of this instant September, which contain the following Accounts from the Forces that went from thence viz. That three Boats had arrived at Crown-Point from Colonel Haviland's Camp the first on the 25th of August, and the other two on the 29th, with 18 French Prisoners, who were taken on board a Schooner of the Enemy's: Her Cable was cut by one of our Shot; and the Wind blowing hard, she was drove on Shore very near the camp: A Sloop of theirs was soon deserted, which fell into the Hands of our Troops; and their Rideau, named the Grand Diable, was afterwards taken by the Schooner and Boats: So that we have now all their Navigation upon Lake Champlain. —— The Captain of the Schooner says, that Gen. Murray had passed Trois Revieres; which agrees with the advices from Quebec; and that Gen. Amherst was at the Rapids about 30 miles above Montreal.

—— On the 1st of Sept, about noon, a Whaleboat arrived at Crown-Point from Isle au Noix, with the following Intelligence, viz. That the Island was deserted by the French the 27th of August: That Col. Haviland took possession of it on the 28th, and found 50 pieces of Cannon, one Mortar, plenty of ammunition and provisions particularly a number of Cattle. Bougainville, who had the command there, went off in the night with 1500 men, it is supposed to Montreal; but

but left 50 men to take care of the baggage, and a letter to Col. Haviland. —— It is said that Montreal was besieged by General Murray. The had no advice of General Amherst having got so far down. —— That Col. Haviland was gone to St. John's, except 400 men left under Col. Thomas at Isle au Noix, —— And that about 50 provincials were killed or wounded. ——

A Letter from Crown-Point Sept. 1.

"I have the pleasure to inform you of the Reduction of the Isle de Noix, by a Letter this Moment receiced from thence: They took Possession the 28th ult in the Morning of a very strong Fortress: M. Bougainville, with 1500 Men left it in the Night, they left 50 Men all their Baggage and their wounded, with a Letter desiring Col. Haviland to take good care of them, and their Effects: We found in the Garrison 50 Pieces of Cannon, 6 of them Brass, 6 Royals, and one large Mortar, 200 Barrels Flour, 100 Pork, 50 Head of Cattle, and considerable Ammunition. —— During the Siege we had 50 Men killed and wounded, all Provincials except 6. —— The Army (except about 400 Men) embarked for St. John's the 30th ult. —— I hope in my next to give a good Account of Montreal."

Another Letter from the same Date, says, ——

"On August 28th in the Morning the strong; Fortress at Isle de Noix was quitted: Bougainville, the French Commander there, desired the Commander of the English Army to take very good Care of the Gentlemen and Things left there —— it is said, that he was sent for to Montreal, and that he went off with 1500 Men to assist against General Murray; when our People say had heard firing upon the Enemy those 5 Days. —— There was taken on Nut-Island 50 well People, and all their Sick and Wounded, 50 Head of Cattle, and a considerable Quanty of Salt Provisions. On the 30th of August our People set off for St. John's in high Spirits; and they don't expect to meet with much Difficulty there.

From General Amherst, Army.

Tuesday Morning last a Gentleman, arrived in Town from Albany who informs, that he left that Place on Thursday last, and that Major Prescot came in there the Sunday before, on his Way to New-York, dispatched on an Express for his Excellency General Amherst, in order to embark immediately on board the Packet there bound to Great Britain: —— Major Prescot brought the most agreeable Intelligence viz. That the General with his Army arrived before the Fortress at La Gallette on the 18th of August; and having besieged in 6 Days, he on the 25th sent a perremptory Summons, demanding an immediate Surrender of the Garrison to His Brittanic Majesty's Forces, to prevent Sword in Hand: —— Which Demand was in a few Minutes complied with, and possession taken of that important Post, with all the Artillery, Stores, and Ammunition, with between 4 and 500 Prisoners of War, who were on the Road to Albany: We lost but 9 or 10 Men in the whole Attempt. —— That the General having taking proper Measures for the Security of the Place proceeded with his main Army the next Day for Montreal; before which Place it was thought he would arrive in 3 or 4 Days. —— We also hear that the Snow Ontario commanded by Commodore Loring, before La Gallette surrendered had the Misfortune to run ashore within Cannon Shot of the Fort, and was much battered by the Fire of the Enemy, but it was hoped she would be got off: The Commander was slightly wounded in the Thigh.

    BOSTON Sept. 15. The Courier from Albany last Friday, bro't an authentic Account of General Amherst's Proceedings to the 26th of August, and are as follow, viz.

    That on the 10th the Army embarked, and having crossed the Lake Ontario arrived at Oswegatchie on the 16th: At Day Break of the 17th, our Row Gallies engaged one of the Enemy's Vessels, which struck to them by 7 in the Morning: She was called the Ottawawa, mounted 10 twelve pounders, and carried 100 Men, Officers included, and commanded by Mons. de la Broquery: in the Engagement we had only one Man killed, and one wounded, the Enemy had thirteen of both.

    Oswegatchie which is a very good Indian Settlement with a Block house Fort, was abandoned, the Enemy being posted on an Island between 4 and 5 Miles further down the River, where they were reported to be strongly fortified. The General ordered both Shores to be reconnoitred; and the 18th a Part of the Army passed doen on each Coast, and after some opposition by a smart Cannonading, the Fort was compleatly Invested; so that none of the Garrison could Escape. The four following Days were employed in raising Batteries, which being finished, on the Morning of the 23d, the Army began in concert with the Shipping, to fire on the Fort; this lasted till the 25th in the Afternoon when the French beat a Parley, desiring to know what Terms the General would grant them? whose answer was, That the Garrison should be Prisoners of War. ⸺ That every Thing in, and depending on the Fort should be delivered in it's present State, and that He should give them but 10 Minutes to accept of, or dissent from those Proposals. The accordingly yielded to these Conditions, and His Majesty's Troops are now on Possession of Fort Levis.

Our loss on this Occasion has been very inconsiderable, that of the Enemy (whose Garrison consisted of about 300 Men) about 12 killed, and 40 Wounded. Mons. Pouchot the fame Gentleman that was last year taken at Niagara, had the Command of them.

The Courier informs, That an account was received at Albany before he came away, that the Army under Col. Haviland had taken posession of St. John's and Chamblee, the enemy having abandoned those posts, on the approach of the army, and in their flight had destroyed every Settlement between St. John's and Montreal, as Mons. Bougainville had received positive orders to abandon every post, and immediately join the French army at Montreal; at which place their whole force is now collected. ⸺ That a communication has been opened between General Murray and Col. Haviland, and that the former had sent express orders to the latter to join him with all possible dispatches, and not even to wait for ammunition or provisions, as he had enough to supply an army of 30,000 men.

An Officer that was sent out with a party to harrass the rear guard of the enemy when they abandoned Chablee, was wounded, but got back to Crown-Point, says, that he heard the report of upwards of 70 cannon, which he supposed were discharged by Gen. Murray's army against Momtreal.

Our Troops were well and in high spirit and doubts not in a short time to make an entire conquest of the whole country of Canada.

The Courier left Albany last Monday noon, at which time the troops from South-Carolina, under Col. Montgomery, were marching into that place.

NEW-YORK Sept. 15. By Capt. Holmes from Georgia we have advice that the garrison of Fort Loudoun capitulated with the Indians, and were conducted to Fort Prince George.

We hear that Col. Haviland's army has joined General Murray's on the Island of Montreal.

By letters from Pittsburgh, on the 28th ult. we learn that all was well there: That Presque Isle and Venango were well secured, and well supplied; that the Indians were very sincere and hearty in their friendship, going constantly with our convoys, and daily delivering up prisoners and bringing in deserters.

CANADA SURRENDERS.

By an Express that came to Town last Wednesday afternoon, with dispatches to his Excellency from Isle au Noix and Crown-Point, by the was of No. Four, we have the joyful news of the surrender of the City of Montreal to the British arms, on the 8th of September last, in the evening, and therewith the surrender of Canada. ——— The garrison and troops prisoners of war, to be sent to France, and not serve against the English during the war: The peasants to remain in their lands, and not to trade with the Indians on pain of death. ——— This account being sent to in haste by the commanding officer at Isle au Noix, the next day after Montreal surrendered, is all we can as yet learn. ——— It was wrote to a Gentleman at Crown-Point, who received it on the 12th, and immediately sent it hither by express. ——— A more particular account of the glorious conquest is every moment expected.

The above account is confirmed by a Gentleman who came to town last Saturday morning from Albany, but bro't no further particulars.

To allude to the beginning of the celebrated Mr. Allison's Cato, "The great, the important day is now come:" —— A day big, not indeed with the fate of Rome, or British America, but made forever illustrious by the British arms, and signal by the fall of the American Cartage. The reduction of Canada is no longer problematical; but a certain fact! And our enemies, who a few years since, threatened to "drive us all into the Sea," are now many of them to be transported beyond it themselves, in the land of slavery; their mother country: while the rest are to become subjects of Great Britain. —— So graciously and with such an outstretched arm, Heaven appeared for: —— Hail the happy day! and thank to Him, who has thus subdued our cruel, proud and insulting enemies under us! On receiving the above agreeable intelligence, on Wednesday last, the guns of the batteries in town were discharged, at night were bonfires, &c. —— And cheerfulness appeared in the countenance of every one.

We hear from Albany, that upon surrender of the city of Montreal, upward of 300 French ladies of distinction, came and implor'd the protection of General Amherst, who was pleas'd to order proper care to be taken of them, and all their jewels, rings, &c. to be returned.

We learn from New-York, that the articles of the capitulation of Fort Loudoun was that the garrison should be safely conducted to Fort Prince George, which was truly observed; and that there was a likelihood of peace with the Indians.

When the enemy abandoned the Isle of Noix, they left on the Island 50 pieces of cannon, and several mortars all mounted, 1000 rounds shot, 100 Barrels of powder, 50 ditto pork, 50 live cattle, and 60 men as guards to the sick and wounded, and a commissary to deliver us the ammunition, stores, and baggages. &c. the killed and wounded of the enemy were 150; the reason given by the prisoners for their going off, was, that the French were gathering all their troops together at Montreal, to make a Capitulation.

BOSTON Sept. 29. Proceeding of the Army under Gen. Amherst, from the Time they embarked at Oswego the 10th of August, to the happy Reduction of Montreal: viz.

That, arriving the first Night after they set off at the river Sable, they continued there till noon the next day, when, they then again pushed forward, and got to the river l'Assomption, thence they proceeded to bay Noire, from thence to Isle Couchon, Isle Cheverille, and on the 16th landed on Point Auberrie. ——— At 11 this night (the French brig laying about 15 miles off) Col. Williamson and the five row gallys, together with the grenadiers and light infantry, were dispatched to take her which they did at 8 in the morning of the 17th, after a smart fire: In the affair we lost a serjeant of artillery, and two private men; the French had 3 killed and 12 wounded, and we took 100 prisoners. The brig mounted twelve 14 pounders. ——— Embarking from this point, we arrived at Oswegatchie, and encamped on a hill to the eastward of the fort, where we remained till the 18th, when we rowed down towards Isle Royal. ——— here our new acquired brig anchored within cannon shot of the enemy's battery, when a cannoning began: and while they were that employed, our light-infantry and grenadiers got below the fort. ——— On the 18th, at noon, a party was ordered to cut a road to the point on the Eastern shore, which is about 700 yards from the fort. At 5 o'clock this day, Com. Loring and our other vessels, went down to assist the brig, where they amused the enemy, while our works were going on, on the Western side. The 20th of August, at day break, a captain, 2 subalterns, from each regiments, and 160 men, went to make fascines. At noon, Col. Murray, 6 captains, 6 subalterns, and 300 privates, went to take post on the East side of the river, below the fort; and the fascine being ready, a battery was erected. The enemy continuing their cannoade, our ships hauled off from their battery, for it blowing hard, and very rainy.

At 12, Friday the 22d, we marched below the fort, and our rear joined us in their boats, between twelve and one in the morning on Saturday.

The 23d, and at day break our batteries began to fire. At 10 our vessels were ordered down, Capt. Phips in the Mohawk, led, and ran close along side the fort, when he bro't to, with a spring in his cable, and kept up an incessant fire of great guns and small arms, which silenced the enemy much; but their shot at length cut the cable of the Mohawk, who drove down with the stream, and being much damaged, and in want of her anchor, was forced to run aground. Our men in this affair behaved extreamly well. Com. Loring, in the Onondago, and Capt. Sinclair, in the Williamson [the French brig that was] bore down betwixt ten and eleven, but too late to assist the Mohawk: ——— However, they ran close to the fort, poured in their broadsides, and small arms from the tops; our batteries going at the same time, and the enemy not idle with their artillery and musquetry, made very pretty musick. ——— At 3 o'clock, Capt. Sinclair's brig being disabled, was obliged to fall below the fort, and the Commodore getting aground close to it, was sunk by the enemy, whose fire raked him, and dismounted his guns. ——— In this condition, he was obliged to surrender, being wounded withal, and the French attempted several times to go on board to hoist a white flag, and carry our people on shore; but they were as often disappointed, for our battery guns drove their boats into the air, while their crews went to the bottom. ——— At 6 o'clock, Lieut. Penning with a party of grenadiers, in two whale-boats set off coming from the Grand batteries and proceeding through a number of grape shot and small arms as thich as hail getting on board the Onondago, and hoisted the English Colours, but to his misfortune found her full of water. In this exploit he lost 6 grenadiers, and had several wounded. This day being expended, and our ships entirely disabled, our mortars and Hawbitzers played all the night following, every shell falling within the island, which tho' small, was extremely well fortified all round to the water's edge, and commanded by Mons. Pouchot. We have had abundance of rain lately.

Sunday the 24th of August, all our mortars continued playing very smart: —— No likelihood of recovering the Commodore's ship. —— The Mohawk was most horribly torn.

August 25th. All night our mortars played. another new battery which was begun yesterday, will be ready to open to night: And our two vessels are getting ready with all expectation to go up and cover the boats intended for a general storm tomorrow. The enemy kept a brisk fire yesterday and this morning. —— About 4 p. m. the French beat a parlay, and about 7 our grenadiers took possession of the fort. —— The enemy had killed and wounded about 80: We had near 50 who were killed and wounded.

26th and 27th employ'd in destroying our batteries, and repairing the damages of the fort.

28th, Still employ'd in repairing the fort, and endeavouring to weigh the Onondago and to move our camp to Abbey Picquet's island.

30th This day arrived a party of French Indians, who report General Murray's being near Montreal. —— The stream this day was very strong —— We landed at eve, and waited 'Till Sept. 1st. When we put off again, and passed the Rapids, or Long Falls, and encamped three leagues from Lake St. Francis.

Tuesday 2d Sept. Received orders, in case of an attack, to land, and charge any enemy that presents themselves to us, and the party so landing to make an obstinate resistance, as they might depend on being supported. Sept. 3, being bad weather, lay by.

Sept. 4th, Set off, and crossed Lake St. Francis, and about 11 o'clock arrived at the town of Gaspey. Here we again passed large falls, and lost an officer and about 85 men, at Bloody Point, and a great number of boats. About 2 o'clock, we passed the Cedar Town, and 11 at night landed on Le Isle Perrot, close to Montreal Island. —— The country very thickly settled. This island has five hundred families on it.

Sept. 5. Lay by all day to repair our damages. ——— Great number of inhabitants took the oath of allegiance, and are put in the peaceable possession of their farms. ——— No soldier to plunder under pain of death. ——— The Indians yesterday took near 400 prisoners off the island of Montreal; and the Indian Sachem who commanded the party, told them, that they were in there power, they had orders from the English General not to kill any of them, but carry them to their farms, adding, that the French always told them to kill the English when they took them. On this occasion the Indians killed but one man who attempted to runaway.

About 5 o'clock this day, Lieutenant Elliott arrived from Col. Haviland, with an account of l'Isle de Soriel being taken; and about 7 o'clock Lieut. Craston arrived from General Murray, when orders were given out to embark at day break.

6th of Sept. The generall beat at day, and the General himself embarked half an hour after, the army rowing by the right four columns. At eleven o'clock we landed on the Isle of Montreal (nine miles from town) fixed our bayonets, and formed: We marched directly for the town, along a most delightful road, very thick inhabited. About 4 o'clock we arrived before the wall of the town, where we formed in battle array, expecting General Levy, with his army, to come out. Some skirmishes happened between the enemy's troops of horse, and our light-infantry. We lay upon our arms all night, getting our cannon up, which on,

Sept. 7. Were posted in proper columns. This day we learned, that Mons. Levy's regulars were on an island the other side of the town to prevent Mr. Murray's landing. ——— At 8 o'clock, a flag of truce came from the city, demanding a suspension of arms till they heard from France: ——— but all the answer they got was, They should have till 12 o'clock to consider; ——— and accordingly they began to capitulate which lasted, Till Sept. 8th, 1760. [We lay upon our arms all night] when Gen. Murray's army landed, and the General came to our camp, together with several of his officers. About the same time arrived at our camp, Major Christie, from Col. Haviland's army ——— The capitulation being finished, the grenadiers and light infantry marched into the town, commanded by Colonel Haldeman, in the following order of prosession, viz.

1. A twelve pounder with a flag; and a detachment of royal artillery.

2. grenadiers of the line, commanded by Col. Massey.

3. The light infantry of the line, commanded by Col. Amherst. Each with a band of musick before them. ——— And the eldest ensign in Generals Amherst's army, to take possession of the colours of the eight French regiments.

Sept. 9th 1760, Camp before Montreal. The colours of Shirley's and Pepperrell's regiments lost at Oswego [1756] were marched out of Montreal by a detachment of grenadiers and a band of musick, and marched down the right of our line, to headquarters, where they were lodged.

General orders: ——— Camp before Montreal Sept. 9, 1760. Purole. ——— King George, ——— and Canada. ———

The General sees with infinite pleasure, the success that has crowned indefatigable efforts of his Majesty's troops, and faithful subjects in America. ——— The Marquis de Vaudreuille has capitulated; the troops of France in Canada have laid down their arms, and are not to serve during the war; the whole country submits to the dominion of Great Britain. The three armies are instituted to the General's thanks on this Occasion, and he assures them, that he will take the first opportunity of acquainting his Majesty with the zeal and bravery, which has always been exacted by the officers and soldiers of the regulars and Provincial troops, and also by his faithful Indian allies.

The General is confident, when the troops are informed that this country is the King's they will not disgrace themselves by the least appearance on inhumanity, or by unsoldierlike behaviour, in taking any plunder, more especially as the Canadians become now British subjects and will feel good effects of his Majesty's Protection.

Besides the contents of the above Journal, we can further informs the public, that as soon as the army commanded by General Amherst landed on the Island of Montreal, most of the Peasants laid down their arms, and left Mons. Vaudreuille and Levy to obtain the best terms they could for them. That out Indians under the command of Sir William Johnson, behaved so well, that they were looked upon to be under as much command as the regulars; that they advanced near the town, and dismounted some Gentlemen that came out with Levy and Vandreuille to reconnoitre our army, but killed none of them, that the Indians formerly in the French interest, and who no doubt, have butchered many innocent English subjects in this and neighbouring provinces, were vastly complaisant, and hoisted a union flag in sight of Montreal sometime before General Amherst arrived there; that Major Berry was immediately sent home in the Diana frigate from Montreal, via St. Lawrence river, with the important news: that the French regulars and others would not swear allegiance, were sent down the river to be transported to Old France; that the Canadians have the exercise of their religion under their own Priests, during good behaviour; that Governor Murray is to command at Quebec with 4000 soldiers; General Gage appointed Governor of Montreal, to be with 2500 men, at that place; That Pedro Vaudreuille, the Governor's brother with Mr. St. Piere, who escaped out of town, and were supposed to be gone by the way Outawaw river, thence go thro' Lake Huron, passing Detroit and crossing the west end of Lake Erie to proceed to the Missisippi, a circuit greatly west of Niagara, Fort du Quesne, &c. And that Col. Schuyler, with 4000 men were returning by the way of Oswego.

BOSTON Sept. 29. The following Authentic Account of the surrender of Canada is published by Authority.

On the 31st od August in the Morning, General

Amherst left Fort Levis, now Fort William Augustus, and proceeded from Station to Station until he arrived at Montreal on the 6thth of September, in the Evening. In this Passage the Army sustained a loss of 88 Men drowned, and 20 Battoes of the Regiments, 17 Artillery, with some artillery Stores, 17 Whale-boats and one Row-Galley, staved by the Violence of the Current and the broken Waves, in passing the Rapids.

The Inhabitants of the Settlements through which the Army passed, abandoned their Houses, and run into the Woods; the General sent after them; some were taken, and others came in their own accord. They were disarmed and had the Oath of Allegiance tendered to them, which they readily took; they were then put in quiet possession of their Habitation, with which treatment they were no less surprized than happy.

The Troops being formed, and the light Artillery brought up, the Army lay on their Arms the Night of the 6th. On the 7th in the Morning two Officers came to an advanced Post, with a letter from the Marquis de Vaudreuille, refering to what one of them, Col. Bougainville, had to say. The conversation ended with a Cession of Arms till 12 o'Clock, when the Proposals were brought in: Soon after the General returned them, with the Terms he was willing to grant; which both The Marquis de Vaudreuille and Mons. Levy, the French General, were very strenuous to have softened. This occasion'd sundry Letters to pass during the Day as well as Night (when the Army again lay on their Arms) but as the General would not on any Account deviate from his original Conditions, and instead on an immediate Answer, M. de Vaudreuille, soon after Day Break, notified the General that he had determined to accept them. Two Setts of Articles were accordingly signed by General Amherst and the Marquis de Vaudreuille, and exchanged on the 8th of September; when Col. Haldeman, with the Grenadiers and Light-Infantry of the Army, took Possession of one of the Gates of the Town.

By the Articles of Capitulation the French Troops are to lay down their Arms, and not serve during the Continuance of the present War, and are to be sent back to Old France; as are also the Governor and principal Officers of the Legislature of the whole Country, which is entirely yielded to the Dominion of His Majesty.

Governor Murray, with the Troops from Quebec, landed below the Town on the 7th, and Colonel Haviland, with his Corps, arrived on the 8th, at the South Shore, opposite General Amherst's Corps.

Last Friday being appointed to be observed as a Day of general rejoicing for the entire Reduction of Canada: At Noon his Excellency the Governor accompanied with the Lieutenant Governor the Gentlemen of the Council, and several other Gentlemen of the Town, preceded by the Troops of Horse Guards and guarded by the Company of Cadets, went from Province House to the Council Chamber, when his Excellency received the Compliments of the Gentlemen on this happy Occasion: After which, on a signal given, the Guns at Castle William were discharged to the number of 63, which were followed by the Guns of several Ships in the Harbour. The Troops of Horse Guards, the Regiment of Militia and the Company of Cadets being drawn up before the Council-Chamber performed their rejoicing fire.

———— From thence his Excellency with the Lieut. Governor, the Gentlemen of the Council, several Members of the House of Representatives, and many of the principal Gentlemen of the Town, guarded by the Company of Cadets, then went to Faneuil Hall, where a public Dinner for 150 Persons was provided. After Dinner his Excellency and the Company went to the Concert-Hall, on the Invitation of the Managers, and were entertained with a Concert of Musick. In the Evening his Excellency, &c. went to the Council Chamber, when, upon signal given, the Guns of the Batteries were fired to the Number of 30, and fine Fireworks were play'd off from a Scaffold erected in King Street before the Chamber; in the intervals of which his Majesty's Health and many other loyal Healths were drank: The Gallery of the Council Chamber was adorned with transparent Paintings: the whole Town was Illuminated; there were two large Bonfires erected with Scaffolding 5 Stories high on the two principal Hills of the Town, and another of the same Structure on a Hill in Charlestown; and there was a great Variety of Fireworks, (besides the public) play'd off in different Parts of Town. In short there were all possible Expressions of that universal Joy which this happy and glorious Event diffused through that loyal and grateful People.

OCTOBER 1760

BOSTON Oct. 6. By Capt. Duff who arrived here last Saturday from Halifax we learn, that on Sunday the 21st of Sept. 2 ships and 7 or 8 sloops, arrived there from Louisbourg, with cannon and warlike stores, taken from that garrison: They bro't advice that the demolishing of the fortification and works of that place goes on briskly, and were in hopes of compleating the whole very soon. ——— Capt. Byron, in the Fame, with the Archilles, Scarbourough, &c. were gone to the Bay of Gaspee, in quest of a number of French storeships that are there, or expected them from France about this time.

We learn from Montreal, that the Articles of capitulation were many, but we can't yet favour our readers with them; however, the most material were inserted in our last; ——— The right of nominating a Bishop to be in the King of England, though strongly insisted on to be the right of the French King: ——— The regular troops look on the severe articles which bind them not to serve against his Majesty or his Allies during the war, as a great indignity, which they strove hard toward off, but could not, and were obliged, to comply, though the officers say to their ruin; and were told by the General, that the barbarous and inhuman manner in which they had prosecuted the war, was the reason such terms (which military men call very hard) were imposed upon them: ——— The conduct and behaviour, of the General is admired by all, in so prudently conducting, and gloriously finishing this important campaign, without the effusion of blood: may such beneficence indelibly impress the noble principles of christian love and charity in the breast of our catholic enemies, who have died their garments in the blood of the innocent, and seem'd to have delighted in nothing more than in massacreing and scalping: —— The General forbid any depredations on the inhabitants, so that little or no harm has been done to them by the army, not even the Savages, not more than would be done by such an army in our country; such a regulation becomes the noble spirit of free born Englishmen! tho' it is much better Treatment than the enemy had deserved, indeed had reason to expect.

The prisoners taken at Fort Levy, on the Isle Royal, in the River St. Lawrence, are arrived at New-York.

NEW-YORK Oct. 6. Letter received at Williamsburg, from Col. Byed, who marched with the Virginia forces to the relief of Fort Loudoun, Informs for a certainty, that notwithstanding the capitulation, the garrison of the fortress had not marched 15 miles from the fort, when they were most treacherously surprized by a large party of Indians, and all officers (except Captain Stuart) killed, with about 25 of the privates, the rest were made prisoners, and were dispersed thro' the nation. The Little Carpenter gave ever thing he could command, to save Captain Stuart; and having left the Indians under pretence of hunting, he conducted him safe to Major Lewis, who was on Holston river, with an advanced party of Virginians.

General Monckton in his letter to Gov. Sharpe of Maryland, says. "That for the support of his Majesty's rights on Lake Erie and Ohio River it will be absolutely necessary, that the Province should furnish at least 200 men, with a proportionate number of commissioned and non commissioned officers, who, together with the provintial troops in the pay of the neighbouring Colonies, may be employed in garrisoning his Majesty' s forts in that department." "Such, Gentlemen," said the Governor to the Assembly, are the contents of Gen. Monckton's letter, which it is my duty to recommend to your immediate consideration and as the service that you are desired to provide for, is so essential, and the General's requisition may be so easily complied with, I flatter myself you will most chearfully embrace the opportunity that is now given you of contributing towards the preservation of his Majesty's rights in this part of America, and of removing, in some degree, the unfavourable opinion, which the measures that have for some time been unhappily pursued here, have inclined many, besides his Majesty's Generals on the continent, to entertain of the people of Maryland.

Since our last, great part of Col. Montgomery's Highlanders, who lately arrived here from South Carolina, and went up to Albany, returned hither from above, on their way to Halifax.

A few days since arrived here from Albany, the prisoners (amounting to 300) that were taken at Fort Levi, on the Isle Royale, with the commander Monsieur Pouchet. And Sunday last all the Canadians taken among those prisoners, embarked for Albany, thence to proceed to Montreal, intending to take oath of allegiance, and to resume their former possessions.

PHILADELPHIA Oct. 9. Extract of a letter from Fort-Bedford, September 26, 1760.

"I am sorry I have no better news to communicate, than the fresh instance of want of sincerity and humanity in the Cherokees, who, instead of fulfilling the Terms of the capitulation of Fort Loudoun, by conducting the garrison to Fort Prince George, as they had engaged to do, fell upon the unaware, butchered the commanding officer in the most cruel manner, killed all the officers except Capr. Stuart, put to death 25 soldiers on the spot, and dispersed the rest (above 200) among the towns, to be made slaves or sacrifices. They reserved Capt. Stuart, in order to make use of him towards the surrender of that Garrison, but the Little Carpenter purchased him of the Indians that had him, and has bro't him, with three other white men, to Col. Byrd. You may depend on this as fact. The Express that passed here yesterday in his way to Fort Pitt brought me a letter from Major Irwin dated the 15th instant, at Sayer's Mill, where Col. Byrd is encamped, waiting for orders from Williamsburg. It is thought they will kill all the prisoners they now have, if the garrison of Port Prince George does not surrender, and that if it does they will put the whole to death, when they have them in their power. God keep them out of their hands."

CHARLESTOWN S. Carolina Oct. 11. This morning the Cherokee prisoners taken at Little Keeohwee by the Hon. Col. Montgomery's detachment (being 11 women and 17 children, the idiot found at Sugar-Town and the fellow made prisoner a few hours before the action at Etchowih) set out hence, escorted by a party of our new regiment, to be exchanged at Ninety-Six if the Cherokees will bring their prisoners thither (as they have pretended) for this purpose.

According to our last advices from North-Carolina, they have raised 4 companies of provincials for the protection of the frontiers of that province, for which provisions is made to the first of December next: Two of them were at Fort Dobbs and the others on the way thither; but whether they are complete, we do not learn.

BOSTON Oct. 13. Extract of a letter from Paris July 21, 1760.

Letters from America mentions the gallant behaviour (in the late action near Quebec) of an Irish serjeant in Bragg's regiment. ———— The poor fellow, it appears, had received a shot in the breast which rendered him unable to retreat into the capital with the rest of the troops, he accordingly was left in the field of battle, and near him an English volunteer, lying on the ground, who had received a dangerous wound in his leg. Not long after the engagement the savage Indians, as is their custom began to scalp and strip the dead, and six of these wretches approaching the volunteer, with an intent to serve him in this inhuman manner, the serjeant collected what strength he could, and with his halbert levelled two of them with one blow, and weak as he was, killed another soon after, when the three remaining savage cowards took to flight. ———— The serjeant seeing the part of a French regiment near he called to then in English, and begged their assistance from the barbarous Indians; he was luckily understood by the commanding officer, who humanely ordered him and the volunteer to be taken care of, and the next day sent to Quebec to protect them from the resentment of the Canadians, who had vowed vengeance against the serjeant.

BOSTON Oct. 13. By a Gentleman who came to town last Wednesday in 17 days from Quebec, and 12 from Montreal, by way of Crown-Point, we learn that M. Vaudreuil and Levy, and all the French regulars with their officers, a number of merchants and other inhabitants at Montreal and parts adjacent, that had not complied with the articles of capitulation, were gone from thence with their moveable effects to Quebec, where a number of transports are provided, in order for a general embarkation from thence to France.

——— That Major Elliot was appointed to command at Bay of Chaleurs and Gaspee, and other places down the river, and was to proceed thither with a number of troops to take possession; the capitulation included in it, as we hear, not only all Canada, but likewise all the territories thereof depending. ——— And, that Major Rogers with a large body of Rangers were gone upon a distant expodition towards Lake Superior.

BOSTON Oct. 20. We learn from Quebec that a Chaplain in the garrison was highly serviceable in the late battle on the heights of Abraham, by riding into the ranks whom engaged, and bringing off several wounded officers, which otherwise might have been left to the barbarous sacrifice of a scalping party.

CHARLESTOWN S. Carolina Oct. 22. The following are the most authentic and material advices received from the Cherokee country, viz. That it was Round O's brother who seized and carried off Capt. Stewart from the field of blood, where so many of our countrymen and friends were so treacherously butchered by the perfidious savages, and who delivered him to the Little Carpenter then at Fort Loudoun. ——— Judd's Friend exerted himself much that day for our favour, and prevented the massacre from becoming almost general; He went around the field, ordering and calling the Indians to desists, and by the representation, he made to them, stopt the further progress and effects of their barbarous and brutal rage. He declares it as his opinion and resolution, that if they can now obtain a peace, there never shall be more war as long as he and the Old Warrior live ——— On the 26th of last month the British colours were displayed all day and night at Nookasee, where there was a meeting of war 2000 Cherokees, about 1400 who were men, and a talk was delivered by Ocunnahstatah and Judd's Friend for a peace with their brothers, the white men; which talk was reported by same head-men and agreed to by all present, the 9th inst. at Sugar-Town. Orders were given, that no white man [British] coming into the nation, should be interrupted, but allowed freely to pass and repass. This great alteration in the talk sent them by our Governor and Col. Byrd. ——— The whole crop this year in all the Cherokee towns, is not sufficient to supply them three months. Many of that nation, among whom are nearly all the people of the middle settlements and lower towns, who were the most severely chastised and scourged by his Majesty's troops commanded by Col. Montgomery, are now almost naked and in want of every necessary. There is therefore, on the whole, little reason to doubt of the sincerity of their request for peace.

We hear that upward of one half of the Royals encamped at Congarees are sick, and will be bro't to town, where preparations are made for their reception.

Extract of a Letter from Augusta Oct. 9, 1760.

A few days ago arrived ten Chactaws, with a scalp of one Chactaw, of the French party, as a satisfaction for a pack horseman lately killed by them. Duvall's Landlord, with 40 of his nation (Creeks) and one Chactaw, went very near the fort in Chactaw country, killed a fellow and a wench of the French party, and fired at the fort till the French obliged them to retire by their cannon. Duvall's Landlord declared, that while he came to get a man to follow him, he will continue a war against the Choctaws in the French interest; proposed being down before now if nothing more happened, and as he has not come, we conclude the Choctaws followed the party for satisfaction.

About 180 Royal Scots are come down sick from the camp at Congarees, and are lodged in the Barracks.

The distance from Virginia camp to the country of the Cherokees Indians is said to be only 5 days ride.

Fort Prince George, Oct. 10. The Indians seem very desirous of a peace, and are gone up to bring the prisoners down to Ninety-Six to exchange, agreeable to the Governor's answer to their talk by Macnamar. There are some white savages among them, greater Villains than the Indians themselves, who let no opportunity slip of informing them of every thing they see or hear, and how affairs go in the settlements.

BOSTON Oct. 27. Saturday last arrived Captain Bradford in 26 days from Quebec, and 15 from Isle of Coudre, by him we learn that they are between 4 and 5000 French to be sent to France, who would not take the oath of allegiance, and that five transports, with a number of them on board, had got down the river as far as the Isle of Coudre, in their way to France: That the Repulse and Racehorse frigates, and a large cat, had gone to the Bay of Chaleurs, to take off the inhabitants there, having carried with them a French officer, with orders from Gov. Vaudreuil to disband all the Regulars and make void all commissions; but that if they should not tamely submit, 2 or 3 schooners, with between 3 or 400 Regulars, which went under there convoy, would soon compel them to do it: —— That the garrison had more wood in the city that they could consume this season: —— That the articles of capitulation sent by Mons. Vaudreuil to General Amherst, while in Montreal, consisted of 62 numbers, 15 of which the General rejected; and that Capt. Deming, of this town, in going from Quebec to Montreal, had the misfortue to fall overboard and was drowned. —— And that a number of French deserters, with some English who had been in the enemy's service, having got a boat proceeded down the river a considerable way, where they met Capt. Jenkins in a schooner from this place bound up to Quebec, of whom they artfully begged a passage to Coudre, which being granted them they got on board, when after being some time, and finding themselves too strong for the crew they took possession of the vessel and stood away to Gaspee, but unluckily for them, off that place they met with an English frigate, who retook the vessel, and after taking out the deserters allowed her to proceed on her voyage to Quebec, where she is safe arrived: ———

We learn from Louisbourg, that the works in the front of that place were all blown up, and levelled to that nothing but a beach was to be seen; but that the whole was not yet demolished a fortnight ago.

BOSTON Oct. 27. Province of Massachusetts-Bay. Deserted from his Majesty's Storeship Crown, under the Command of Joseph Mead, Esq; now lying in Piscatagua River, to the following Mem, viz.

William Bachop, 21 Years of Age, 5 Feet 6 or 7 Inches high, of a brown Complexion, with a Scar on his left Cheek and wears a Wig or Cap. smooth faced.

John Tingay, 30 Years of Age, 5 Feet 7 Inches high, black Complexion, pitted with with the Small-Pox, wears a Wig or Cap, rather thin jaw'd and pale-faced.

William Gardner, 23 Years of Age 5 Feet 6 Inches high, of a fair Complexion, pitted with the Small-Pox, with a Cut from Brow to Chin on the Right Cheek, and wears his Hair, if not cut off since deserted.

Michael Cockran, 24 Years of Age, 5 Feet high, black Complexion.

Lawrence Hustmer, alias Hasilin, 23 Years of Age, 5 Feet 4 Inches high, dark Complexion, pitted with the Small-pox, thick made, wears a Wig, &c.

Richard Tirstman, 22 Years of Age, fair Complexion, and a little pitted with the Small-Pox, 5 Feet 7 Inches high, sharp faced, with an Aqualian Nose.

Charles Mc'Roy, 22 Years of Age, 5 Feet 4½ Inches high, fresh Complexion, thick made, wears his Hair, if not cut off since deserted.

George Harrison, 21, Years of Age, 5 Feet 4½ Inches high, a brown Complexion, stutters in his Speech, has light brown Hair, if not cut off since deserted.

John Paterson, 28 Years of Age, 5 Feet 8 Inches high, brown Complexion, well made, wears black Hair, pitted with the Small-Pox & fresh Complexion.

Charles Mathews, 30 Years of Age, 5 Feet 7 Inches high fair Complexion, red Hair, with Marks of two Cuts on the Right Arm, he wears a Cap or Hat.

John Wild aged 24 Years, 5 Feet 6½ Inches high, brown Complexion, thin made, with a scar on his Right Ancle, with flat Cheeks and smooth Face.

William Dodds, aged 23 Years, 5 Feet 6 Inches high, brown Complexion, thick made, pitted a little with the Small-Pox and wears his own Hair.

John Pettegrew, 23 Years of Age, 5 Feet 3 Inches high, dark brown Complexion, with a smooth Countenance, and wears a Hat or Wig.

George Oar, 27 Years of Age, 5 Feet 7½ Inches high, pale Complexion, pitted with the Small-Pox, with his own Hair, if not cut off since deserted, hollow thin jawed.

Thomas Lambert, 22 Years of Age, 5 Feet 8 Inches and a half high, dark Complexion, pitted with the Small-Pox, well made, and wears his own Hair.

Frederick Newman, 30 Years of Age 5 Feet 7 Inches and a half high brown Complexion much pitted with the Small-Pox, a rough Appearance, and marked under the Jaw as if he formerly had a scurfulous Disorders.

Daniel Ripper, 30 Years of Age, 5 Feet 4 Inches and a half, black and pale Complexion, with a Scar on his left Cheek, wears his own curly Hair.

Thomas Hall, Carpenter's Crew, 27 Years of Age, 5 Feet 7 Inches & half high, pale Complexion, with a Scar on his right Jaw, wear a Wig or Cap.

Captain Mead promises a Reward for each and every of the said Men that shall be brought him to said Ship, the Sum of Forty Shillings English Value, according yo current Exchange between that Place and England.

And as it is possible that some or all of said

Deserters may have come into this Province: All Masters of Vessels and others within the same, are therefore hereby cautioned against receiving, harbouring, or concealing any of them, as they would avoid the penalty of the Law. And all Magistrates and other Civil Officers within the Province, are required to be aiding and assisting in securing any of the said Men, that they may be returned to said Ship.

By his Excellency's Command,

A. Oliver Secr.

NEW-YORK Oct. 27. Brigadier General Monckton, has by a letter to the Governor of Virginia, desired to be assisted with 300 Men from that Dominion, to help to garrison and maintain the Posts which we have, in the Course of this successful War taken from the French on the Ohio.

NOVEMBER 1760

CHARLESTOWN S. Carolina Nov. 5, 1760. Extract of a Letter from Capt. Stuart, to his Honor the Governor dated at the Virginia Camp at Sayer's, 30 miles W. of the Great Kanawa.

"Agreeable to the terms stipulated, the garrison marched out of Fort Loudoun on Saturday the 19th of August, with their arms, drums, &c. about seven in the morning. As we passed through Tomawthly and Tequo, the Indians behaved with great civility. Our people being very weak and unused to exercise we encamped in a Savannah about two miles from Talico by Cane-Creek. Oucannostita, Judd's Friend, the Chote Prince, and other Indians, who had all day accompanied us, all left on one pretence or other at night, which gave me some uneasiness. At day break on the 10th we prepared to march; the advanced guard, a serjeant and 12 men marched off, with orders not to pass the verge of the Savannah till they should see the whole body in motion; the people were getting ready when a soldier came and told me he saw several Indians on the other side of the Creek. I ran that way to make what discovery I could, and saw several naked Indians running to surround us. I called to the people to stand their arms, but at that very instant two guns were fired from the enemy, and followed from all quarters, which with the war-whoop, they they threw the men into utmost confusion, and made it in vain to attempt giving directions. The Indians had crept within 200 yards of us, in a long grass, and met the men as they ran in disorder, at every quarter. One soldier, the interpreter, and my servant, were all that remained with me on the spot where we encamped; we snatch'd up soldier's muskets and discharged them; my servant put one of my pistols in his hand, when almost at the same instant, we were both seized, pinioned, and hurried out of the field; in the struggle my pistol went off. —— Capt. Demere, Lieut. Adamson, Ensign Bogges and Wintle, were kill'd at the first onset; besides them, 3 serjeants, 23 privates and 3 women were kill'd; 7 of the advanced guard crossed Talico river, and made off for the creek nation; they were pursued, but not overtaken; the rest of the garrison are prisoners dispersed in the Cherokee towns, trimmed and painted like Indians. The fellow who took me returned to the field and brought me my horse, and then carried me to the Little Carpenter, who received me with great joy, and gave me the fellow his rifle and all his clothes except what he had on, as a ransom for me. —— The night before the ammunition was to be delivered, it was agreed between Capt. Demere and me to bury a part of it, which was done about midnight and I Imagine nobody was privy there to but Capt. Demere, the gunner the person that dug the hole, and myself; but Mrs. Gloster, Capt. Demere's house-keeper, by some means became acquainted with it, which was like to prove fatal to me, for she was no sooner taken than she declared the secret, intending to recommend herself to the Indians; luckily she could not explain herself without an Interpreter, and the trader called for that purpose, had the presence of mind enough to tell the Indians, that it was done without any consent or knowledge, which saved my life. About 2 hours after I was at Carpenter's, who lived in Capt. Demere;s house; Oucannossota, 8 Indians, and Capt. Demere's servant came and dug up the powder, viz. 10 bags: the whole they got from us 23 bags, with ball an provisions.

 On the 27th of Aug. I was sent for to Chote, where Oucannossota and the Standing Turkey communicated to me their plan for taking Fort Prince George, and invited me to a general meeting of the warriors at Chote next day, I accordingly went, when it was agreed that all the people able to carry arms, should set out on the 6th Instant. (Sept) Messengers were the same day dispatched to the Valley and all the middle settlements, who were all to join their forces at Stickney Old-Town, and they were to carry 6 cannon and 2 cohorns that were in the fort, which the white people were to manage. I was put in mind of the obligation I owed in saving my life, and that I must go to Keowee with them, and write such letters to the officers as they should direct. I was much, troubled at my situation, and determined from that instant to make myself escape or perish in the attempt. I informed the Carpenter of all that had passed, who only answered "he was well apprized of all schemes," and added, "you have such good reason to confide in their promises that you will certainly comply with their request, and persuade the garrison to do as you did, and then may expect to be served as you were," I informed him my intention to escape, and asked if he would assist me, to which he said he would, and only waited for his Brother's return from Chote to concert the measure. The same evening he had intelligence that the Standing-Turkey's intentions were, in case they should get the garrison of Fort Prince George in their power, to make but one execution of them; "for" said he, 'we cannot maintain so many; and if the officers of the fort are obstanate, we will try if they can bear to see their countrymen burnt." —— There was no time to be lost, we fixed the 30th of August in the morning for setting off for Virginia; The Carpenter gave out he was going to hunt for 5 days, and that I was going with him to eat venison. On the 29th I went to Chote, and saw a boy who with one of Capt. Demere's company were bro't in to Settoguo. An hour after their arrival the poor wretched soldier was burnt, and the boy saved to give intelligence.

"I made it my business to find out some of our people, and told them, as I had reason, that they must never expect to return to their own country without being severely punished if they gave the least assistance to the Indians; I likewise found out a packhorseman, the only person in the nation that knew how to carry down the great guns, and whom the Indians depended for that purpose; I encouraged him to make his

escape, which he promised to do. This was all that was in my power to disconcert their measures. ——— August 30th in the morning, I set out with Attakullakulla his brother and wife, two young fellows that were not in the secret, and a wench, with my servant, one Johnston a soldier and Shoery the interpreter. The Carpenter communicated his design to Tistoey of Keowee; the Wolf and Willanawaw, who were not to declare the secret till the 6th, the day destined for setting off against Fort Prince George. The 8th inst. we met with Major Lewis, who had been detaches by Col. Byrd with 300 men to scout on Holsson's river, in hopes of meeting with and relieving any of our garrison who might be endeavoring to escape this way. Yesterday the 14th I got to this camp, and have met with the most hospitable treatment from Col. Byrd and his officers, who have supplied me and my people with every necessary, as we were destitute of every thing. I am not yet able to prosecute my journey; as soon as I am I will proceed to Williamsburg, at the Colonel's desire and thence take the speediest and shortest opportunity to get to Charlestown.   John Stuart."
    Camp at Sawyer's 15th Sept. 1760.
    The packhorseman mentioned in Capt. Stuart's letter, as the only man in the nation who knew how to carry down the great guns from Fort Loudoun, is one of the 13, who we are credibly informed, effected their escape from the Cherokees, and are got to Fort Prince George. That 7 of the advanced guard likewise mentioned in that letter, who ran off for the Creek nation, were taken prisoners, after being out 14 days, and reduced to the greatest straits for provisions.
    BOSTON Nov. 10. Extract of a letter from South Carolina, dated October 4, 1760.
    "Our Friends at Fort Prince George are in deplorable circumstances, the fort being blockaded night and day by the Cherokees, who declare they will have it at all event. 'Tis certain by the last accounts, they were within a few days march of it, with part of the artillery they found at Fort Loudoun. A regiment is immediately to be raised, as provisions were made for

that purpose some time since, and 7 companies of rangers are to be compleated forthwith to succour Fort Prince George, the garrison being greatly distressed for provisions." ―――

NEW-YORK Nov. 10. Last Wednesday night the Honourable General Monckton arrived at Philadelphia from the Ohio.

Wednesday last Capt. Baffet arrived here in 21 days from Quebec: He had a very agreeable weather down the river, and the whole passage throughout. Before he sailed Lord Colvin in a 74 gun ship with 10 transports having Frenchmen on board, sail'd for England, and M. Vaudreuil, Levy, and other Gentlemen were soon to set sail for France in an English ship they obtain'd permission to purchase at Quebec; many of the French Inhabitants who had left Quebec during the siege, were returned and got possession of their Houses; A large ship from England by some accident was lost within a few miles of Quebec, and many of the crew drowned; And as Capt. Baffet come down the river, he met a large sloop from Philadelphia going up that had been 57 days at sea.

PHILADELPHIA Nov. 13. Extract of a Letter from Charlestown S, Carolina, dated Oct. 24, 1760.

"This day an Express arrived here from Major Thompson of the Rangers, with Letters to the Governor dated the 8th Inst. at 96, where the Major was arrived, after delivering at Fort Prince George, near 6000 lbs. of jerked Beef, and about 3000 lbs. of Flour. He met with no disturbance from the Indians of whom he saw several Parties, who scamper'd off as soon as they observed the Number of the Detachment. The Letter from Mr. Miln, Commanding Officer at Fort Prince George, is dated the 15th and confirms the former accounts of the alterations in the behaviour of the Indians, and the distressed state they were in from so large a proportion of their Towns, Corn, and other Provisions, Clothing, &c. being destroyed by the Detachment of his Majesty's Troops last Summer. Fort Prince George has got a large supply of Firewood, while Major Thompson was there; and Mr. Miln says, he is resolved, on no Event to give up the Fort, but will rather perish in it, with those that will stick by him, than put any faith in the promises of the Savages; having the fate of the Promises of the unfortunate Garrison of Fort Loudoun so recent in Memory."

On the 16th ult. Major Rogers, and Captain Brehem, and Engineer, arrived at Pittsburgh, in 33 Days from Montreal with Dispatches from General Monckton; and on the 18th in the morning the Major and the Engineer returned from Presque Isle, with a Detachment of the Royal Americans Commanded by Capt. Donald Campbell, who are to join a Body of Rogers Rangers on Lake Erie, and to proceed to take possession of the French Forts at Detroit, and Michillimachinac; these, with all their Dependencies being particularly mention'd in the capitulation of Canada.

BOSTON Nov. 17. Yesterday Capt. Tozer, who sail'd from hence for Quebec about 3 months since put back here: He was obliged to put into Louisbourgh by stress of the weather, from which place he sailed for the river 38 days ago, but meeting with contrary winds and bad weather, in which he received considerable damage he was obliged to return hither.

NEW-YORK Nov. 17. Saturday last Col. Vaughan, arrived here from England with two Regiments: They sailed from thence in Company with Captain Lawrence, under convoy of the Sterling Castle, and Dover. Some of these Vessels are come into the Harbour.

    Province of Massachusetts-Bay
    By His Excellency the Governor,

Whereas it has been represented to me by the Commanding Officer at Fort Frederick in St. John's River, that sixteen Deserters from Fort Cumberland, having put into said River by stress of weather had surrendered themselves to said Officer, and agreed to do Duty there and assist in wooding the Garrison but that Nine of the said men viz. Abel Makcomber, George Makcomber, Thomas Sheppard. Josiah Barret, Nataniel Grey, Solomon Jones, James Baker, Robert Smith and William Merrian, had again deserted the service; carrying the Boat with them, that had been provided for wooding the Garrison; thereby greatly distressing them as they had no other were into transport for their wood.

I do therefore hereby require all Officers throughout the Province, to use their utmost endeavours that each and every of the Offenders aforesaid may be apprehended; and I desire all His Majesty's good Subjects to give information of any Persons suspected on good Grounds to be of the Number of said Offenders, that so they may be brought before lawful Authority, in order to their being examined and proceeded with according to Law.

Given under my Hand at Boston, the 22d Day of November, 1760, in the thirty fourth Year of his Majesty's Reign.   Fra. Bernard.

By his Excellency's Command, A. Oliver Secr.

BOSTON Nov. 24. By the Courier from Albany last week we learned, that his Excellency Gen. Amherst was still there, but 'twas tho't he would soon embark for New-York as most of his baggage was already shipped on board a vessel for this place: ——— That a number of the provincials have been discharged, and 'twas said the rest would also be dismissed in a few days.

NEW-YORK Nov. 24. The following Intelligence we have from the Virginia party on the waters of Kaoawa, dated Oct. 7. viz. That they have met with many difficulties since Col. Montgomery's Retreat, which rendered it impossible for them to oppose the whole Body of Cherokees, with so small force; but that Humanity obliges them to remain on their Hunting Ground, to endeavour to recover the Prisoners among them, amounting to upward of 300: That through Byrd's former Acquaintance with some Indians, our People had so far gained the Confidence of some of the Head Warriors, that they ventured to come to their Camp, to treat of a Peace, and had been dismissed with Presents: that they had agreed to deliver up, on the 21st ult. all our People, and chief Murderers, provided they withdrew their Army immediately after, returned the Cherokees taken by Colonel Montgomery, and procured then the King's Pardon for their Rebellion; And that they were likewise to deliver up Fort Loudoun in the same condition they got it. ———

Whether they intended to be sincere or not, Time only would discover; but it was thought they were certainly coming down.

NEW-YORK Nov. 24. We hear that 500 soldiers lately arrived under convoy of the Dover are to be quarter'd on Long Island, the rest in Jerseys, &c. and that some of the transports lately arrived, will carry the French prisoners to Old France, instead of the vessels intended for that purpose.

CHARLESTOWN S. Carolina Nov. 29. Extract of a Letter from Fort Prince George Nov. 5, 1760. Human affairs are always subject to Vicissitudes, but I believe they happen no where more frequent or strange than with us ——— one day we are firmly persuaded, that peace is at hand, and our troubles and apprehensions at an end ——— and so, visa versa. In this perplexed state, it is now clear to me, that the Cherokees are not in reality disposed to accommodate matters with us; that declaring they were, and promising to bring down their prisoners, was all pretence, to amuse and deceive us, as they did Col. Montgomery when he came up here, to gain time, and if possible to induce us to prevent Col. Byrd's proceeding towards their Country, or, at least, to delay his nearer approach, until they might accomplish their designs against the Fort, which at present is likely to be invested again, and nearly in the same disadvangeous Circumstances it has been in twice before.

The Cherokees are better politicians than we generally imagine; either they have amused us, in order to discover what was doing in Carolina and on the side of Virginia, and take their measures accordingly; and with a view to keep us inactive, 'till their messengers dispatched to different Indian nations and to the French, should return and inform them what dependance they might have on those allies, especially the latter, and agreeable thereto continue the war or conclude a peace: The talk from Col. Byrd, and the apprehension that his troops would soon be in Chotih after them, terrified and disposed them, even when they were meditating our destruction, to take the latter resolution, and avail themselves of the humane and merciful disposition of out Governor; but at that very time, the French arrived in the nation, and encouraged the party for war, and Col. Byrd remaining in the camp, whence they first heard from him, their fears of being chastised from that quarter were off, and every thing taken an unhappy turn, whether for them or us time must discover.

I shall now set down what intelligence I can give you. Nov. 18 we received advice by a faithful hand, from the middle Settlements, that with the ten Frenchmen (who arrived at Chotih you have been acquainted with) came Lewis Lentiniac the French officer, who in Governor Glen's Time, pretended to have had an affair with his commandant at the Albahama fort, which made it necessary for him to desert and seek protection in Charlestown, which he accordingly obtained: That as soon as he arrived at Chotih, an invitation was sent to Sorowith, and he went accordingly; that as soon as Sorowith arrived at Chotih, Lentiniac presented him with a box of paint and some other things, which he accepted; that he afterwards made great professions of friendship to him, and encouraged him to carry on the war against us, promised his assistance, &c. and presented him with a bloody hatchet, which he eagerly took up, struck it with all his might into a stump, declaring that thus deep would he strike it into every Englishman while he lived. that he danced the war-dance, and was joined by may other Indians, and again declar'd that while he lived he never would be at peace with the English; that Sorowith after this, marked out the form and size of this fort, describing its situation and strength, and gave an account of what goods, ammunition, &c. were in it, and proposed to come down immediately. with the great guns from Fort Loudoun, to take it; but that Lentiniac said, those guns would not do. I'll go and fetch more men and better guns that will soon reduce it; and when we have taken it, the fort, mem, guns, ammunitions and goods, shall be at your disposal; that this was readily agreed to; and that as a proof of his sincerity, he proposed to leave the ten men that he had brought with him, in Chotih; that he accordingly left them, and was gone to fetch the men and guns, and promised to return in a few weeks.

We are likewise informed, that the 6 fellows from Estahtowih, are actually gone out to war, that 30 Warriors are gone immediately from the middle Settlements on the same design: ——— Just after day light this morning, the wench that was sent to Estahtowih in the night of the 3d inst. for intelligence, returned, having been obliged to steal herself away last night: All she brings is that Serowih had issued orders that all woman coming into this fort shall be shot, so that from this day we may look upon our communication to be cut off; that to day he was to divide his ammunition and had sent runners to Chotih for more, that yesterday he took out and shook a string of black beads to her and bid her go and tell this; that some of the creek Indians were arrived at Toogalooh, 40 miles from hence, who had sent two runners to Estahtowih last night, but she could not learn this business, and that Serowih had delivered all the letters he had to Lentiniac, opened, read, and interpreted them so as would best suit his purpose, telling the Indians they were very bad.

About noon a fellow who was riding about the hills near Keeowee, observing some women sitting on their horses with some corn, came down, took a bag of it from one of them, and bro't it over to us, pretending friendship, and told us (which no doubt he would have us believe) that the Young Warrior hath bro't a good talk from the Over Hills: That the Great-Warrior and Judd's Friend are to come down with the prisoners when they are collected together (which I suppose will be when they have harnessed them to the great guns intended to take this fort; for, I do not believe they will gather them for any other purpose unless for a general massacre): ——— That Little Carpenter with 16 young fellows was returned to Col. Byrd's camp, and Willanahwa with 40 more; That Serowih had sent off three fellows to the Middle Settlements for more ammunition, and some guns, which he had left behind, probably the great guns from Fort Loudoun: That some Creek at Toogalooh had last night sent 4 messages to Estahtowih, with an invitation to the Cherokees to come out to hunt and talk with them; being asked what number of Creeks were there, he answered eight: And that the Old Warrior of Estahtowih, with other warriors, and some Creeks, would be here tomorrow to give a good talk.

CHARLESTOWN South-Carolina, November 29, 1760.
Fort Prince George Nov. 6, 1760.

On the 1st instant John Welsh came in here from the Middle Settlements, and informed me, that Louis Lautiniac, a Frenchman born, who was a cadet in Capt. Nelson's independent company, thereafter a trader from Carolina among the Cherokees, and now a French officer, arrived very lately at Chote with some presents from the French to these Indians. He immediately sent down for Sailowe or the Young warrior of Estatoe, who obey'd the Summons and delivered to him two letters which were in his hands, written by me to Judd's Friend and Oucannostata. Lautiniac being master both of the English and Cherokee tongues, interpreted these letters as best suited his own interest; and having and having presented Sailowe with a box of paints, which was accepted, he pull'd out a bloody hatches, drove it into a log, and cried out. Where is the man that will take that up for the French? Sailowe immediately seized the hatchet, saying, I am not tired of war yet, I will give them, the English, more of it, and danced the wardance, after which all the others took up the hatchet, and declared in favour of the French. Leautiniac enquired if they could give him a plan of this fort, or an account how it was situated; what force was had in their opinion, &c. To which they gave as true answers as they could, adding, that we had plenty of ammunition, if he could but take it. He answered then that they alone should have the fort, and all that should be taken in it, for neither he nor his people would touch any of the powder, adding, that he would go off, down the river Tenasse, to Fort L'Assomption, and bring cannon and more of his men to come against this fort; and as proof of his determination design to return, left the two Frenchmen which accompanied him, as a pledge thereof, which he assured them should be in 3 weeks from that time furthest. Welsh likewise informs me, that the French commander of Fort L'Assomption sent an invitation to the Standing Turkey, Judd's Friend, Oucannostata, Sailowe, &c. to come to his fort, but, if they accepted the invitation he knew not. He likewise informed me, that some Indians were gone to Col. Byrd with three white prisoners, and that after the Cherokees had declared in favour of the French, a runner was dispatched to bring them back; but whether he overtook them or not he was not certain."

According to our letters from Congarees, Ninety-six, and Fort Prince George, received this week, our affairs in the Cherokee nation have again a bad appearance, and all the pains taken by his honour our Lieut. Governor, in order to bring about a piece, or gain time effectually to chastise our savage enemy, are likely to be defeated, by the arrival of some Frenchmen in that Nation,&c. And we have cause to apprehend that Fort P. George will again be soon invested.

The accounts of the Shawanese joining the Cherokees are confirmed.

It is expected, on good grounds, that the southern parts of the North-American continent will be very speedily the theatre of some interesting and long wished for events.

Some letters from Philadelphia mentions a report, that the Famous Major Rogers will be appointed to succeed the late Paul Demere in the command of one of his Majesty's independent companies here.

DECEMBER 1760

NEW-YORK Dec. 1. Wednesday last his Excellency General Amherst, The Conqueror of Canada, came to town from Albany, attended by several Gentlemen: On his arrival the guns in Fort George were discharged; in the evening the city was handsomely illuminated. --- And on Thursday the Corporation waited on his Excellency with a cordial Address, and at the same time presented him with the freedom of the city in a gold box.

We hear that eight companies of the independents lately arrived from England, are ordered to South-Carolina, and, 'tis reported, three companies of O'Farrel's and two of Forbe's are also ordered thither; and that the transports from Europe are preparing to receive them.

By Capt. M'Alpine just arrived from Charlestown S. Carolina, we have the public prints of the place, till the 5th instant, tho' the accounts are very long, contain nothing remarkable, more than have been already published. The Indians professed great inclination for peace, but their real design were variously tho't of; no dependence being to be plac'd on a people who have given such flagrant & recent proof of their disregard to the most solemn engagements.

NEW-YORK Dec. 5. By His Excellency Jeffrey Amherst, Ecq; Major General and Commander in Chief of all his Majesty's Forces in North-America &c. &c. &c.

Whereas Peter Van Brugh Livingston, Lewis Morris, jun'r of the City of New-York, Esqs; have by the Memorial of the 15th of March 1760, represented to me, that by virtue of Orders and Instructions received from Major General Shirley (whilst he had the Command of His Majesty's Forces in America) to contract with and engage sundry Seamen, Carpenters, Smiths, and others for the services of the Campaign 1756, they had accordingly contracted with sundry Seamen, Carpenters and others, to serve His Majesty's, on, and near Lake Ontario; and that by these contracts their Wages were to run on, during their Captivity, and until their return Home.

That those Debts accrued among these Contracts, after the reduction of Oswego, on the 14th August 1756, the Memorialists had not yet framed any accompt, many of their Creditors being long after that Time, and some of them still Prisoners: nor for the same Reason, had any Application ever being made to the Crown for the Discharge of these Debts.

Wherefore in behalf of themselves and their Creditors, upon the aforementioned Contracts, the Memorialists most earnestly beseeched, That I would appoint some proper Person, to state, examine and discharge, the several demands depending upon those Contracts, or to detect such other Steps, as might give Face to the more anxious and needy sufferers.

The Transactions being so long prior to my being honoured with the Chief Command of His Majesty's Forces, I did not think myself sufficiently authorized to comply with the Memorialist's Request, and yet, being desirous of obtaining for them and their Creditors the relief which I thought them entitled to, I for that purpose transmitted their Memorial to His Majesty's principal Secretary of State, who has caused the same to be laid before the Right Honourable the Lord Commissioners of the Treasury, who have since signified to me their Pleasure, that I should appoint proper persons to liquidate and settle the aforesaid Demands, and that I would cause such of them to be discharged, as should appear to me to be well founded.

In Pursuance of these Commands, there are to Warn and give Notice to all Seamen, Carpenters, Smiths, &c. that have any claims on the afore mentioned Peter Van Brugh Livingston and Lewis Morris jun. Esqs; under the before mentioned Contracts, from the Reduction of Oswego, until their return to the Colonies, that they do, on, or before the 15th day of Janusry 1761, ensuing, either of themselves personally, their legal Representatives, or Attorneys, bring their claims to Lieut. Colonel Robertson the Deputy Quarter-Master General in the City of New-York, who is authorized to receive and examine the same, In order that such as shall appear to be properly supported and well founded, may be discharged agreeable to the Intention of His Majesty signed to me as aforesaid.

But whereas sundry of these Claimants, by being Seamen and perhaps absent, will not have it in their power to make their appearance, by the time above stated; I do therefore, in order to procure them the like Satisfaction, with the other Artificers, prolong the Appearance of those that may happen to be in that case for three Months; on every Wednesday in each Week, during the same, they may in like manner as the others, make Applications to the said Lieut. Col. Robertson, and deliver over to him, their Claims for Examination, in order to receive the Satisfaction that shall be found to be due thereupon.

Given under my Hand at Head Quarters, in New-York this third day of December, 1760.

By His Excellency's Command,   Jeff. Amherst.
    J. Appy.

Boston Dec. 8. Wednesday last arrived the Ship Alexander, Capt. Aiken, from London; and from the public Print of the 7th of October, we have the following advices.

London Gazette Extraordinary.
Whitehall, Oct. 6, 1760.

Early yesterday morning Major Barré and Capt. Dean arrived here from North America, with dispatches from Major General Amherst, Lord Colville, and Brigadier General Murray, to the right Honourable Mr. Secretary Pitt.

Copy of a Letter from Major General Amherst to the Right Hon. Mr. Secretary Pitt, dated Camp at Montreal, 8th of September 1760.

On the 26th of August, I did myself the honor of writing to you, by Capt. Prescott, to give you an account of the progress of his Majesty's arms to that time; from which I have proceeded to this place.

From the 26th to the 30th, I was employed in repairing some part of the fort, mending Battoes, and fitting out vessels, besides making such preparations, as I judged essentially necessary for the passage of the army down the river.

On the 31st I set out, rowed 24 miles, and encamped on the Isle of Chat; the rapids were more frightful than dangerous.

Sept. 1. I passed the Long Saut, marched covering parties on shore, the boats were obliged to row in single file, and keep at some distance, this took up great time, though the current of the river was violent. The rapids were full of broken waves, the battoes took in water, a corporal and three men of the Royal Highlanders were drowned: I encamped at Johnson's Point, 14 miles from the Isle of Chat. I sent parties forward on the Lake; Sir William Johnson soon went to an Indian village, Asquesashna, to assure them of protection on their good behaviour.

2d. I rowed 24 miles down Lake St. Francis and encamped at Point au Beau det. M. La Corne, with a party, had been here, and at the Indian village. Very violent wind and rain came on at night; luckily our boats were in sheltered coves.

3d. The bad weather continuing. the army halted, a scouting party brought in a prisoner from the Cedars.

4th. The army was in their boats soon after day-break; the weather was favorable for passing the worse part of the river, but I am sorry to acquaint you, the rapids were the occasion of 84 men being drowned. We lost likewise 29 battoes of regiments, 17 artillery, with some artillery and stores; 17 whale boats, and one row galley were saved; the guns, with some stores and provisions were saved; I encamped this night at the Isle Perrot, about two miles from the river, with the regulars. It was too late for the greater part of the artillery and provincials to proceed there, and they encamped on the river side.

5th. The inhabitants of the island had all run

into the woods, and abandoned their houses, some were taken and some came in: I had the oath of allegiance tendered to them, and I put them in quiet possession of their houses; and they seemed as much surprized with their treatment, as they were happy with it. The necessary repairs of the boats put it out of our power to proceed that day. The remains of the artillery and provincial regiments joined me.

6th. The army was in their boats soon after day-break; I rowed in four columns by the right as I intended to land on my left, at la Chine, on the island of Montreal, about three leagues from my last camp; the weather was favorable and I landed without opposition; some flying parties ran into Montreal, after a few shots: To make the most of the day I could, I marched on: The parties had broke up one bridge, which was soon repaired; and, after a march of two leagues, I formed the troops on a plain before Montreal, where we lay the night on our arms, and I got up two 12 pounders, five 3 pounders of light infantry, I left the New-York and two Connecticut regiment for the security of the boats at La Chine.

7th. In the morning, two officers came to an advanced post with a letter from the Marquis de Vaudreuil (A) referring me to what one of them, le Colonel Bougainville, had to say. The conversation ended with a cessation of arms till twelve o'clock, at which time the proposals came: I returned mine, and wrote the Marquis de Vaudreuille (B) this was followed by another letter from the Governor (C): I sent my answer (D) I then received a letter from M. de Levis (E), which I answered (F). The troops lay on their arms all night, and soon after day I had a letter from the Marquis de Vaudreuil (G) which I answered (H) and sent Major Abecrombie into the town, to bring me the articles of capitulation, signed by the Marquis de Vaudreuil, of which I had sent him a duplication signed by me (I); and Colonel Haldimand, with the grenadiers and light infantry of the army, has taken possession of a post, and will proceed tomorrow in fulfilling the articles of capitulation. I thought it better, from the number of battalions, to oblige them not to serve during the present war, than to incumber England with them as prisoners of war. I shall do myself the honour of sending the colours of the battalion to you by the next occasion.

General Murray, with the troops from Quebec, landed below the town yesterday, and Colonel Haviland with his corps (that took possession of the Isle au Noix, which the enemy abandoned on the 28th) is this day arrived at the South shore opposite my camp. I should not do justice to General Murray and Col. Haviland, if I did not assure you they have executed the orders I gave them to the utmost of my wishes, I must likewise beg leave to say, I am obliged to brigadier General Gage for his assistance he has given me; and I have taken the liberty to give in publick orders, my assurances to the three armies, that I would take the first opportunity of acquainting the King with the zeal and bravery which has always been exerted by the officers and soldiers of the English and Provincial troops, as also by his Majesty's faithful Indian allies.

Sir William Johnson has taken unwearing pains in keeping the indians in humane bounds; and I have the pleasure to assure you, that not a peasant, woman or child has been hurt by them, or a house burnt, since I entered what was the enemy's country.

A compleat list of artillery, arms, ammunition, stores, &c. in the several posts, as well as those of Montreal, shall be made out, which I shall transmit to you: Time does not permit this at present to be done.

I am now to acknowledge the honour of receiving, on the 30th of August, your duplicate of the 14th, which your letter of June 20th of June, inclosing of the Instructions to Lord Colvill of the 20th of June. The assurance you are pleased to give me of his Majesty's approbation, on the receipt of my several dispatches make me very happy.

I shall now use my utmost endeavours for settling every thing in this country to keep a sure possession of it; and I shall immediately dispose of the troops in such manner, that I may compleatly finish the forts that were begun last year: and as far as the season will permit me, I shall repair or erect such forts or posts, as may be necessary for the strengthening and insuring the future command of the lakes, with the possession of every part of the South side of the river St. Lawrence.

I inclose to you, Sir a copy of the articles of capitulation, with copies of all the letters that have passed, from your full information of the whole transaction.

I Imagine there may be many particulars you may like to know in what has passed since I dispatched Capt. Prescott; and I now sent Major Barré, with this, that you may receive all the intelligence I can give you of the apparent state of every thing in this country. I am, &c.
          Jeff. Amherst.

(A)

Montreal Sept. 7, 1760.

Sir,
I send your Excellency M. de Bouganville, Col. of foot, accompanied by M. de Lac, Captain in the regiment de la Reine; you may rely on all that Colonel shall say to your Excellency in my name. I have the honour, Vaudreuil.

(B)

Sir, Camp before Montreal Sept. 7, 1760.
I am to thank your Excellency for the letter you honoured me with this morning by Colonel Bouganville, since which the terms of capitulation which you demand have been delivered to me. I send them back to your Excellency with those I have resolved to grant you; and there only remains for me to desire that your Excellency will take a determination as soon as possible, and I shall make no alteration in them. If your Excellency accepts of these conditions you may be assured that I will take care that they shall be duly executed, and that I shall take a particular pleasure to alleviate your fate as much as possible, by procuring to you and your suite, all the conveniences that depend on me. I have the honor to be &c.

                              Jeff. Amherst.
                (C)
                    Montreal, Sept. 7, 1760.
   Sir,
   I have received the letter your Excellency has
honoured me with this day, as well as the answer to the articles which I had caused to be
proposed to you by M. de Bouganville.
   I send the said Colonel back to your excellency
and I persuade myself that you will allow him
to make by word of mouth, a representation to
your Excellency, which I cannot dispense with
myself from making.
               I have the honour to be, &c.
                              Vaudreuil.
                (D)
             Camp before Montreal Sept. 7, 1760.
   Sir,
Major Abacrombie has this moment delivered to me
the letter with which your Excellency has honoured me, in answer to that which I had address
to you, with the conditions on which I expect
that Canada shall surrender: I have already had
the honour to inform your Excellency, that I
should not make any alterations in them. I cannot deviate from the resolution: Your Excellency
will therefore be pleased to take a determination immediately and acquaint me of your answer,
whether you will accept them or not.
               I have the honor to be, &c.
                              Jeff. Amherst.
                (E)
                    Montreal, Sept. 7, 1760.
   Sir,
I sent to your Excellency M. de Lapase, assistant
quarter master to the army, on the subject; of
the too rigorous articles which you impose on
the troops by the capitulation, and to which it
would not be possible for us to subscribe; he
pleased to consider the severity of that article.
   I flatter myself, that you will be pleased to
give an ear to the representation that officers
will make to you on my part and to have regard
to them.   I have the honour to be &c.
     (Signed)   Le Chevalier de Levis.
                (F)

Camp before Montreal Sept. 7, 1760.
Sir,
The letter which you have sent me by M. de Lapase has this instant been delivered to me: all I have to say in answer to it, is, that I cannot alter in the least the conditions which I have offered to the Marquis de Vaudreuil; and I expect his definitive answer by the bearer on his return: on every other occasion, I shall be glad to convince you of the consideration with which I am, &c.   Jeff. Amherst.
(G)
Montreal, Sept. 8, 1760.
Sir,
I have determined to accept the conditions which your Excellency proposes, In consequence whereof, I desire you will come to a determination with regard to the measures to be taken relative to the signing of the said articles.
I have the honor to be &c.
(Sign)   Vaudreuil.
(H)
Camp before Montreal Sept. 8, 1760.
Sir,
In order to fulfil so much the sooner, I would propose that you should sign the article which I sent yesterday to your Excellency, and that you would send them back to me by Col. Abocrombie, that a duplicate may be made of them immediately, which I shall sign and sent to your Excellency.

I repeat here the assurance of the desire I have to procure to your Excellency, and to the officers and troops under your command, all possible conveniences and protection, for which I reckon that you will judge it proper, that I should cause possession to be taken of all the gates, and place guards immediately after, the reciprocal signature of the capitulation: However I leave this to your own convenience, since propose it only with a view of maintaining good order, and to prevent, with the greater certainty, any thing against the good faith, and the terms of capitulation; in order to which I shall give the command of these troops to Col. Haldimand, who I am persuaded will be agreeable by you.

>I have the honor to be, &c.
>Jeff. Amherst.

(I)

Camp before Montreal Sept. 8, 1760.

Sir,
I have just sent to your Excellency, by Major Abecrombie a duplicate of the capitulation, which you have signed this morning; and in conformity thereto, and to the letters which have passed between us, I likewise send Col. Haldimand to take possession of one of the Gates of the town; in order to enforce the observation of good order, and prevent difference on both sides.

I flatter myself that you will have room to be fully satisfied with my choice of the said Colonel on this occasion,

>I have the honor to be, &c.
>Jeff. Amherst.

Articles of Capitulation between His Excellency General Amherst, Commander and Chief of his Britannic Majesty's Troops and Forces in North-America and his Excellency the Marquis de Vaudreuill, Grand Croix of the Royal and Military order of St. Louis, Governor and Lieutenant General for the King in Canada.

Art. I. Twenty-four hours after the signing of the present capitulation, the English General shall cause the troops of his Britannic Majesty to take possession of the gate, of the town of Montreal, and the English garrison shall not come into the place, till after the French troops shall have evacuated it.

The whole Garrison of Montreal must lay down their arms and shall not serve during the present war. Immediately after signing the present capitulation, the King's troops shall take possession necessary to preserve good order in the town.

Art. II. The troops, and militia, who are in garrison in the town of Montreal, shall go out by the gate of   with all honours of war, six pieces of cannon, and one mortar, which shall be put on board the vessel where the Marquis de Vaudreuil shall embark, with ten rounds for each piece. The same shall be granted to the garrison at Trois Rivieres, as to the honours of war.

Art. III. The troops and militia who are in garrison in the fort of Jaques Cartier, and the island of St. Helen, and the other forts shall be treated in the same manner, and shall have the same honours; and these troops shall go to Montreal or Trois Rivieres, or Quebec, to be there embarked for the first seaport in France by the shortest way. The troops who are in our posts, situated on our frontiers, on the side of Acadia, at Detroit, Michillimakinac, and other posts, shall enjoy the same honours, and be treated in the same manner.

All these troops are not to serve during the present war, and shall likewisr lay down their arms. The rest is granted.

Art. IV. The militia, after being out of the above towns, forts, and posts, shall return to their homes, without being molested, on any pretence whatever on account of their having carried arms. Granted.

Art. V The troops who keep the field shall raise their camp, and march, drums beating, with their arms, baggage and artillery, to join the garrison of Montreal, and shall be treated in every respect the same. Those troops as well as others must lay down their arms.

Art. VI. The subjects of his Britannick Majesty, and his most Christian Majesty, soldiers, militia, or seamen, who shall have deserted, or left the service of their Sovereign, and carried arms in North-America, shall be, on both sides, pardoned for their crime; they shall be be respectively, returned to their country; if not, each shall remain where he is, without being sought after, or molested.   Refused.

Art. VII. The magazines, the artillery, firelocks, sabres, ammunition of war, and in general every thing that belongs to his Most Christian Majesty, as well in the town of Montreal, and Trois Riviere, as in forts, and posts mentioned in the third article, shall be delivered up according to exact inventories, to the commissaries, who shall be appointed to receive the same in the name of his Britannick Majesty. ——

Duplicates of the said inventories shall be given to the Marquis de Vaudreuil.

This is every thing that can be asked in this article.

Art. VIII. The officers, soldiers, Militia, seamen, and even the Indians, detained on account of their wounds or sickness as well in the hospital as in private houses, shall enjoy the privileges of the cartel, and be treated accordingly.

The sick and wounded shall be treated the same as our people.

Art. IX. The English General shall engage to send back to their own homes the Indians and Moraigans, who make part of his armies immediately after signing of the present capitulation. And in the mean time, in order to prevent all disorders on the part of those who may not be gone away, the said General shall give safe guards to such persons as shall desire them, in the town as in country.

The first is refused. There never had been any cruelty committed by the Indians in our army; and good order shall be preserved.

Art. X. His Britannick Majesty's General shall be answerable for all the disorders on the part of his troops, and shall oblige them to pay the damages they may do, as well in towns as in country.

Answered by the preceeding Article.

Art. XI. The English General shall not oblige the Marquis de Vaudreuil, to leave the town of Montreal before the   and no person shall be lodged in his house till he is gone. The Chavalier Levis, commander of the land forces; the principal officers and major of the land forces, and the artillery, and commissaries of war, shall also remain in Montreal to the said day, and shall keep their lodgings there. The same shall be observed with regard to M. Bigot, Intendant, and commissaries of Marines, and writers whom the said Bigot shall have occasion for; and no person shall be lodged at the Intendants house before he shall be gone.

The Marquis de Vaudreuil, and all those gentlemen, shall be masters of their houses and shall embark when the King's ships shall be ready to sail for Europe, and all possible conveniencies granted them.

Art. XII. The most convenient vessel that can be found shall be appointed to carry the Marquis de Vaudreuil, by the straitest passage to the first seaport in France. The necessary accommodations shall be made for him. The Marquis de Vaudreuil, M. de Rigaud governor of Montreal and suit of this General. ―――― This vessel shall be properly victualled at the expence of his Britannick Majesty; and the Marquis de Vaudreuil shall take with him his papers, without there being examined; and his equipages, plate, baggage, and also those of his suite.

Granted, except the archives, which shall be necessary for the Government of the country.

Art. XIII. If before, or after, the Embarkation of the Marquis de Vaudreuil, news of peace should arrive, and that, by the treaty, Canada should remain to his most Christian Majesty, the Marquis de Vaudreuil shall return to Quebec or Montreal, every thing shall return to its former state under the domination of his most Christian Majesty, and the present capitulation shall become null and of no effect.

Whatever the King may have done on this subject, shall be obeyed.

Art. XIV. Two ships may be appointed to carry to France le Chevalier de Levis, the principal officers and the staff of the land forces, the engineers, officers of the Artillery, and their suite. Those vessels shall likewise be well victualled, and necessary accommodations provided in them. The said officers shall take with them their papers, without being examined, and also their equipages and baggage. Such of said officers as shall be married, shall have liberty to take with them their wives and children, who shall also be victualled.

Granted except that the Marquis de Vaudreuil, and all officers of whatever rank they may be shall faithfully deliver up to us all charts and plans of the country.

Art. XV. A vessel also shall be appointed for the passage of M. Bigot the intendant with his suite: in which vessel the proper accommodations shall be made for him, and the persons he shall take with him: he shall likewise embark with his papers, which shall not be examined, his equipages, plate and baggage, and those of his suite. This vessel shall also be victualled as before mentioned.

Granted with the same reserve, as in the preceeding Articles.

Art. XVI. The English General shall also under the necessary and most convenient vessels to carry to France Mr. de Longueuil, Governor of Trois Rivieres, the staff of the colony, and the commissary of marines, they shall embark therein, their family, servants, baggage, and equipage; and they shall be properly victualled during the passage, at the expence of his Britannick Majesty.   Granted.

Art. XVII, The officers and soldiers, as well as the land forces, as of the colony, and also the marine officers and seamen, who are in the colony, shall be likewise embarked for France, and sufficient and convenient vessels shall be appointed for them. The land and sea officers who shall be married, shall take with them families, and all of them shall have sacks and baggage. These vessels shall be properly and sufficiently victualled at the expence of his Britannick Majesty.   Granted.

Art. XVIII. The officers, soldiers, and the followers of the troops, who shall have their baggage in the fields, may send for it before they depart, without any hindrance molestation.
                                                          Granted.

Art. XIX. An hospital ship shall be provided by the English General, for such of the wounded and sick officers, soldiers and seamen, and shall be in condition to be carried to France, and said likewise be victualled at the expence of his Britannick Majesty.

It shall be the same with regard to the other sick and wounded officers, soldiers and sailors, as soon as they shall be recovered. They shall be at liberty to carry with them their wives, children, servants and baggage; and the said soldiers and sailors shall not be solicited nor forced to enter into the service of his Britannick Majesty.   Granted.

Art. XX. A commissary, and one of the King's writers shall be left to take care of the hospitals, and of whatever may relate to the service of his Most Christian Majesty.   Granted.

Art. XXI. The English General shall also provide ships for carrying to France the officers of the Supreme council of justice, police, admiralty, and all other officers, having commissions or brevets from his most Christian Majesty, for them, their families, servants, and equipages, as well as for other officers: and they shall likewise be victualled at the Expence of his Britannick Majesty. They shall however, be at liberty to stay in the colony, if they think proper, to settle their affairs, or to withdraw to France, when ever they think fit.

Granted: But if they have papers relating to the government of the country, they are to be delivered to us.

Art. XXII. If there are any military officers whose affairs should require their presence in the colony till next year, they shall have the liberty to stay in it after having obtained the permission of the Marquis de Vaudreuil for that purpose, and without being reputed prisoners of war.

All those whose private affairs shall require their stay in the country, and who shall have the Marquis de Vaudreuil's leave for so doing, shall be allowed to remain till their affairs are settled.

Art. XXIII. The commissary for the King'sprovisions, shall be at liberty to stay in Canada till next year, in order to be enable to answer the debts he has contracted in the colony, on account of what he has furnished; but if he should prefer to go to France this year, he shall be obliged to leave till next year a person to transact his business. This private person shall preserve, and have liberty to carry off all his papers, without being inspected. His clerks shall have leave to stay in the colony, or go to France and in the last case, a passage and subsistance shall be allowed them on board the ships of his Britannick Majesty, for them, their families, and their baggage.

            Granted.

Art. XXIV. The provisions, and other kind of stores which shall be found in the magazines of the commissary, as well as in the towns of Montreal; and Trois Rivieres, as in the country, shall be preserved to him, the said provisions belonging to him and not the King, and he shall be at liberty to sell them, to the French or English.

Every thing that is actually in the magazines destined for the use of the troops, is to be delivered to the English Commissary for the king's forces.

Art. XXV. A Passage to France shall likewise be granted on board of his Britannick Majesty's ships, as well as victuals to the officers of the India Company as shall be willing to go thither, and they shall take with them their families, servants and baggage. The chief agent of the said company, in case he should chuse to go to France, shall be allowed to leave such persons as he shall think proper till next year, to settle the affairs of the said company, and to recover such sums as are due them. The said chief agent shall keep possession of the papers belonging to the said company, and shall not be liable to inspection.   Granted.

Art. XXVI. The said company shall be maintained in the property of Everlatines and Castorre, which they may have in the town of Montreal; they shall not be touched under any pretence whatever, and the necessary facilities shall be given to the chief agent, to send, this year his castors to France on board his Britannick Majesty's ships, paying the freight on the same footing as the English would pay it.

Granted, with regard to what may be granted to the company, or to private persons; but if his most Christian Majesty has any share in it, that must become the property of the King.

Art. XXVII. The free exercise of the Catholick, Apostolick and Roman religion, shall subsist entire; in such manner that all the states and the people of the towns and countries, places and distant posts, shall continue to assemble in the churches, and to frequent the sacraments as heretofore, without being molested in any manner directly or indirectly.

These people shall be obliged, by the English government, to pay their priests, the tithes and all the taxes they were used to pay, upon the government of his Most Christian Majesty.

Granted, as to the free exercise of their religion. The obligation of paying the tithes to the priests, will depend on the King's Pleasure.

Art. XXVIII. The chapter, priest, curates and missionaries, shall continue with an entire liberty, their exercise and functions of their cures, in the parishes of the town and country.

Granted.

Art. XXIX. The Grand Vicars, named by the Chapter to administer to the diocese during the vacancy of the episcopal see, shall have liberty to dwell in the towns, or country parishes as they shall think proper. They shall at all times be free to visit the different parishes of the diocese, with the ordinary ceremonies, and exercise all jurisdiction they exercised under the French domination. They shall enjoy the same rights in case of death of the future Bishop, of which mention will be made in the following article.

Granted, except what regards the following articles.

Art. XXX. If by the treaty of peace Canada should remain in the power of his Britannick Majesty, his Most Christian Majesty shall continue to name the Bishop of the colony, who shall always be of the Roman communion, and under whose authority the people shall exercise the Roman religion.   Refused.

Art. XXXI. The Bishop, shall, in case of need, establish new parishes, and provide for the rebuilding of his cathedral and his episcopal palace; and, in the mean time, he shall have liberty to dwell in the towns or parishes, as he shall judge proper. He shall be at liberty to visit his diocese with the ordinary ceremonies, and exercise all the jurisdiction which his predecessor exercised under the French dominion, save that oath of fidelity, or a promise to do nothing contrary to his Britannick Majesty's service may be required on him.

This Article comprised under the foregoing.

Art. XXXII. The communities of Nuns shall be preserved in their constitutions and privileges. They shall continue to observe their rules. They shall be exempted from lodging any military, and it shall be forbid to trouble them in their religious exercises, or to enter their monasteries: Safeguards shall ever be given them, if they desire.   Granted.

Art. XXXIII. The preceding article shall likewise be executed with regard to the communities of Jesuits and Recolets and the house of Priests of Saint Sulpice at Montreal. These last, and the Jesuits, shall preserve their rights to nominate to certain curacies and missions Heretofore.

Refused, till the King's pleasure be known.

Art. XXXIV. All the communities, and all the priests, shall preserve their movables, the property and revenue of the seignories, and other estates which they possess in the colony, of what nature soever they may be. And the same estates shall be preserved in their privileges, rights, honours, and exemptions.   Granted.

Art. XXXV. If the cannons, priest, missionaries, the priests of the Seminary of the foreign missions, and of St. Sulpice, as well as the Jesuits and Recolets, chuse to go to France, passage shall be granted in his Britannick Majesty's ships: And they shall all have leave to sell, in whole or in part, the estates and moveables which they possess in the colonies, either to the French or to the English, without the least hindrance or obstacle from the British Government.

They may take with them, or send to France, the produce, of what nature soever it be, of said goods sold, paying the freight, as mentioned in the 26th article. And such of the said priests who chuse to go this year, shall be victualled during the passage, at the expence of his Britannick Majesty; and shall take with them their baggage.

They shall be masters to dispose of their estates, & to send the produce thereof, as well as their persons, and all that belongs to them to France.

Art. XXXVI. If, by the treaty of peace, Canada remains to his Britannick Majesty, all of the French, Canadians, Acadians, Merchants, and other persons, shall desire to go to France, they shall likewise have leave from the English General, ——— both the one or the other shall take with them their families, servants, and baggage.

Granted.

Art. XXXVII. The lords of manors, the military and civil officers, the Canadians as well in the towns as in country, the French settled on trading in the whole extent of the colony of Canada, and all other persons whatsoever, shall preserve the entire peaceable property and possession of their goods, noble and ignoble, movable and immoveable, merchandizes, furs, and other effects even their ships; they shall not be touched, nor the least damaged done to them, on any pretence whatsoever.

They shall have liberty to keep, let, or sell them, as well to the French as to the English, to take away the produce of them, in bills of exchange, furs, specie, or other returns, wherever they shall judge proper to go to France, paying the freight, as in the 26th article.

They shall also have their furrs which are in the posts above, and which belong to them, and may be on the way to Montreal. And for this purpose they shall have leave to send this year, or the next, canoes, fitted out, to fetch such of the said furrs as shall have remained in those posts.   Granted; as in the 26th article.

Art. XXXVIII. All the people who have left Acadia, and who shall be found in Canada, including the frontiers of Canada, on the side of Acadia, shall have the same treatment as the Canadians, and shall enjoy the same privileges.

The King is to dispose of his ancient Subjects: In the mean time they shall enjoy the same privileges as the Canadians.

Art. XXXIX. None of the Canadians, Acadians, or French, who are now in Canada, and on the side of Acadia, Detroit, Michilimakinac, and other places and other posts of the countries above, the married and unmarried soldiers remaining in Canada, shall be carried on transports into thr English colonies or to old England, and they shall not be troubled for having carried arms.

Granted, except with regard to the Canadians.

Art. XL. The savages, or Indian allies of his most Christian Majesty, shall be maintained in the lands they inhabit, if they chuse to remain there; they shall not be molested on any pretence whatsoever, for having carried arms, and served his most Christian Majesty. They shall have, as well as the French, liberty of religion, and shall keep their missionaries. The actual vicars general, and the bishop, when the episcopal see shall be filled, shall have leave to send to them new missionaries when they shall judge it necessary.

Granted except the last article, which has been already refused.

Art. XLI. The French Canadians, and Acadians, of what state and condition soever, who shall remain in the colony, shall not be forced to take up arms against his most Christian Majesty of his allies, directly or indirectly, on any occasion whatsoever. —— The British government shall only require of them an exact neutrality.

They become subjects of the King.

Art. XLII. The French and Canadians shall continue to be governed according to the custom of Paris, and the laws and usage established for this country: and they shall not be subject to any other imposts than those which were established under the French dominion.

Answered, by the preceding articles, and particularly by the last.

Art. XLIII. The papers of the Government shall remain, without exception, in the power of the Marquis de Vaudreuil, and shall go to France with him. These papers shall not be examined on any pretence whatsoever.

Granted, with the reserve already made.

Art. XLIV. The papers of the intendancy of the

officers of comptrollers of the marine, of ancient and new treasuries, of the King's Magazines, of the office of the revenues and forges of St. Maurice, shall remain in the power of M. Bigot, the intendant, and they shall be embarked for France in the same vessel with him. These papers shall not be examined.

The same as to this article.

Art. XLV. The registers, and other papers of the supreme council of Quebec, of the Prevoste, and admiralty of said city; those of the royal jurisdictions of Trois Rivieres, and of Montreal; those of the Seigneurials jurisdictions of the colony; minutes of the acts of the notaries of the towns and of the countries; and in general, the acts, and other papers that may serve to prove the estates and fortunes of the citizens, shall remain in the colony, in the rolls of the jurisdiction of which those papers depend.

Granted.

Art. XLVI. The inhabitants and merchants shall enjoy all the privileges of trade, under the same favours and conditions, granted to the subjects of his Britannick Majesty, as well in the countries above, as in the interior colonies.

Granted.

Art. XLVII. The negroes & Panis of both sexes shall remain in their quality of slaves, in the Possession of the French and Canadians to whom they belong; they shall be at liberty to keep them in their service in the colony or to sell them, and they may also continue to bring them up in the Roman religion.

Granted except those who shall have been made prisoners.

Art. XLVIII. The Marquis de Vaudreuil, the general and staff officers of the different places of the colony; the military and civil officers, and all other persons, who shall leave the colony, or who are already absent, shall have leave to name and appoint attorneys to act for them, and in their name, in the administration of their effects, moveable and immoveable until the peace. And if, by the treaty between the two Crowns, Canada does not return under the French dominion these officers and other persons, or attorneys for them, shall have leave to sell their manors, houses, and other estates, their movables, effects, &c. to carry away, or send to France, the produce, either in bills of exchange, specie, furrs, or other returns, as is mentioned in the 37th article.   Granted.

Art. XLIX. The inhabitants and other persons who shall have suffered any damage in their goods, movable or immovable, which remains at Quebec, under the faith of the capitulation of the city, may make their representation to the British Government, who shall render them due justice, against the persons to whom it shall belong.   Granted.

Art. L. and last. The present capitulation shall be inviolably executed in all its articles, and bond side on both sides, notwithstanding any infractions, and any other pretence with regard to the preceeding capitulation, and without making any use of reprisals.   Granted.

P. S. Art. LI. The English General shall engage, in case any Indians remain after the surrender of this town, to prevent their coming into the town; and that they do not in any manner insult the subjects of the Most Christian Majesty.

Care shall be taken, that the Indians do not insult any of the subjects of his Most Christian Majesty.

Art. LII. That troops and other subjects of his most Christian Majesty, who are to go to France, shall be embarked, at latest fifteen days after the signing of the present capitulation.   Answered by the eleventh article.

Art. LIII. The troops and other subjects of his most Christian Majesty, who are to go to France, shall remain lodged and encamped in the town of Montreal, and other posts which they now occupy, till they shall be embarked for their departure: passports however shall be granted to those who shall want them for the different places of the colony, to take care of their affairs.   Granted.

Art. LIV. All the officers and soldiers of the troops in the service of France, who are prisoners in New-England, and who were taken in

Canada shall be sent back, as soon as possible to France, where their ransom or exchange shall be treated of, agreeable to the cartel; and if any of these officers have affairs in Canada, they shall have leave to come there. Granted.

Art. LV. As to the officers of the militia, the militia and the Acadians, who are prisoners in New-England, they shall be sent back to their country.

Done in Montreal, Sept. 8, 1760.

Vaudreuil.

Granted; except what regard the Acadians. done in the camp before Montreal, the 8th of Sept. Jeff. Amherst.

BOSTON Dec. 8. Extract of a letter from the Honourable Brigadier General Murray, to the Right Honourable Mr. Secretary Pitt, dated at Contrecoeur, nine leagues from Montreal, August 24, 1760.

Before I set out from Quebec, I did myself the honour to transmit a plan of operation I had proposed for the corps under my command this campaign; I have hitherto adhered to it, and it has succeeded beyond my most sanguine expectations.

M. de Levis has for a month, done me, and still does me the honour to watch our motions, with the gross of his army; and tho' I have no tiding of Gen. Amherst, I cannot doubt of his being well advanced, unless he had found his route impracticable, which indeed I am told difficult: I am confident he has not yet had any interruption from the enemy, their post at Galet excepted.

The Manifesto I have published to the Canadians have had desired effects: most of the parishes on the south shore, as far as the river Sorrel, have submitted to his Majesty, and taken the oath of neutrality.

As I advanced with the detachment of the Quebec garrison, which sailed a fortnight before the arrival of the two regiments from Louisbourg, the French army kept pace with me, abandoning every post in their rear: I therefore sent orders to Lord Rollo to disarm and swear all the inhabitants on the north shore, whenever it could be done without retarding his junction with me. The winds proved frequently contrary, and put it in his power to accept of the submission of most of the parishes on the shores as far as Trois Rivieres, which though the Capital of the government of the same name, is no more than an open struggling village.

I found that the inhabitants of the parish of Sorrel had deserted their habitation and in arms; I was therefore under the cruel necessity of burning the greatest part of these poor unhappy peoples houses. I pray God this example may suffice, for my nature revolt when this becomes a necessary part of my duty.

Colonel Fraser makes me hope that I shall not be distressed much for fuel in the winter; but for fear he may have miscalculated, I have ordered him to strengthen the post at Jaques Quartier and des Chambeaux, which are excellent passes, and an effectual barrier; betwixt which and Quebec. I can safely canton two thousand men in the houses of the inhabitants. This will save fuel, and be more comfortable for the troops than if they were crowded in the ruins of Quebec; but I flatter myself this expedient will not be necessary, and that Montreal and its neighbourhood will be the winter quarters of the part of the troops. You may be assured, Sir, I shall do my utmost to make it so; I am positive I shall be well seconded by the officers, and I flatter myself the soldiers have some confidence in their leader.

If Mr. Amherst does approach, success is certain; should he not, I apprehend I must be very cautious. I have a great country to maintain; the inhabitants are brave and numerous, and never can be depended upon, until the colony is entirely subdued, and the French troops and government removed. In every attempt I make, I shall therefore look upon the preservation of the conquered already made, as the principal object: I am sensible of what importance it is in Great-Britain at this juncture, and that no prospect of glory, however flattering, should put it to the least risque.

I am now, Sir, to make an apology for the

incorrectness of bad writing of this letter; the effects of last winter has lamed me; it is with difficulty I can write at present; and I flatter myself you will pardon my involuntary errors, as I left my secretary at Quebec.

I have the honour to be &c.   Ja. Murray.

P. S. We are now entirely master of the navigation from Quebec to Montreal; it is perfectly safe for vessels not drawing above 11 feet of water; there has not any accident happened to any of our fleet; and we have from this place, for a first rate to Montreal.

CHARLESTOWN S. Carolina Dec. 10. Letters by the last vessel from London inform us, that as there has been no agent from this province in Great-Britain since the departure of the Hon. James Wright Esq; his Excellency Governor Pownall had applied in behalf of South-Carolina for a share of the 200,000 pounds, Ster. Granted by parliament for the provinces in North-America who had sent troops last year against the common enemy, judging this province was well intitled thereto, from the great expence it had been put in that year.

PHILADELPHIA Dec. 11. On Monday last came to town from Pittsburg, the Hon. John St. Clair, deputy quarter master general of his Majesty's forces in North-America and several other Gentlemen. ——— All quiet in that quarter, and the garrison very healthy.

NEW-YORK Dec. 15. On further advices by the express from South-Carolina are, that the Creek and Shawanese, join'd with the Cherokees, are supposed to make their numbers 5 or 6000, some say 7 or 8000, who intend to lay siege to Fort Prince George, and destroy all the country before them. That the regulars under the command of Major Hamilton (about 5 or 600) were at Congarees, and the Carolina provincials amounted to 1500. That tho' it might seem strange that the Province of Carolina could not raise a force sufficient to repel such an enemy, yet in fact it was so, near two thirds of the inhabitants being Negroes, who require a large number of whites to keep them in proper subjection ——— That the Indians had fully rebuilt their towns and houses destroy'd by Colonel Montgomery, and had sufficient supplies of corn and provisions (to which some of our own people contributed) so that they were in a condition to carry on the war, and in disposition to do it with the utmost fury. ——— That they greatly despise the English, and treated their threats with contempt; especially since Colonel Byrd, with his army, notwithstanding his menaces, was so far from being likely to molest them, that they were retired, to winter in Augusta county. The Indians refused to accept the prisoners of their own nation, in exchange for ours, with great contempt.

BOSTON Dec. 22. Since our last several vessels have arrived here from Nova Scotia having on board a number of officers and soldiers belonging to this Province, which have been in his Majesty's service in the garrisons in those parts, and lately relieved by some of his Majesty's regular troops: The other Provincials who have been discharged there and at Louisbourg, are daily expected up.

Charlestown S. Carolina Dec. 26. Letters from Augusta dated the 22d ult. bring no favourable accounts of the present disposition of the Creek Indians. The Long Warrior of Coweta informed, that a great number of Creeks and Cherokees were to have a meeting about the middle of this month, in the forks of Okonih river, which he thinks portends no good.

The Wolf was on his way to Savannah, in consequence of the invitation given him by Governor Ellis, and repeated by Lieut Governor Wright.

Joseph Cornel, who arrived at Augusta the 31st from the Upper-Creeks, says, that the Indians are insolent to the last degree, and publickly threatened to cut off the trades in the Spring. That the Wolf continues our Friend, but he believes it would not be in his power to prevent the French and Cherokee parties striking a blow soon. That the Mortar continued indefatigable in behalf of the Cherokee; and his brother declared he would kill the English traders as well in the nation as on the road to Augusta; and that the Wolf desires him (Cornel) if he, on his way down, should meet any traders going up, to stop them.

BOSTON Dec. 29. Province of Massachusetts-Bay At a Council held in the Council Chamber in Boston 19th Decenber 19th 1760. Present His Excellency the Governor.

Whereas diverse Persons who had beating orders for raising Men for the last Campaign, received Money out of the Treasury to pay the Bounty to such Men as should inlist under them, and gave Bond for the same:

Advised, and Ordered, That the Treasurer do not pay the Wages of such Officers, who received Money as aforesaid, until they shall have taken up their Bond: And that the Treasurer make demand of all such Persons who received Money as aforesaid, and did not proceed in the Service, who have not accounted thereof: and that he cause the bond of all such to be put in Suit who shall not account with him in ten Days after Demand. Copy examined.

A. Oliver Sec'ry.

The Province Treasurer, in Obedience to the above Order, hereby notifies all concerned, who received Money out of the Treasury, as Bounty for raising Men at the last Expedition that they come and settle their Bonds with the Governor in Council, and pay the Ballance that may respectively be due from them into the Treasury; otherwise the Wages of the Officers who went in Expedition will be stopt: and the Bonds of these who did not go in the Expedition will be put in suit in ten Days.

CHARLESTOWN S. Carolina Dec. 30. Yesterday four Chicasahs came to Town from Augusta, with a Talk from Piamongo, the Chief of that Nation, in Answer to one that his Honor the Lieut. Governor sent him.

Letters from Augusta, dated the 22d Instant, bring no favourable Accounts of the present Disposition of the Creek Nation.

Letters from the Camp at Congarees dated the 26th instant, say all is well there, but that several of the Men have deserted.

FULLNAME INDEX

All names appear as they were originally published

ABACROMBIE, Maj 278
ABECROMBIE, Maj 275 280
ABENTHIN, 150 Mathew 149
ABOCROMBIE, Col 279
ADAMSON, James 212 Lt 260
AIKEN, Capt 273
ALLEN, Lt 40 Peter 227
ALLIOTT, Mr 58
ALLISON, Mr 239
AMHERST, 222-223 225 Col 244 Gen 1 5 9 11 16-20 23 33 36 39-40 43 51-52 56 74 83 85 88-89 106-107 111 113 115-116 124 126-127 137 145-146 153 162 164 168 173 183 185 199 204 207 209-210 214-215 217 219 221 234-236 239-240 245-247 255 265 271 293 Jeff 273 277-280 293 Jeffrey 271 Maj Gen 273 Mr 294 William 215
ANDERSON, Capt 199
ANDREWS, Capt 200
ANSTRUTHER, 41 110 112
ANSTRUTHERS, 225
APPY, J 273
ARBURTHNOT, Col 26 200
ARBUTHNOT, Lt Col 3 73
ARCHIBALD, Capt 172 183
ATKIN, Edmond 50 Edmund 34 Mr 7 35 50 61-62 68 133
ATLEE, Capt 200
ATWOOD, Capt 28 John 28
AUSTRUTHER, 223
AVERY, Ens 66-67

AXSON, Joseph 96 Mr 115
AYRES, Lt Col 56
BACHOP, William 256
BACKHOUSE, Lt 22
BAFFET, Capt 263
BAGLEY, Col 53 55
BAKER, James 264
BALTON, Mathew 227
BARBUT, Capt 217 Ens 171
BARKER, Ens 171
BARNS, 20
BARRE, Maj 273 277
BARRET, Josiah 264
BARRY, Maj 29 38 40 87
BASSET, Lt 172
BEACH, James 90
BEHG, Samuel 117
BELL, Capt 196 Mr 151
BELLERRE, Mons 191
BENUFALEN, M 2
BERNARD, Fra 265 Francis 185 204 206 Gov 134
BERRY, Maj 245
BIDDLE, Capt 199
BIGLOW, John 227
BIGOT, M 282-283 291
BIRD, Capt 41
BLAKE, Capt 54
BLODGET, Samuel 57
BOCANVILLE, Mons 37
BOCCANVILLE, Mons 54
BOGGES, Ens 260
BOND, Maj 76
BONNEAU, Mons 192
BOONE, Mr 134 Thomas 134 185
BORKLAMARE, Mons 44
BOSOMWORTH, Mr 144 Mrs 140 144
BOUCANVILLE, Mons 87
BOUCHER, Francis 220

BOUGAINVILLE, 234 Col
   246 275 M 235 M De
   112 114 Mons 237
BOUGANVILLE, Col 277 M
   De 277-278 Mons 145
BOUQUET, Col 199 207
BOURLAMAQUE, M De 107
BOURLIMAC, Mons 183
BOURNE, Capt 26
BRADDOCK, Gen 45
BRADFORD, Capt 255
BRADSTREET, Humphrey 185
BRAGDON, 201
BRAGG, 40 110 112 252
BRANNON, Mr 117
BRATTLE, Wm 93 156
BRAY, Capt 29
BREHEM, Capt 264
BREWER, Capt 199 232
BROCKBACK, William 69
BROQUERY, Mons De La 236
BROWN, Capt 179 182 John
   195 Lt 171
BULL, Brig Gen 51
   William 128
BURBANK, 43
BURNARD, Capt 69
BURTON, Brig Gen 37 87
   Col 41 223 226 Grig
   Gen 38
BUSHEE, Mons 132
BUTLER, Lt 124 127 Mr
   117
BYRD, 190 265 Col 9 120
   250 254 262 266-268
   270 296
BYRON, Capt 249
CALDER, Lt 41 168 175
CALHOON, Mr 120 Patrick
   189
CAMARON, Ens 41
CAMERON, Capt 172
CAMORON, Duncan 172
CAMPBELL, Alexander 41
   172 Archibald 41 172
   Donald 264 John 172
   Lt 172 216 Maj 23
CARLETON, Col 101 103
CARLSON, R 13

CARLTON, Col 29 38 40 79
   87
CARRY, Maj 216
CASTLE, Capt 69
CASTORRE, 286
CATBURN, Lt 171
CHAMBERLAN, 190
CHARTRES, Capt 172
CHAVEGNIER, M 72
CHEVELETTE, Col 59
CHEVIELETTE, 71
CHEVILLETTE, Col 63
CHRISTIAN, Capt 52
CHRISTIE, Maj 244
CHURCH, Mr 57
CLAP, Col 26
CLAPHAM, Capt 199
CLEMENT, Capt 69
CLERMENS, Lt 172
CLOUSTON, Capt 201
COBB, Capt 126
COCK, Lt 172
COCKBURN, Lt 40
COCKRAN, Michael 256
COFINE, Ens 172
COL, Montgomery 178
COLBURN, Capt Lt 171
COLLINS, Giles 129
COLMAN, Capt 32
COLVILLE, Commodore Lord
   54 Lord 131 214 273
COLVIN, Lord 263
CONTADES, M 91
CONVAY, Capt 172
CONYER, Miles 69
COOPER, Lt 40
CORNEL, Joseph 296
COSNAN, Capt 41
COURTONNE, Jerone 181 Mr
   182
COX, Lt 161 192
COYTMORE, Capt 134 Lt
   114 118 123 138
CRASTON, Lt 243
CRAWLEY, 201
CROWDIN, Capt 227 Thomas
   227
CUMMINGS, Leonard 26
CURRY, Capt 40

CURTIS, Capt 3
DAINTY, Ens 41
DALLING, Maj 171 223
DANK, Capt 82 102
DAVID, Joseph 3 Lt 172
DAVIS, 119
DDELANCEY, James 206
DEAN, Capt 169 225 273
DEFORGE, Peter 227
DELABROITZ, Capt 90
DELABTAT, Mons 57
DELANCEY, James 33
DEMERE, Capt 15 47 115 164 180 212-213 260-261 Paul 116-117 211 270
DEMING, Capt 255
DEMPSEY, Mr 181
DENORMANDEI, 199
DETIN, Capt 203
DOAKE, Capt 145
DOBBS, Gov 90
DODD, Gov 51
DODDS, William 257
DOGHARTY, Mr 151
DONALD, Capt Lt 172 Mr M 151
DONOLLY, 166
DORELL, 78
DORRINGTON, Capt 131
DOUGLAS, 139 James 109 John 41
DOWNING, John 164
DRATTON, Wiliam 96
DRAYTON, Wn 96
DUFF, Capt 249
DUGEON, Capt 77
EDDINGTON, Ens 189
EDGERSON, Ens 40
ELCHINER, Mr 35
ELLIOT, 77 Maj 253 Mr 76
ELLIOTT, Lt 243 Mr 114 Samuel 144
ELLIS, Gov 7 16 48 61 68 90 136 140 143 146 167 175 296 Mr 62 144
ERVIN, Lt 171
EUSHION, Ens 172
EVANS, Barabas 227 Lt 40

EVER, Lt 172
EVERLATINES, 286
FAIRFAX, Ens 40
FASH, Capt 172 Lt 172
FASSFAIL, Lt 171
FAUQUIER, Gov 181
FAYER, Alexander 172
FITCH, Gov 137
FLEMING, Capt 52
FLETCHER, Lt 2 74
FORBES, 271 Gen 45 Lt 172
FORD, Capt 10 Mr 144
FORESTER, Lt 172
FORTES, Lt 172
FORTISCUE, Lt 140
FOSTER, William 96
FRANKS, William 181
FRASER, 41 Alesander 172 Alexander Simon Sr 172 Alexander Sr 172 Col 172 223 294 Malcolm 172 Malcomb 41 Malcon 172 Simon Jr 172
FRAST, Thomas 220
FRAZER, Alexander 41 Capt 41
FRYE, Col 4 Joseph 132
FURLONG, Capt 36 38
GAGE, 32-33 Brig 1 Brig Gen 56 Col 215 Gen 20 22 245 276
GARDINER, Capt 124
GARDNER, Capt 40 216-217 220 William 256
GEORGE, King 210
GEORGE II, King 28 156 206
GERMAIN, Pere 73 120
GERMAN, 139-140
GERMANY, Mr 122
GIBSON, Lt 172
GILLIVRAY, Mr 138
GILMER, Ens 171
GIST, Capt 136
GLADWIN, Maj 201 228
GLEGG, Capt 219
GLEN, Gov 267

GLOSTER, Mrs 260
GLOVER, Capt 144
GODWIN, Maj 199
GOFFE, Col 200
GOGHAM, Mr 193
GOLPHIN, Mr 194
GONEDY, Mr 75
GOODWIN, Maj 172 Phineus 227
GORDON, Ens 172 John 227 Peter 189
GORE, Lt 40
GORHAM, Capt 41 83
GOWELL, Capt 168
GRANT, Col 55 James 164 Lt 41 67 172 Lt Col 186 Maj 45 71 74 89
GRAY, Capt 227 Mr 144
GREATRAKERS, Capt 218 220
GREDUEDY, Mr 150
GREGORSON, Alex 172 Ens 41
GREY, Nataniel 264
GRIFFIN, John 185
GRINMAN, Capt 138
GRINNAN, Capt 189
CUNNINGHAM, Charles M 96
HAGLER, Indian King 8
HALDEMAN, Col 244 246
HALDIMAN, Col 56
HALDIMAND, Col 275 279-280
HALE, Capt 218 John 109 Lt Col 39
HALFBREED TOM, 178
HALL, Thomas 257
HALLOWEL, Benj 228
HALLOWELL, Benj 157 Capt 157 201
HAMILTON, Ens 171 Fredrick 207 James 62 Lt 192 Maj 295
HARRIS, Job 168
HARRISON, George 256
HARTETT, Capt 217 Mons 216
HARVEY, Capt 28 30
HASILIN, Lawrence 256

HATCH, Capt 69
HAVILAND, Col 191 209-210 216 234-235 237-238 243-244 247 276
HAZZEN, Capt 60 172 223
HEATHERS, 2nd Lt 172
HENFIELD, Ens 172
HEWES, Capt 16-17
HILL, Ens 172
HOAR, Col 26
HOLBORT, Ebenezer 62
HOLLAND, Capt 41
HOLMES, Adm 110 164 Capt 238 Lt 230 Rear-admiral 106
HOOPER, Robert 227
HOPKINS, Sgt Maj 2
HOPSON, 41 81
HOWARD, Lt 17 Mr 19
HOWARTH, Col 51
HOWE, Col 110 112
HUFFREY, Maj 172
HUGHES, Richard 181
HUSTMER, Lawrence 256
HUTCHIN, Ens 16 19
HUTCHINS, Ens 17 20
HUTCHINSON, T 138 156-157 Thomas 155-156
HYRNE, H 96
INCE, Capt 171 183 224
INDIAN, Atakilla-kulla 96 Atakulla-kulla 94 114 Attakullakulla 262 Capt Jacob 157 213 Capt Jo---ny 8 Cayanquilliqoa 121 Chenallotochee 75-77 Chenohe 95 Chifquatalone 95 Chista 95 Christanah 95 Cilina-ka 35 Connasoratah 95 Duvall's Landlord 254 Eallitahe 95 Fool Harry 143 146 Great Warrior 211-212 268 James Horn 3 Joseph Marie Zachebrsen 149 Judd's Friend 253-254

INDIAN (cont.)
259 268-270 Judge's
Friend 14 Katacroe 95
Kehowret Zachetien
149 Kettagusta 35 96
Kilcannokeh 96 King
Hagler 8 Little
Carpenter 59 69-71
76-77 92 94 114 117-
118 152 154 163-164
179-180 196 250 253
260 268 Malachi 16
Motoi 35 Ned 3
Nicholoche 95
Occactota 76
Occonastata 196
Oconi-ker 35
Oconnastota 75
Oconoeca 96
Oconostota 96
Ocummastota 35
Ocunnahstatah 254
Ocunnastorah 180
Ocunnastota 47-48 58
Ocunnatota 123 Old
Ceasar 35 Old Hop 35
48 117 Otacitte 57-58
Otassite 95-96
Oucannossota 260
Oucannostata 269-270
Oucannostita 259
Oucatah 35 Oucha 95
Oulasta 35 Ousanatah
95 Ousanolitah Of
Cowetche 95
Ousanolitah Of Jore
95 Pilot Sowomoog 3
Quarrasattahe 95
Rattlesnake Sam 121
Rogguery 50 Round O
57 253 Round-o 53
Sailowe 269-270
Santoeste 95 Scalp-
jack 97 Scoliloski 35
Scrawney 16 Serowih
268 Skaliloske 95
Skiagusta 95 Solomon
3 Sorowith 267 Spring
Warrior 35

INDIAN (cont.)
Sympoyassee 146
Tallochama 95 The
Carpenter 261-262 The
Chote Prince 259 The
Gun Merchant 16 The
Gun-merchant 175-176
182 193 The King 35
The Lieutenant 16 The
Little Carpenter 14
The Mankiller 53 57
The Miser 175 The
Mortan 193 The Mortar
16 78 97 124 175 296
The Mortar Of Oakehoy
182 The Old Stump 177
The Old Warrior 254
The Old Warrior Of
Estahtowih 269 The
Raven 58 76 151 The
Raven Of Estahtowih
179 The Standing
Turkey 151 260-261
270 The Tobacco Eater
34-35 51 The Wolf 182
262 296 The Wolfe
151-152 The Young
Twin 8 The Young
Warrior 196 268 The
Young Warrior Of
Estatoe 269 Tiftie 76
Tiftoe 35 75-76 154
Tiftowee 178-179
Tistoey Of Keowee 262
Tistowe 163 Togulki
16 Tony 35 95
Totaiah-hoi 95
Waohatch 95
Willanahwa 268
Willanawaw 262
Woahatchee 35 48
Woeyah 95 Yahoulah 35
INGLISH, Capt 217
IRWIN, Maj 251
ISTOR, 45 John 44
JACOBS, 43
JEFFERSON, 195
JEFFRIES, Lt 41
JENKINS, 138 Capt 255

JOHNSON, Capt 165 231
    Gen 8 183 215 John
    181 Sir William 15 62
    166 204 245 274 276
    Sir Wm 210 214
    William 40 119
JOHNSTON, 262
JONES, Daniel 93 Ens 41
    Lt 41 Solomon 264
KELLY, 124
KEMPLE, Lt 41
KENDAL, 26
KENNEDY, 40 110 223-224
    Capt 74 115-116 Lt 10
KEPPLE, Capt 171
LAC, M De 277
LACORNE, M 274 Mons 42
LAKE, Mr 219
LAMBERT, Thomas 257
LAPASE, M De 278-279
LASCELLES, 110 112 183
    223
LAUTINIAC, Louis 269
LAWRENCE, 41 Capt 264
    Gen 218
LAWTRIDGE, Capt 40
LEAUTINIAC, 269
LEBLANC, Paul 131
LEIVEREX, John 227
LENTINIAC, 268 Lewis 267
LESLIE, Capt 216
LEVEY, Mons 42
LEVI, Chevalier De 221-222 Mons 233
LEVIS, Chavalier 282
    Chevalier De 278 M De 275 293
LEVY, 43 Gen 243 Gen De
    197 M 88 253 263 M De
    113 170 Mons 19 38 55
    184 227 234 245-246
    Mr 31
LEWIS, Lt 172 Maj 250
    262
LINDSAY, John 128
LISON, Lt 192
LITTLETON, Gov 57 90
    William Henry 94

LIVINGSTON, Peter Van
    Brugh 271-272
LLOYD, Maj 138
LOCKHART, Lt 171
LONGE, Mons 183
LONGUEIL, Mr De 284
LONGVILLE, Mons 231
LORING, Capt 44 56-57
    Com 240-241 Commodore
    74 204 236
LOTTERIDGE, Capt 42
LUCAS, 191
LYSAGHT, Ens 171
LYSALT, Lt 172
LYTTLETON, Gov 97 124
    128 William 114
    William Henry 96
M'ALPIN, Lt 225
M'ALPINE, Capt 271
M'CDONALD, Donald 223
M'CORMICK, Lt 231-232
M'KENNON, 189
M'LAMORE, Charles 211
M'NEIL, Capt 199
MACCORSSON, Capt 171
MACFARLAND, Capt 227
MACKAY, Ens 172
MACKELLAR, Maj 224
MACKELLER, Maj 172
MACNAMAR, 255
MAILLARD, Rev Mr 130-131
MAITLAND, Capt 172 Maj
    226
MAKCOMBER, Abel 264
    George 264
MAKEY, Lt 171
MALCOM, John 220
MANTLAND, Maj 220
MARSTON, Mr 46
MARTURIN, Lt 40
MASON, Lt 40
MATHEWS, Charles 257
MAUSFELL, Capt 40
MAW, Ens 172
MAXWELL, Lt Jr 40 Lt Sr
    40 171
MAY, Lt 192
MAYHEW, Capt 3

MC'ROY, Charles 256
MCBEAN, Donald 172
MCCARTNEY, Capt 146 162
MCCLOUD, Capt 54
MCCULLOUGH, George 181
MCDANIEL, Lt 41
MCDONALD, Capt 41 Hector 172 Lt 41
MCDONALDS, Ens 172
MCINTOSH, Lachlan 181
MCKENSEY, Ens 41
MCMARTON, Lt 189
MCNEAL, Donald 172 Lt 41
MEAD, Capt 257 Joseph 256
MELEAD, 172
MENZIER, Robert 172
MERCER, Col 207 Hugh 199
MERRIAN, William 264
MILBANKS, Capt 29
MILE, Mr 213
MILES, 166 Capt 200
MILIN, Ens 123 Mr 150-151
MILLBANK, Capt 40
MILLER, Capt 161
MILLS, Ens 171
MILN, Mr 263
MITCHELL, William 181
MOCK, 153
MOCKTON, 41
MOLTON, 35
MOMTRESOR, John 127
MONCHTON, Gen 29
MONCK, 144
MONCKTON, 41-42 Brig 40 101 104-105 110 Brig Gen 38 61 87 111 258 Gen 29-31 54 79 83 86 109 165 192 209-210 226 250 263-264 Rob 109
MONNEYPENNY, Ens 171
MONRO, J 189
MONTCALM, 10 30 41-43 89 Gen 31 36 111 Lt Gen 38 87 M 74 86 111 184 Marquis De 100 102 Mons 19 28-29 39 90

MONTGOMERY, 25 32-33 144 214 Capt 182 Col 89 128 144 153 162 165 167 179 181 185 188 194-196 207 213 228 238 251-252 254 265-266 296 Ens 171
MONTREFOR, Mr 124
MONTRESOR, Lt 127 226
MORIN, M 8
MORRIS, Lewis Jr 271-272
MORRISON, Capt 186 189 195
MORTON, Capt 5
MOSS, John 217
MUNROE, Henry 172
MURPHY, Simon 227
MURRAY, 150 Brig 19 38 104 106 110 112 Brig Gen 88 127 273 293 Col 43 240 Dr 149 Gen 11 17-18 54 82 124-125 169-170 183 207 209-210 216-217 219 232-235 237-238 242 244 276 Gov 201 245 247 Ja 226 295 James 220 Lord John 56
NEGRO, Abraham 117 154 185 213 Tom 181
NELSON, Capt 269 Eli 227
NEVIN, Lt 41
NEWMAN, Frederick 257
NICHOLS, Capt 17
NOBLE, Capt 232-233
NORTH, Capt 153 George 134
NORTON, George 227
O'FARREL, 271
O'NEAL, Capt 189
OAR, George 257
OGDEN, Capt 27 65-66
OLIVER, A 28 34 52 69 149 156 206 258 265 297 Hon Mr Secretary 205 Secretary 137
ONOTIO, (Gov Of Canada) 121
OTWAY, 40 81 110 183

OTWAY (cont.)
223-224
PAINE, Capt 56 Timothy 227
PARKER, Capt 26
PATERSON, John 257
PATTEN, Capt 157
PAUL, Capt 4
PEGAN, Jonathan 227
PEIN, Solomon 227
PENNING, Lt 241
PEPPERRELL, 244
PERCIVAL, Lt 100
PETTEGREW, John 257
PHILLIPS, Ens 230
PHIPPS, Lt 171
PHIPS, Capt 241
PICKNEY, Ens 172
PICQUET, Abbey 242
PIKE, Joseph 192
PINFORN, Lt 41
PITT, Mr 46 Mr Secretary 100 220 273 293 Secretary 109
POUCHET, Mons 251
POUCHOT, Mons 237 242
POWELS, 71
POWNALL, Gov 155-157 295 T 25 28 34 Thomas 27 93 128 147-148
PREBBLE, Col 153
PRESCOT, Maj 235-236
PRESCOTT, 29 Capt 273 277
PRIDEAUX, 33 56 Gen 6
PRIDIOUS, Gen 8
RAE, Mr 139 William 181
RAMESAY, Mons 40
RAMSAY, Mons 88 Mons De 42
RATCLIFFE, 150 Richard 149
REED, Capt 135
REID, 50 John 34
RENCH, Capt 209
RICHARDSON, 71 Col 77 152
RIGAUD, M De 283
RIPPER, Daniel 257

ROBERTS, Capt 10 John 181
ROBERTSON, Lt Col 273 William 172
ROBINSON, Col 56 William 181
ROGERS, 4 10 14 65 Maj 9 13 20 23 27 43 51 55 60 64 66-67 91 98 116 120 160 165 173 191 199-200 209 230 253 264 270
ROGGLE, Col 227
ROLLO, Lord 53 293
ROSE, Arthur 172
ROSS, Capt 41 John 181 Lt 40
ROUSE, Capt 17
ROYALL, Col 45
RUGGLES, Brig 43 209 Brig Gen 216 Col 56
RUNDLE, 201
RUSSEL, Capt 44
RUXTON, Lt 40
SAINT-LUKE, Gen 192
SAINT CLAIR, John 295 Lt Gen 56
SAINT PIERE, Mr 245
SAUNDER, Adm 54
SAUNDERS, Adm 6 11 30
SAWYER, 262
SAYER, 251 259
SCHOMBERG, Capt 27 220 225 Henry 131
SCHUYLER, Col 245
SCOMBERG, Capt 169 Henry 130
SCOT, Col 59
SCOTT, 2nd Lt 172 Maj 41
SEAL, Ens 171
SHARPE, Gov 250
SHAW, Lt 41
SHELDING, William 26
SHEPHERD, Ens 171
SHEPPARD, Thomas 264
SHERIFF, Lt 172
SHIENNIT, 45 Thomas 44
SHIRLEY, 244 Maj Gen 271
SHOERY, 262

SIMPSON, Decon 57
SINCLAIR, Capt 187 241
SINGLETAN, Benjamin 63
SINGLETON, Lt Col 91 Maj 78
SKEEN, Lt 40
SKEY, Capt 172
SMALL, Capt 227
SMALLAGE, Capt 126-127
SMITH, Capt 40 Robert 264
SOUNDERS, Vice Adm 100
SOURIE, Edward 227
SOUTHERLAND, Capt 187
SPAN, Capt 40
SPANN, Capt 171
SPITALL, Maj 29
SPITTAL, Maj 61 Rig Maj 40
STANWIX, Gen 8-9 12 120 Maj-gen 136
STARKS, Lt 230
STEEL, Ens 41 172
STEPHENSON, Lt 172
STEWARD, Ens 140
STEWART, Capt 253
STOBO, Maj 19
STOTT, Capt 53
STRETFORD, Lt 172
STUART, Capt 14 57 213 250-251 259 Charles 172 Ens 172 John 212 262
SWANTON, Commodore 169 225
TAFTS, Capt 227
TAGGART, Capt 168
TAPLEY, Maj 3
TATLER, William 57
TAYLOR, James 227
THOMAS, Col 235
THOMPSON, Maj 263
TINGAY, John 256
TIRSTMAN, Richard 256
TOBLER, Capt 138 Ulric 120
TOTTINGHAM, Ens 41
TOWHSHEND, Brig 38
TOWNSEND, 41 Gen 29

TOWNSHEND, 223 225 Brig 42 104-106 Gen 54 109 Geo 114
TOZER, Capt 264
TRESTS, Jacob 138
TRUTT, Robert 227
TUCKER, Capt 181
TURNER, 138 Lt 67
TUTE, 43 Capt 139-140
VADREUIL, Monsieurs 75
VANDREUIL, Mons 19 173
VANN, John 48
VAUDREIUL, Monsieur 90
VAUDREUIL, 43 277-278 293 Gen 55 Gov 255 M 253 263 Marquis De 279 Marquis De 275 282-283 285 291 Mons 38 40 90 141 Mr 89
VAUDREUILE, Marquis De 290
VAUDREUILL, M 88 Marquis De 280
VAUDREUILLE, Marquis De 244 246 275 Mons 145 245 Pedro 245
VAUGHAN, Col 264
VEAL, William 15
VIATER, Lt 171
VOTANG, Com 169
W-------N, Col 10
WADDEL, Maj 77
WADDELL, Col 135
WAGGONFIELD, 50 Mr 35
WALES, Prince Of 28
WALSH, Col 171
WALTER, Maj 228
WALTERS, 207
WARBURTON, 41 81
WEBB, 40 111 223 Lt 178
WELCH, 152
WELSH, John 269
WESTON, Capt 28
WHETCOMB, Col 227
WHITE, S 34
WHITMAN, Capt 207
WHITMORE, 41 81 Brig Gen 130 Edw 30 Gen 131 217 Gov 29 53

WILD, John 257
WILLARD, Mr 168
WILLIAM, Capt 14
WILLIAMS, Capt 13 188-
  189 John 227 Mrs 98
WILLIAMSON, Col 59 240
  Mr 196
WILSON, Mr 195
WINTLE, Ens 260
WOLFE, 42 85 Gen 1 4 6-7
  9-10 16-20 28-32 36-
  41 72 86-87 89 91

WOLFE (cont.)
  94 109-110 115-116
  197-198 James 108 Maj
  Gen 100
WOOD, Ens 165 231
WRIGHT, James 295 Joseph
  175 Lt Gov 296
  Magarett 220
WYLY, Justice 92
YORK, Joseph 185
YOUNG, Col 172-173 184-
  185 Henry 144

Other Heritage Books by the author:

1767 Chronicle

Boston, the Red Coats, and the Homespun Patriots, 1766-1775

Central Colonies Chronicle: The Freeman, the Servants, and the Government, 1722-1732

French and Indian War Notices Abstracted from Colonial Newspapers
Volume 1: 1754-1755
Volume 2: 1756-1757
Volume 3: January 1, 1758 to September 17, 1759
Volume 4: September 17, 1759 to December 30, 1760
Volume 5: January 1, 1761 to January 17, 1793

Jolly Old England

Journal of Occurrences: Patriot Propaganda on the British Occupation of Boston, 1768-1769

Newspaper Datelines of the American Revolution
Volume 1: April 18, 1775 to November 1, 1775
Volume 2: November 1, 1775 to April 30, 1776
Volume 3: May 1, 1776 to November 1, 1776
Volume 4: November 1, 1776 to January 30, 1777

Pontiac's Conspiracy and Other Indian Affairs: Notices Abstracted from Colonial Newspapers, 1763-1765